CLAUDIA SCOTT is Professor of Public Policy, Victoria University of Wellington, New Zealand, and the Australia and New Zealand School of Government (ANZSOG). She is the author of many articles and monographs in the areas of health and social policy, tax policy and local government. Her books include *Public and Private Roles in Health Care: Reform Experiences in Seven OECD Countries*; *The Family and Government Policy in New Zealand* (with Peggy Koopman-Boyden); *Local and Regional Government in New Zealand: Function and Finance*; *Fiscal Interactions in a Metropolitan Area* (with K Greene and W. Neenan); and *Forecasting Local Government Spending*.

KAREN BAEHLER is Senior Lecturer at the School of Government, Victoria University, Wellington, New Zealand. She is co-author, with William Galston, of *Rural Development in the United States: Connecting Theory, Practice, and Possibilities*, as well as various articles and papers on public policy and public management.

ANZSOG Program on Government, Politics and Public Management

The Australia and New Zealand School of Government (ANZSOG) is a network initiative of ten jurisdictions and 13 universities. Established in 2003, ANZSOG represents a new and exciting prospect for the development of world-class research and teaching in the public and community sectors.

ANZSOG has announced an extensive research program that promotes innovative and cutting-edge research in partnership with academia and the public sector (see www.anzsog.edu.au). In association with UNSW Press, ANZSOG has undertaken to publish a series of books on contemporary issues in Australian government, politics and public management. Titles in this program will promote high-quality research on topics of interest to a broad readership (academic, professional, students and general readers) and will include teaching texts relevant to the ANZSOG consortia in the areas of government, politics and public management.

Series editors are Professor John Wanna and Professor RAW Rhodes, Research School of Social Sciences, Australian National University, Canberra.

Recent titles include:
- *Terms of Trust: Arguments over Ethics in Australian Government* by John Uhr
- *Yes, Premier: Political Leadership in Australia's States and Territories* edited by John Wanna and Paul Williams
- *Westminster Legacies: Democracy and Responsible Government in Asia and the Pacific* edited by Haig Patapan, John Wanna and Patrick Weller
- *The Australian Electoral System: Origins, Variation and Consequences* by David M Farrell and Ian McAllister
- *Cabinet Government in Australia, 1901–2006: Practice, Principles, Performance* by Patrick Weller
- *Power without Responsibility: Ministerial Staffers in Australian Governments from Whitlam to Howard* by Anne Tiernan
- *Australian Foreign Policy in the Age of Terror* edited by Carl Ungerer
- *Calculating Political Risk* by Catherine Althaus
- *In Government We Trust: The Paradox of the Market State* by Warwick Funnell, Robert Jupe and Jane Andrew
- *Evidence for Policy and Decision-Making* edited by George Argyrous
- *Policy in Action: The Challenge of Service Delivery* by John Wanna, Benoît Freyens and John Butcher.

ADDING VALUE TO
POLICY ANALYSIS AND ADVICE

CLAUDIA SCOTT
KAREN BAEHLER

*To my family and to those who design and deliver
quality public policies and services. – CDS*

*To my parents, Fred and Marjorie Good,
with love and gratitude. – KJB*

A UNSW Press book
Published by
University of New South Wales Press Ltd
University of New South Wales
Sydney NSW 2052
AUSTRALIA
www.unswpress.com.au

© Claudia Scott & Karen Baehler 2010
First published 2010

National Library of Australia
Cataloguing-in-Publication entry

Author: Scott, Claudia D. (Claudia Devita), 1945–
Title: Adding value to policy analysis and advice/Claudia Scott,
Karen Baehler.
ISBN: 978 086840 859 0 (pbk.)
Notes: Includes index.
        Bibliography.
Subjects: Policy sciences.
        Political planning – Australia.
        Political planning – New Zealand.
        Policy scientists – Australia.
        Policy scientists – New Zealand.
        Australia – Politics and government.
        New Zealand – Politics and government.
Other Authors/Contributors: Baehler, Karen.
Dewey Number: 320.994

Design Di Quick
Printed and bound by CPI Group (UK) Ltd,
Croydon, CR0 4YY

CONTENTS

PREFACE

High-quality policy advice underpins good government and governance, and is typically a feature of high-performing governments. The contribution of advisers and analysts through their influence on and contribution to decision-making and deliberation on policy issues is widely recognised. This book examines how policy advisory systems in Australia and New Zealand operate, and how they can create value for decision-makers and citizens.

A specific impetus for preparing the book was our role in designing and teaching the core policy course, Designing Public Policy and Programs, for the Australia and New Zealand School of Government (ANZSOG), which serves mid-career public servants studying for a Masters of Public Administration (Executive).

ANZSOG is a consortium of governments and participating universities conceived as a world-class institution with a mission to enhance the breadth and depth of policy and management skills in those destined to be leaders in the public sectors of member jurisdictions. Our students are interested in policy systems, models and frameworks, policy tools, methods and practices, and bring with them many valuable ideas about how the public service can improve its performance. In addition to our students, the audience for this book includes managers and policy advisers in government organisations, citizens, stakeholders and students, as well as those who contribute and observe policy-making from further afield.

Teaching active and committed public servants from different jurisdictions in Australia and New Zealand has been a challenging and rewarding experience. Many participants in the course hold positions in strategic or operational management or policy roles. The cross-jurisdictional nature of the group – it began in 2003 with five jurisdictions and grew to ten by 2010 – offers a rich and stimulating environment for sharing ideas, experiences and reflections across jurisdictional and organisational boundaries.

Since the format of the course is intensive (four and a half days), we adopted a highly readable guide to applied problem-solving by Eugene Bardach (2009), which has served us well in our courses for over a decade. We supplemented this with extensive readings from the academic and practitioner literatures.

Some books were concerned with understanding policy processes and institutions; others with policy analysis and advising as professional activities; and others with the content of policy. Many, as ours does, seek to provide information and insights on both policy theory and policy practice.

Some approaches focus on policy process; others on the content of policy. Some models are state-centric and others client- or adviser-centric; some give an 'inside government' perspective on policy, while others look outwards, giving attention to non-state actors, international forces, shocks and other drivers of policy change and outcomes. As the book progressed, we concluded that what was needed was not a new model but rather an integrative approach that builds on existing work and fosters better connections between theory and practice.

The integrative approach offers new insights about policy systems and practices in Australia and New Zealand. This approach adopts a systems perspective on policy development, which draws together and links up elements both 'inside' and 'outside' of government. We believe that enhancing the quality and performance of the public sector advisory system is a challenge to which public sector policy advisers can contribute – but alongside others.

Our book speaks to governments but also to private individuals, organisations, and stakeholders, all of whom are integral parts of the policy system. It provides advice on analysing simple and complex problems, and considers some strategies for enhancing the performance and capability of the policy advisory system.

Acknowledgments

We wish to express our thanks and support to our colleagues and students at the Australia and New Zealand School of Government and at Victoria University of Wellington, New Zealand, and to international and local academics and practitioners who have provided comment and review on our work.

We acknowledge valuable research assistance from Frances Leather and Helen Gilbert and the contribution of our editor Janet Hughes. We thank Glenn Withers for his incisive review of the manuscript and the team at UNSW Press for their contribution and advice regarding editorial, design and production matters.

INTRODUCTION

The practice of policy advising is as old as government. The figure of the advisor to the ruler appears repeatedly in story, with the wily vizier in Middle-Eastern tales reflecting the influence of the role, while the likes of Tolkien's Wormtongue caricature its potential for mischief. The policy practitioners who design and evaluate policy proposals and proffer advice to governments nowadays may be less colourful, but it remains unwise to underestimate the reach and importance of their work. Public policy affects all of us, and an effective advisory system is essential to good government and governance. This book is about policy analysis and advice, and their contribution to the work of governments and the well-being of communities.

Good governments can respond to internal and external events with strategic vision and leadership, helping their jurisdictions adapt to and shape the future. They commonly rely on public service policy professionals for assistance in designing and evaluating policy options, and for help in understanding the likely impacts, costs, risks and consequences of government intervention. The value of the work of policy practitioners thus comes from their understanding of the complexities of issues and problems in the real world and their ability to design practical solutions to those problems.

Good public service policy work cannot turn a corrupt and incompetent oligarchy into a thriving democracy, but where constitutional fundamentals are sound, it can help support the wise and well-informed exercise of democratic powers. It can also expand and multiply the connections between representatives and their electorates, ensure that sound information and evidence support policy design, and tailor policy to the specific context. This book is about ways to ensure that policy practice delivers in all these respects.

AUSTRALIA AND NEW ZEALAND

Australia and New Zealand share a long tradition of practicality, adaptability, and innovation. The two countries have developed over a century from colonies to semi-sovereign constitutional monarchies; this attests to their people's capacity for inventing new institutions for new circumstances, and incrementally building new paradigms of representative democracy.

Policy advisory practices in Australia and New Zealand are modelled after the Westminster tradition, in which apolitical, professional public servant advisers supply 'frank and fearless' advice, while also responding to the priorities and strategic directions of the government of the day. In both countries, however, various forces have eroded the centrality of public sector advisers and their monopoly over the design and delivery of policy advice.

Approaches to policy analysis in Australia and New Zealand need updating for an era in which many former fixtures of antipodean history are gone or under threat, including village-style politics, Westminster and Whitehall conventions, exclusive sovereignty over domestic policy, predominant social consensus, policy problems amenable to government solutions, and the public service's near-monopoly on advice to government. The challenges for policy analysis and advice have grown with social diversity, globalisation and decentralisation, and high-stakes politics, forcing almost every industry from software to supermarkets to reinvent themselves. Why should public policy analysis and advising be any different?

While we address specific issues in the Westminster-style advisory systems of Australia and New Zealand, we believe our approach to policy analysis and advisory practice has a wider potential application. Governments everywhere continue to need reliable sources of high-quality, sophisticated policy advice on addressing complex problems and seizing equally complex opportunities. The profession or field of policy analysis and advising appears not to be filling this niche to everyone's satisfaction.

CHANGING POLICY ENVIRONMENT

An agile and inventive public policy response has never been so necessary. The nature of policy issues themselves is changing, with the rise of 'wicked issues' – big, intractable issues that cut across sectoral and jurisdictional boundaries. The nature of these problems and the mandate of governments to respond to them are contested, never mind the solution; and they resist definitive resolution, needing instead to be managed on multiple fronts for long periods and perhaps indefinitely.

The components of such complex problems are diverse and not always easily separated out, and more and more policy work is being done in teams assembled within agencies or across multiple agencies in order to marshal all the necessary kinds of expertise. Moreover, various kinds of partnerships between the public and private and community sectors are often involved in the search for creative and innovative responses to complex real-world issues.

Such complex and pervasive challenges have encouraged governments to adopt 'whole-of-government' policy development, to align policies and to foster collaborations between the public, private and voluntary sectors in pursuit of apt and enduring solutions. There is pressure on governments to lift their performance because public services, including policy, are increasingly contested by other suppliers. It has become very clear that public policy is not just about governments, and that governments and their institutions function as part of a wider policy system.

At the same time expectations of government and of democracy are rising, as citizens demand responses to their wants and needs. Governments are under pressure to deliver policies that will improve the well-being of people, communities and whole nations. Individuals, communities and interest groups are expecting more meaningful engagement in policy development, and indeed it can be essential to successful policy design and implementation.

Political pressures in a media-conscious world tend to encourage policy designed for the pursuit of quick results with short-term benefits, treating symptoms when the complex underlying causes call for longer-term strategies. Governments are therefore attempting to improve their strategic management to incorporate the kinds of timeframes demanded by complex policy challenges.

Our response to all these challenges is not to develop a wholly new model of policy-making, but rather to suggest an approach to policy analysis and advising that combines and builds on the strengths of existing theory and practice, in an effort to overcome oversights and limitations.

THEORY AND PRACTICE

The nature and proper conduct of policy work is debated extensively. It has been portrayed both as a scientific, technocratic exercise and as a merely ancillary craft, subordinated to politics. We would argue that good policy work draws together elements of the arts, the humanities and the sciences, in ways that are both creative and rigorous. While policy analysis often adopts social science methods, its problemsolving orientation means that it draws upon many disciplines and subject areas, and devises practical solutions with the creativity of the arts and the pragmatic purposefulness of the crafts.

Adding value to policy analysis and advising is about much more than technical efficiency and effectiveness, though these have their place. It requires clear strategic direction, and a good understanding of the overarching policy system, which embraces not just governments and their advisers but many other actors, institutions and influences. It needs room and incentives for creativity and innovation, to respond to new issues and to old issues in new ways. And it needs to reconcile political imperatives with policy purposes, recognising that they are a permanent and legitimate part of the policy environment rather than an occasional impediment.

There are various schools of thought on how to improve policy-making and policy outcomes in the contemporary environment. Some models rest on the conviction that better processes will lead to better outcomes. Others argue for a fundamentally different focus – on deliberative democracy, for example, on policy networks, or on evidence-based policy. All of these developments are clearly desirable; they recognise various opportunities or deficits and contribute to solutions. But none provides a comprehensive solution in and of itself.

We argue that practitioners have no need for yet another Copernican Policy Revolution. Instead we propose in this book a working synthesis of existing techniques for analysing policy problems, and a more open and receptive approach to solutions, with a view to adding value to policy practice.

SYSTEMS APPROACH

We approach policy development by viewing policy problems, policy solutions, and policy-making processes from a systems perspective. We believe there is more scope to connect up actors and institutions on the inside and outside of government, the inner and outer reaches of the policy system, more closely together – the former including the political dimension of cabinets and caucuses as well as the work of the public sector agencies, and the latter covering pretty well everything and everyone that can affect or be affected by public policy.

This approach lends itself to tackling more complex problems, which increasingly involves drawing on international as well as local information, expertise and evidence, and on sources outside of government, including the public. Placing governments at the centre of public policy-making and distinguishing rigidly between 'inside' and 'outside' dimensions has become inappropriate in a connected world. Many countries are wrestling with similar complex issues, and information and policy ideas can be transferred almost instantaneously and often beneficially. Sharing experiences across borders can also help judge when to borrow policies, and when to craft home-grown solutions.

We call for a crafting approach to the nuts and bolts of policy analysis and advising, as detailed in the central chapters of this book, in the interests of fitness for purpose. This means assembling frameworks, processes, and tools for the particular context and purpose of each policy task. It means openness to contributions from outside the formal policy system, involving for example NGOs, peak bodies and citizens in policy development, and less resort to routine solutions. It means abandoning the default assumption that government knows best, and recognising that in many situations a government is unlikely to procure satisfactory outcomes working on its own.

We also advocate deeper connections between the strategy, policy and operational areas of government – in the interests of policy alignment, but also because effective policy is not procured simply by the advisory component of the policy system. The best of policy solutions can fail for lack of correspondingly good governance, leadership, strategy, management or implementation.

PERFORMANCE AND CAPABILITY ISSUES

This book also considers the issues regarding quality and value in policy analysis and advising, and explores strategies for expanding the knowledge, skills and capabilities needed to lift policy capability and performance. Public-sector advisory systems have been criticised by the governments they serve for declining policy capacity and capability, which raises important issues about what constitutes quality and value in policy work, and how it can be judged or recognised. At issue here is the proper relationship between governments and advisers, but also much more. We argue that capability should not be approached in terms of the public sector advisory institutions alone, but from a much wider perspective that embraces the whole policy system, recognising that policy performance is inextricable from performance in other areas of government – strategy, management, implementation and governance.

Indeed there has been public concern about the quality of leadership and governance, and citizens have become less confident in and trusting of governments and their institutions. Accusations of short-termism and lack of responsiveness are contributing to pressure on governments to lift their game. Some governments are trying to be more proactive and innovative in their pursuit of policies to improve economic, social and environmental outcomes. We would argue that a systems perspective is needed to maximise the chances of such initiative being rewarded with the desired results; any deficiency in the capability and effectiveness of any part of the public policy system can limit the ability of governments to address policy challenges.

OVERVIEW

Chapter 1 explores the nature and environment of public policy advisory work. Chapter 2 sets out a systems perspective on the world of policy, with its interpenetrating 'inside' (governmental) and 'outside games', and considers some typical policy scenarios. Chapters 3 and 4 look more specifically at policy practice: chapter 3 explores the fundamentals of analysis and advising around the role of government, design of instruments, and focus on public purposes, while chapter 4 discusses three methods for applying the fundamentals. Chapter 5 sets out a crafting approach to policy, providing an approach to selecting policy activities, tools and methods in particular contexts, and discussing elements of good policy practice. Chapter 6 examines issues regarding quality and capability, and explores the implications of a systems perspective for the performance of the policy system as a whole.

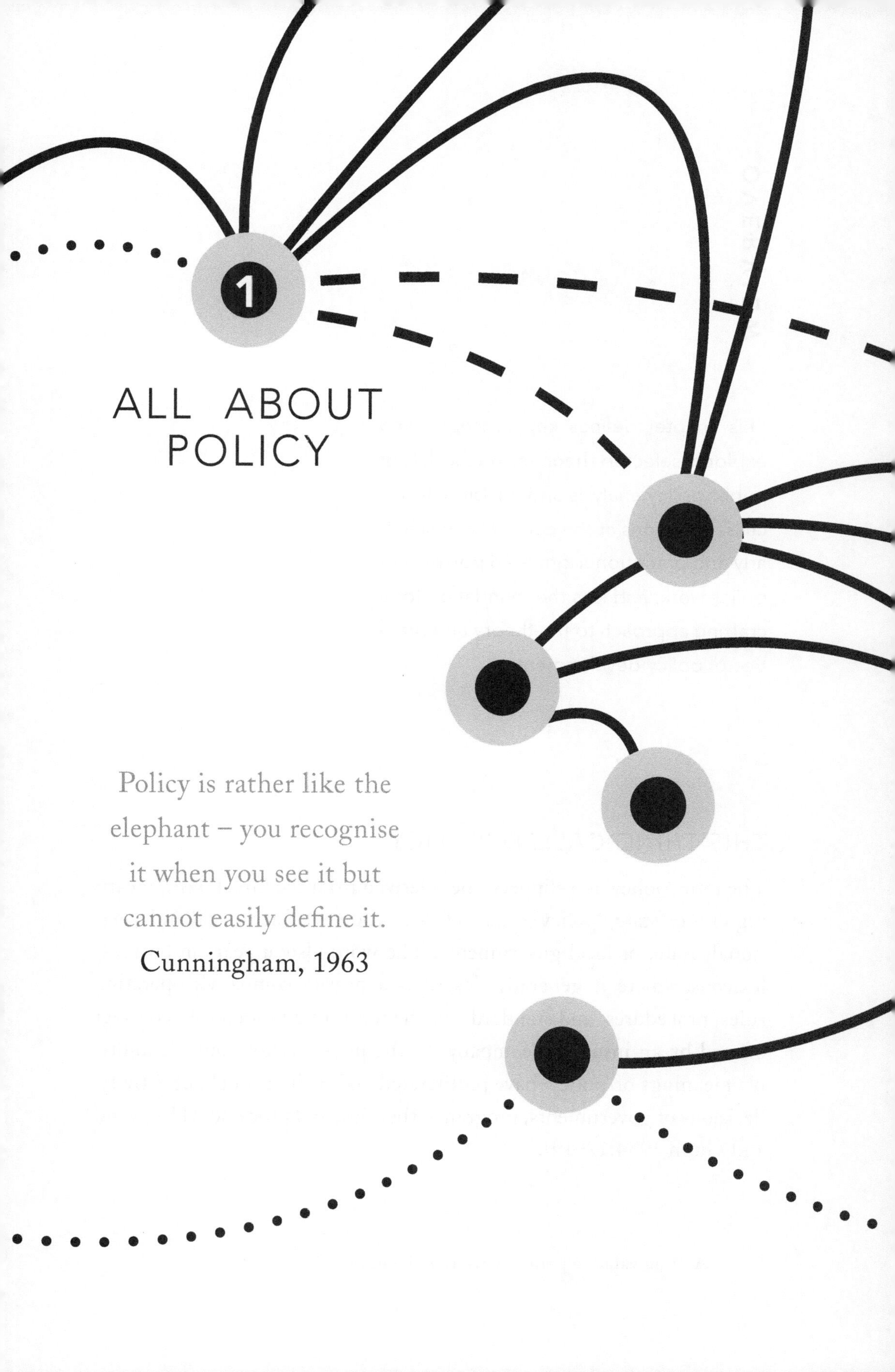

1

ALL ABOUT POLICY

Policy is rather like the elephant – you recognise it when you see it but cannot easily define it.

Cunningham, 1963

This chapter defines key concepts, and explores selected theories and models of public policy analysis and advising. It discusses tensions at the core of both scholarly and practitioner-oriented portraits of policy work, and lays the foundation for a crafting approach to the theory and practice of policy development.

THIS THING CALLED 'POLICY'

The term 'policy' is a slippery one. Derived from the Greek *polis*, meaning city or state, 'policy' often refers to courses of action taken by national, state, or local governments. The word also appears in business lexicons, where it generally describes a private company's operating rules, procedures, and standards, or the terms of an indemnity contract offered by an insurance company. In the public sector context, multiple meanings of 'policy' have proliferated and include a field of activity, decisions of governments, programs, theories, and processes (Hogwood and Gunn 1984:12–19).

All of these definitions have subtle normative implications for how policies would be made and carried through in an ideal democracy. The 'public' component of 'public policy' is sometimes taken to suggest public-mindedness or concern for the public interest, a definition that often implies the need for more participative policy-making. More commonly, 'public' is used to signal public sector ownership – the policies of elected governments. This interpretation tends to focus attention on the internal processes of policy-making and the particular, discrete public programs or measures that are introduced by governments at specific points in time to achieve immediate purposes, such as a policy of using tax credits to stimulate research and development. But policy more broadly understood means a stance or attitude toward a set of related issues. For example, a government might adopt or exhibit a 'wait and see' policy or a 'policy of aggression'.

Policy may be articulated in a statement of position or intention, perhaps in the form of a manifesto or formal document; but policy arises from behaviour as well as intention. A consistent course of action exhibited in response to particular issues amounts to a *de facto* policy, even if it is not articulated or acknowledged as such. So too can inaction constitute *de facto* policy; decisions *not* to act indicate an implicit policy of non-intervention. Policy in both these formal and behavioural senses may erupt suddenly as the result of a change in government or in response to a crisis, or it may emerge gradually over time, subject to frequent modifications.

For the purposes of this book, we understand public policy to be a course of action (or, sometimes, deliberate inaction) taken by a government using its various powers and authorities to shape the world around it. Thus, public policy may refer to specific programs or activities, each of which contains a hypothesis about how a selected policy mechanism is expected to produce desired results, as well as the broader sense of policy as synoptic orientation, strategic direction, or master plan.

This conception of public policy avoids the narrowness of a purely internal, institutional definition obsessed with government machinations. It also avoids the vagueness of an all-inclusive definition encompassing everything done in the name of the public. If public policy simply means whatever governments do, then it must include departmental procurement of pens and pencils; but such a conception risks disconnection from the realities of citizens' lives.

Conversely, if public policy means everything from a community organisation's plans for a local fair to the World Trade Organization's plans for global trade talks, then the term does not lend itself to analytical distinctions. For these reasons, we prefer a conception incorporating the interface between the exercise of government power and authority and the many ways in which government activity influences people and events.

Our understanding of public policy takes its bearings from both means and ends, actions and results. Even before a new policy has been implemented, it consists of both means (the selected instrument) and ends (the purposes to be served). After it has been unleashed, it will be judged on the basis of what was done, how it was done, and what effects were produced.

Thus, public policy is composed of three core elements: (1) the role played by government when it decides to exercise its authority; (2) a particular instrument or set of instruments effecting action, such as regulation, privatisation, or exhortation; and (3) a result, which may be intended or unintended, tacit or expressed, and which includes effects from both formal and *de facto* policy.

Take, for example, a policy of subsidising the arts. Such a policy uses government's spending power (role) to design and implement a grants program (instrument) in order to enrich the lives of citizens by facilitating artistic production (intended result). By contrast, a policy of economic sanctions against an anti-democratic regime in a neighbouring country uses government's coercive power (role) to prohibit economic activity (sanctions as an instrument) in order to put pressure on the neighbouring regime to proceed with elections and improve human rights compliance (intended result).

Not all public policies draw equally from these three elements. A 'pro-Israel' policy, for example, may consist of an authoritative but vague statement of purpose (that is, to support and defend Israel) without clear commitments to particular policy instruments. Minimising the statement of intended results may operate positively rather than negatively. For example, a policy consensus to protect a sensitive wetland from development may be obtained by avoiding clear statements of purpose in order to build a support coalition: if hunters and fishers support preservation for hunting purposes and conservationists want to preserve the area for overall preservation values, then a coalition is more likely to form around *what* should be done than *why*. The resulting policy is likely to be strong on actions and weak on clarity of purpose. Occasionally policy-makers will overstep their official authority by committing to roles and actions that lie outside their powers.

Regardless of the particular mix, all three core elements – role, action, and result – need to be present in some form for a document, statement, or set of activities to count as a public policy. The three core elements of the policy definition link to the three broad domains of policy work, which involve varying degrees of strategic and operational policy, as shown in figure 1.1.

At the top of the triangle, strategic policy shapes government's role in addressing an issue of concern. The process of policy development in this domain orients government's authority and activity relative to the other actors and institutions involved in the issue, and sets an overall strategic direction for public action or inaction. Huge internal and external pressures are brought to bear on government decision-makers in the course of strategic policy-making. Many organisations and individ-

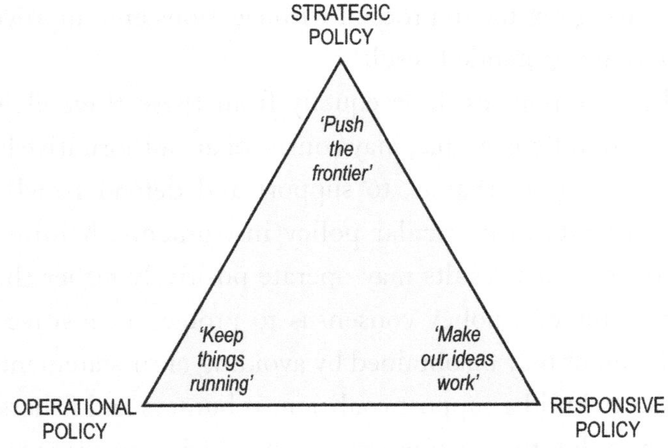

uals vie for influence over high-level decisions regarding the exercise of governmental power.

In this domain, the values of relevance and responsiveness take precedence, and policy work hews closely to the agenda of the government of the day, but at the same time, policy officials act as the eyes and ears of government, spotting potential problems and opportunities and keeping ministers and others well alerted to current and emerging issues.

Overall policy direction is often determined by electoral mandates, coalition agreements, or other political cues, with varying input from policy professionals. Thus, a lot of policy work in reality focuses less on strategic direction-setting and more on the details of program design and implementation planning. We call this responsive policy work, because what the analysts and advisers can recommend is constrained by what they are currently authorised to consider. This type of policy work operates in the domain of responsive policy, on the right side of the triangle, where policy analysis and advice focuses on realising government's predetermined priorities rather than setting those priorities, and designing programs that work rather than influencing what those programs are meant to do. This domain puts a premium on constructive dialogue between policy-oriented staff and those with decision-making power, as well as those whose job it is to implement the policies.

The operational policy domain, on the left of the triangle, is where front-line staff and their managers put policies into practice. When things are going well in this domain, policy analysts and advisers maintain close ties with operational staff, and in the Australian federal context, with state government implementers. They share information about what is and is not working so that programs can be adjusted and redesigned in response to experience and changing conditions. The values of organisational learning, efficiency, and fair treatment of citizens dominate this area of policy, which might be called policy maintenance. Maintenance is a continuous feedback process, because constant changes in the program environment create a need for frequent tune-ups, but this activity is most intense in the early phases of a new program, when inconsistencies and implementation issues need 'debugging'.

In our experience, work in these domains proceeds best when the networks of connections between them are dense, and information flows freely across organisations and jurisdictions.

BRIDGING THE PUBLIC POLICY – PUBLIC MANAGEMENT DIVIDE

Some readers will recognise similarities between the Policy Triangle in figure 1.1 and Mark Moore's (1995) Strategic Management Triangle, a fixture in many public management courses in Australia and New Zealand. Moore advises public managers to divide their attention strategically in three directions: managing 'up' to their political bosses and influential supporters in the authorising environment, managing 'down' to the operational inner workings of the organisation to ensure practical capabilities for action, and managing 'out' toward the people and activities that determine whether a particular public organisation will succeed in its mission of creating and delivering a valuable outcome to the public – what Moore calls 'public value'.

The similarities are not accidental. The link between the Policy Triangle and the Strategic Management Triangle reflects the reality that good governance requires a dense web of connections between policy and management functions to ensure that government's activities are effective, efficient, and aligned with society's fundamental values. Universities like to draw clean lines between disciplines such as public policy and public management, but this does not mean that such lines should be treated as representing real boundaries in the real world.

Mark Moore (1995) offers a definition of public policy that supports such an integrated picture of policy and management. Policy for Moore is a story about creating public value; it is an account of a public enterprise, of what the enterprise does and why. He encourages his main audience, public managers, to strengthen the policies that support their work by participating in formulating, designing, and authorising policy. In Moore's words (1995:55):

> Specifically, the policies that guide an organisation's
> activities must reflect the proper interests and concerns of
> the citizens and their representatives; the story about the
> value to be produced must be rooted in accurate reasoning
> and real experience; and the real operating experience of
> the organisation must be available to the political overseers
> through the development of appropriate accounting systems
> that measure the performance and costs of the organisation's
> performance. It is here that the analytic techniques of policy
> analysis, program evaluation, cost-effectiveness analysis,

and benefit–cost analysis make their major contributions.
Otherwise, the strengths of the political process will not be
exploited, the knowledge and experience of the operating
managers will not be utilised, and the acknowledged
weaknesses of the process will not be challenged.

Admittedly, this understanding narrows policy to the performance of
particular organisations; but Moore balances the inward focus with an
insistence that public managers should look *outside* their organisational
charts and outside government altogether to anticipate new tasks and
challenges. The whole thrust of Moore's book is outward, toward 'initi-
ating and reshaping public sector enterprises in ways that increase their
value to the public in both the short and the long run', even when this
requires 'reducing the claims that government organisations make on
taxpayers and reclaiming the resources ... for alternative public or private uses', which is a polite way of saying that a strenuous public-val-
ue approach might mean some government organisations closing down
programs and even closing their doors (Moore 1995:10).

Moore's definition of policy accords well with our understanding of
it. If policy is a story about creating public value, as Moore argues, then
that story can just as easily be presented as a proposition about how
government may exercise its authority (role) in developing programs
(instruments) to serve public purposes (intended results). Both understandings provide a potential bridge between policy and public management, and between the inside and outside games of policy-making in a
common pursuit of public value.

POLICY LOGIC

Putting luck aside, the success of a policy story heavily depends on the
quality of the fit between policy instruments and policy purposes, and
the capacity of government to marshal the resources needed to oper-

ate these instruments. Thus, a core requirement for value-adding policy work is the ability to assess a policy story's credibility before it goes 'live'. Is the story believable? Could it possibly come true?

Policy stories can be illustrated and assessed using an intervention logic diagram, which maps each step in the plot from initial policy implementation to expected impacts as a chain of causes and effects. Figure 1.2 illustrates the technique by plotting the story behind Australia's 'baby bonus' policy, or Maternity Payment scheme, as it was intended to work.

The hypothesis behind this program is simple. Australia's 'baby bonus', which resembles similar policies in other low-fertility countries, was enacted in 2004 to relieve financial pressure on new parents and encourage higher fertility by giving lump-sum payments to all new parents. The program was a response to widespread concerns about falling birth rates and the problems associated with a rapidly ageing worldwide population. With fewer younger workers available to drive economic growth, many societies are already struggling to finance current pension and medical care costs for elderly citizens, and the gap between needs and available funds is predicted to widen sharply in the near future. Governments alone have the authority and resources to meet a challenge of this scale and scope, and that is where policy comes in.

Intervention logic is a useful tool for unpacking the story or hypothesis behind a policy by showing how a particular policy instrument – for example, cash payments to new parents – is designed to serve a stated policy purpose or result, such as higher fertility rates. The boxes in the middle of an intervention logic diagram represent intermediate steps in the hypothesised chain of causal reasoning from program to intended impact.

The painstaking process of detailing a policy's logic helps clarify policy thinking and exposes weak links in the rationale. Intervention logic clearly shows that the baby bonus scheme is premised on the assump-

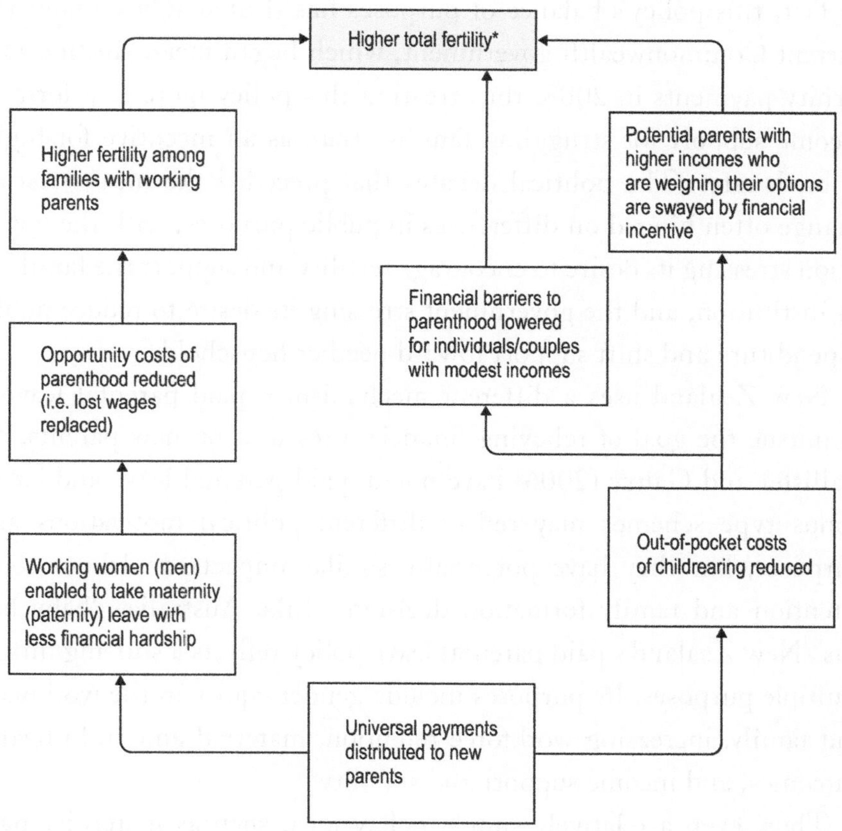

tion that individual fertility decisions are influenced significantly by both opportunity costs and out-of-pocket costs associated with childrearing. If this assumption proves false, then the policy could turn out to be a colossal waste of money, at least as regards boosting birth rates. Before recommending such a policy, officials should learn as much as possible about the factors in real fertility decisions.

The 'baby bonus' might look more promising if assessed against different policy goals and purposes, such as those noted below figure 1.2. In fact, this policy's balance of purposes has shifted subtly under the current Commonwealth government, which began means-testing maternity payments in 2008, thus treating this policy more as a form of income support for struggling families than as an incentive for higher birth rates. The political debates that preceded the means-testing change often hinged on differences in public purposes, with the opposition stressing its desire to encourage fertility and support the family as an institution, and the government stressing its desire to reduce public expenditure and shift support toward needier households.

New Zealand uses a different mechanism – paid parental leave – to pursue the goal of relieving financial pressures on new parents. As Callister and Galtry (2006) have noted, paid parental leave and baby-bonus–type schemes may reflect different political motivations and purposes, but they have potentially similar impacts on labour force retention and family formation decisions. Like Australia's 'baby bonus', New Zealand's paid parental leave policy reflects a shifting mix of multiple purposes. Its purposes include gender equity in the workplace and family, increasing workforce retention, maternal and child health outcomes, and income support and stability.

Thus, even a relatively simple policy idea, such as maternity payments or paid parental leave, often becomes a complex, moving target because of the many potential connections between actions and purposes and the shifting motivations of those who exercise authority. Understanding policies and their evolution requires attention to the subtleties of policy stories as they appear not only in formal statements of intentions and arrangements, but also in tacit goals and exhibited behaviours. Because intervention logic facilitates such understanding, it is one of the core policy-analysis methods discussed later in this book (see chapter 4).

POLICY ANALYSIS AND ADVISING

The profession of policy advising can be traced, in principle, to Plato's idealised republic. Rulers in ancient times and in today's democratically elected governments have always had policy advisers helping them to plan military campaigns, manage alliances, promote trade and commerce, and maintain social order. Once considered a calling or a privilege for the educated elite, policy advising now constitutes an industry that supports a large class of professionals. Our concern in this volume is with the value created by this professional work of policy analysis and advising, which includes many different activities carried out in many different types of organisations, as diverse as the Department of Prime Minister and Cabinet, the state hospitals, and the local schools.

Weimer and Vining (2004) describe policy analysis as 'client-centred advice relevant to public decisions and informed by social values'. The client-centricity of this definition highlights the need for policy work always to take account of, and respond to, the priorities of the employer, whether this be a minister, departmental secretary or chief executive, or board of directors. The inclusion of social values in Weimer and Vining's definition balances such client-centricity with awareness of broader public values. It highlights the fact that making policy nearly always entails taking positions on value-laden issues and designing actions to address them.

The quality of policy advice is determined to some extent by the soundness of the analysis on which it is based, and the accuracy with which its constituent elements are distinguished and described. At the core of policy analysis is evaluation, which Jenkins-Smith (1990) defines as 'a set of techniques and criteria with which to evaluate public policy options and select among them'. Evaluation involves the exercise of judgment; and the considerations that are pertinent when choosing options will include subjective and elusive values as well as objective criteria.

A distinction can be made between the work of policy advisers, who are immediately involved in proffering policy recommendations, and that of policy analysts, who may be involved in various ways in the research, analysis and discussion of policy issues. Policy analysis and policy advising are related but distinct activities; not all advice draws on policy analysis. Both policy analysis and advice are necessarily context specific; in any jurisdiction policy work has its own history, traditions and philosophical inclinations, its particular structures, habits and culture – all of which shape and constrain the roles of policy professionals.

The Greek root of the word *analysis* and the English word itself in its basic acceptance mean breaking something down into its component parts; policy analysis entails dissecting an issue systematically with a view to understanding its component parts and designing an appropriate, effective response to the underlying problem. Advising involves stitching the parts back together again to create a coherent picture of the situation so that sound policy options can be designed and recommendations developed. In the public sector, both policy analysts and advisers help governments develop, evaluate, and implement policy options, and there is considerable overlap and blurring of the boundaries between the two roles. Both are essential.

POLICY AS TOPIC AND DISCIPLINE

Debate has raged for decades about the scope and nature of public policy and policy analysis as topics, the degree to which they are multi-disciplinary or inter-disciplinary endeavours, and whether they constitute their own fields of inquiry or separate disciplines. The hallmark of a discipline is a distinctive and defining theoretical framework. Whether policy analysis can be called a discipline depends then upon its capacity to create distinctive new concepts, frameworks, theories and models that advance our understanding of policy-related matters. It can be argued that policy work more often involves the application of overlapping concepts and frameworks drawn from pre-existing disciplines than it does the invention of new concepts.

Economics is the core discipline when analysis is focused on scarcity, choice and the efficient allocation of resources. Concerns about the distribution of power and the administrative arrangements and institutions of government are better addressed with the tools of political science and public administration. Public management, which evolved out of public administration, concerns the application of generic management techniques to the public-sector context; this has characterised reform agendas in many OECD countries. Within finance ministries, economic and financial perspectives dominate predictably; but in other areas, several different complementary or competing ways of perceiving the nature of issues may apply.

Rather than starting from a particular disciplinary framework, however, policy analysis moves from a presenting problem or issue, to select frameworks and disciplines that are likely to help devise a solution. Policy analysis by its nature is multi-disciplinary, interdisciplinary, and pragmatic – good policy design draws on a wide range of skills and competencies to create new approaches and frameworks as needed from the raw materials of existing disciplines. Given that 'real-world' policy problems 'come in complex bundles rather than separate packages addressed to political scientists, economists, public administrators, and other relevant disciplines and professions' (Dunn 2004:4), there is little choice but to start with problems and then scavenge for the best intellectual resources to address them.

The various tools and methods employed differ in their precision and relative objectivity. Modelling and econometric approaches deliver precise measurement and objectivity, but struggle to prove policy causation. While abstract and theoretical, models may be of considerable use to practitioners; their usefulness should be judged primarily by their ability to improve the understanding of real-world phenomena and to predict the consequences of policy changes. Stakeholder analysis, interviewing, and various qualitative methods involve substantial primary data collection, which is costly, but may provide deeper insights into people's perceptions of issues than theoretical models can furnish. Choosing between methods is not straightforward, although some specific public policy topic areas have developed their own well-established approaches, such as statistical modelling in the transport area. Most of the time, methods are chosen pragmatically, based on the nature of the policy question and the data available.

While the field of public policy resembles the social sciences in its focus on positive analysis of information and evidence, its normative and prescriptive role is defining. This normative component contextualises analysis with a view to delivering and evaluating options for decision-makers and citizens. In other words, policy analysts seek knowledge not for its own sake, as social scientists do, but for its usefulness in informing decisions and improving government. Policy analysis is based substantially on the fruits of positive inquiry, and much of this inquiry may initially be undertaken for academic rather than practical reasons; but ultimately policy analysts will judge the value of information on the basis of its applicability to real problems.

Policy work is frankly concerned with values as well as information and evidence. It must confront competing views about the nature of problems, and then weigh not only the likely consequences of different courses of action, but the value attached to their various potential outcomes. The contribution of a policy analyst to designing policy options is to project their consequences and then make explicit their links with alternative values. Thus, while it is true that policy analysis draws on data, information and evidence, and applies scientific methods, it also combines common-sense knowledge with frameworks and skills associated with the professions and the humanities. Advisers bring evidence-based analytical perspectives to bear on public issues of the day, but they must also take account of the authorising environment with its ideological and political preferences and perspectives, and balance existing policy commitments against information and evidence from international and local experiences.

Despite its thoroughgoing, craftsman-like pragmatism and normative focus, public policy as a field has not escaped the academic culture wars. Alongside the positivist tradition in policy advising, which espouses a detached, value-neutral ethos, post-positivist streams have formed that dispute the very possibility of neutrality. Over the past decade, critical theorists and constructivists have challenged the knowledge and evidence base used in policy analysis, the standing of participants in policy discussion, and the authority behind decision-making. For example, Colebatch (2002:82) promotes a social construction approach to policy work, in which neither 'policy' nor 'problems' are naturally occurring phenomena with an existence independent of the participants in the policy process.

The objective of policy analysis in this view is to forge agreement among stakeholders rather than to prepare a technical analysis to underpin authoritative choice. In a related vein, Frank Fischer has argued for assessing policy performance on the quality of communication within the policy-making process, rather than the quality of analytical practices and products.

THE ROLE OF MODELS

In order to move the field of policy analysis beyond its reputation for opportunistic, magpie-style theory-building and methodology, academics and practitioners have put forward a vast array of models to explain policy development and to guide policy practice. These efforts, in turn, have generated decades-long, self-perpetuating debates in the literature about the relative merits of specific models and the general question of whether models should strive to describe reality, set aspirational ideals for practitioners, or both. The discussion below introduces a few of the models, theories, and frameworks that have influenced our teaching and scholarship over many years, and reflects on the different institutional and country contexts in which they emerged.

A large international literature outlines models, taxonomies and frameworks for public policy and policy work as an activity and process, and the role and values of policy analysts and advisers, and various policy 'styles'. Among many others, Althaus, Bridgman and Davis (2007), Bardach (2009), Colebatch (2002), Considine (2005), Dunn (2004), Fenna (2004), Howlett and Ramesh (2003), Maddison and Dennis (2009), Mayer, van Daalen and Bots (2004), Radin (2000), and Weimer and Vining (2004) have made contributions that we draw upon.

There are two principal variant streams in the scholarly discussion of public policy. One is the 'rational comprehensive' approach, which gives rise to policy cycle models and linear, multi-step models of decision-making and problem solving. The other major stream, which focuses on actors and institutions rather than processes, has come to be called the 'network participatory' category of approaches, reflecting an emphasis on participatory democracy and horizontal networks of influence rather than the vertical exercise of authority.

The two streams do not constitute a binary pairing; their underlying assumptions differ to such an extent that they diverge along multiple dimensions, including emphasis, methodology and logic. Because they are not binary opposites, elements from both approaches may coexist in practice; here, however, we look at the theory.

Policy cycle and stagist models

Policy cycle and stagist models form part of the rational comprehensive stream and set out a series of key phases in the process of developing policy. Some seek to describe in broad strokes the process of policy-making as it actually occurs, while others offer prescriptive guidelines for good practice in applied problem-solving or rational decision-making. The prescriptive literature is commonly used by governments to organise policy work and train officials. Like all models, the policy cycle models radically simplify a more complex reality.

The Australian Policy Handbook by Althaus, Bridgman and Davis (2007) offers an 'Australian policy cycle' model that is intended to be both descriptive and prescriptive. As a descriptive model, it offers a heuristic for breaking down the apparent chaos of policy development into manageable steps in order to study it. Its prescriptive role is justified on the grounds that governments should aim for a more orderly and predictable policy-making process, because more structured processes tend to produce better policy results. The resulting model specifies eight stages as listed below, and encourages users to build in a period of reflection at crucial junctures:

- *identifying issues*: the recognition of a problem as needing attention, so that it joins the government's policy agenda
- *policy analysis*: the assembling of information to frame the issue and understand the problem
- *policy instruments*: determining the appropriate tools and approaches to design a policy response
- *consultation*: a structured process to seek and respond to views about a policy issue from relevant interest groups or individuals, or the community generally
- *co-ordination*: ensuring that politics, policy and administration work together
- *decision*: confirmation of policy by government, usually via a formal resolution of cabinet
- *implementation*: giving expression to the decision through legislation or a program

- *evaluation*: a process to systematically examine the effects of a policy program.

The Australian cycle offers an expanded version of a largely descriptive and explanatory model presented by Howlett and Ramesh (2003) in five steps: agenda-setting, policy formulation, decision-making, implementation, and evaluation. For each of the five steps, the authors canvass a range of theories that can be used to predict and explain how policy will be developed under varying conditions.

Bardach (2009) presents a multi-stage model with similar-sounding steps, but no ambitions to describe reality. His handbook was developed as a general, prescriptive approach to applied problem-solving, building on twenty-five years of conducting policy analysis workshops with graduate students. Its purpose is to help junior analysts organise

Figure 1.3 Althaus, Bridgman and Davis cycle model

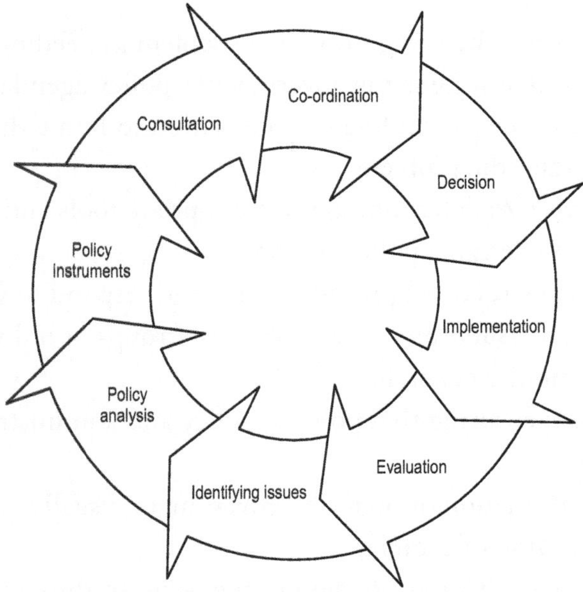

source Althaus, Bridgman and Davis (2007)

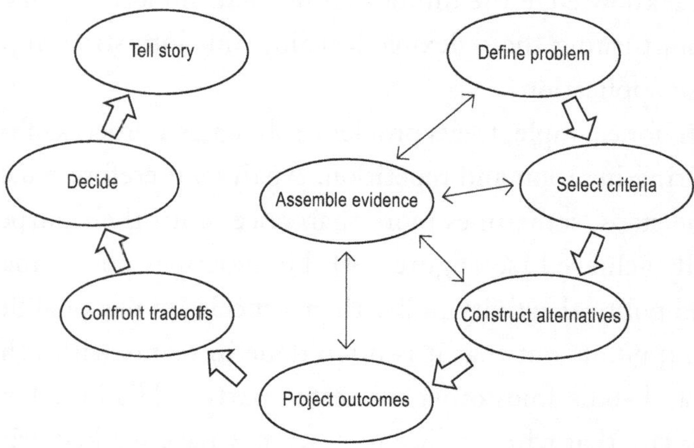

SOURCE Adapted from Bardach (2009)

their thoughts and begin making sense of the formidable issues placed before them.

Bardach sets out eight steps: define the problem; assemble some evidence; construct the alternatives; select the criteria; project the outcomes; confront the trade-offs; decide; and tell your story.

Cycle-based and step-wise models of policy are often scorned for being overly rational, orderly, linear, and therefore unrealistic. The critics argue that both descriptive and prescriptive models need to begin with the policy world as it is, rather than as it should be, so that efforts to understand and improve the system will be based in reality rather than fantasy.

In their defence, the purveyors of the cycle models argue that neither scholars nor practitioners can make much progress when they begin with conceptual pandemonium. Rough heuristics or rules of thumb – such as the stages in an exploratory policy cycle – can aid scholarship and practice by providing just enough conceptual organisation to allow new patterns and new ideas to emerge from the confusion of data.

In addition, it is important to note that the authors of most cycle models openly acknowledge the limitations of their models and discourage readers from turning these flexible learning aids into strict algorithms for practical application.

Bardach, for example, treats problem-solving as a process of trial and error requiring iteration and repetition. Analysts therefore must repeat some of the steps, sometimes more than once, until their purposes are satisfactorily achieved (see figure 1.4). He describes policy analysis as a social and political activity rather than a species of personal decision-making, and points out that it is often done in teams with other professionals and sometimes other interested parties. His broad audience reflects the fact that while policy analysts may have worked principally in government bureaucracies in the past, the clientele for policy advice now spans all sectors, and policy analysis is often undertaken by people employed outside of government.

Bardach places particular emphasis on assembling information and evidence throughout the policy process, rather than treating it as a discrete stage that can be dealt with summarily. He insists on presentation of multiple policy options, which prevents analysts from becoming too enamoured with a single proposal and promotes healthy democratic decision-making processes.

Self-justifying policy analysis is avoided in the eight-step path by requiring analysts to set specific criteria relating to values and intended impacts, as the basis for assessing the outcomes of policy options. These two disciplines – selection of criteria and construction of multiple options – create the shell of an outcomes matrix, which helps analysts to rank particular options against criteria that measure values and impacts.

The 'projecting outcomes' stage of Bardach's model, probably the most difficult to complete, prompts analysts to think about how different policy options are likely to achieve specific results, and reminds them that they are designing policy options for the future rather than the present. The 'decide' and 'tell your story' stages invite policy professionals to put themselves in the shoes of their clients, and call for effective policy communication.

Bardach's model, developed in the US context, is a generic model designed to develop generic problem-solving skills relevant to all settings and policy clients, whether they be cabinets, boards, individuals, or organisations from the private, public, or not-for-profit sectors. The model therefore concentrates on policy development, in contrast with more government-specific models, which extend further down the timeline, with stages covering the client's decision as well as policy implementation and evaluation processes.

The differences between the Australian policy cycle model and Bardach's eight-step approach reflect the particular uses envisaged for them and the policy system contexts in which they were developed. The Althaus, Bridgman and Davis model in its original form was developed as a departmental policy handbook for the Department of the Premier and Cabinet in Queensland. The model was designed to regularise policy processes and routines and encourage co-ordination and alignment between agencies in their policy development.

The authors treat policy-making as a co-operative venture involving politicians, public servants and others in order to foster these connections; their focus on policy process is designed to help public-sector advisers bring a professional approach to decision-making. The policy cycle is supplemented with a set of checklists for developing policy objectives, offering policy advice and managing the policy cycle.

Whereas the Australian model is institutionally based, presuming a highly partisan, time-pressured, quasi-Westminster context of public-sector policy-making, Bardach presumes a plurality of contexts, with policy proposals being generated in multiple sites for multiple clients, many of them not in the public sector. Bardach stops short of the institutional specifics, and focuses on the fundamental features that all or nearly all policy analysis tasks have in common, while Althaus, Bridgman and Davis emphasise the importance of institutional processes for generating good policy advice.

Despite their different origins and orientations, the high degree of similarity between these models is striking. Descriptive, prescriptive, Westminster-based, USA-based, generic and specific models all boil down to variations on the basic steps of applied problem-solving familiar to engineers, doctors, and policy officials alike. In plain language, these steps include identifying a problem, determining possible solutions to the problem, assessing the solutions, deciding between them, and monitoring the results.

Network participatory approaches

Where cycle or stage models are shaped by the context and the process of the policy-making task – the setting and the plot, if you will – network participatory approaches focus on the actors in a policy system.

Howlett and Ramesh (2003), for example, offer a model of the policy system that traces the interactions between various actors and institutions of the state, society and the international system. The state includes political (elected) representatives and the public sector. The social sphere comprises the media, business, community and other interest groups. The international system includes international organisations, policy experiences from other countries, and policy instruments such as international agreements and treaties.

The heart of the policy subsystem in the Howlett and Ramesh model is the *interest network* of actors who are intimately involved in the policy process and resulting policies and programs. *Discourse communities* are groups that are more loosely involved, but still maintain an interest in policy outputs and outcomes, usually motivated more by subject in-

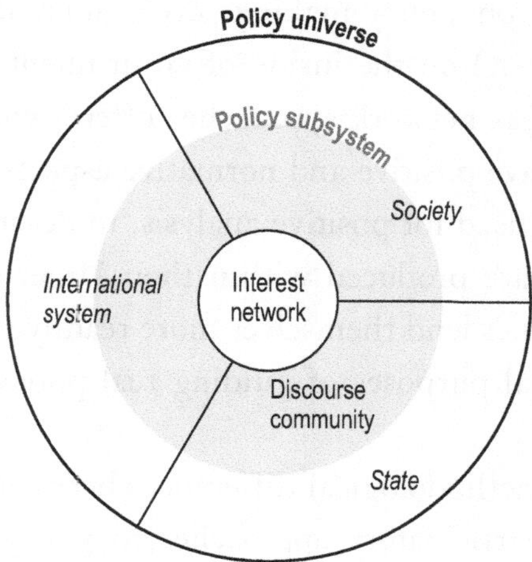

SOURCE Howlett and Ramesh (2003)

terest than personal or institutional interest; they play bit parts to the interest networks' principal roles.

Sabatier's Advocacy Coalition Framework is a model of the policy process dominated by interest groups, which are organised into policy communities within a specific policy domain. Sources of changes to policy settings include variability in socioeconomic conditions and technology as well as shifting government coalitions (Sabatier 1988). Reflecting a US context, this model suggests that policy development and change are determined principally by advocacy coalitions of elite opinion – by particularly focused types of networks, in other words.

Policy networks facilitate more and less formal interactions among policy analysts, decision-makers, citizens and other stakeholder groups, and provide a means of forging consensus on policy settings. Models of the network kind vary in the prominence they accord to government organisations relative to business, international and not-for-profit organisations, the media and other influences (Howlett & Ramesh 2003).

A comparison of cycle and network approaches to policy shows different perspectives on policy-making: cycle approaches focus largely (but not exclusively) on the inside-of-government policy world and its processes, whereas network approaches offer a wider systems view. Both approaches have positive and normative aspects, but the network approach is largely used for positive analysis, to describe how and why particular policies are produced within their larger contexts. In contrast, cycle approaches lend themselves more readily to normative analysis for the practical purposes of guiding real policy choices and designs.

There are also methodological differences between the rational linear and network participatory approaches to policy. Not surprisingly, most rational approaches to policy attach a high value to assembling information and evidence in problem-solving, while network participatory approaches call for a more discursive and argumentative approach, valuing communication between actors and institutions, and seeking common understandings of policy problems, more than objective evidence, as a basis for negotiating agreement on policy solutions.

Critics of the rationalist approach typically object that step-wise, prescriptive models give an unduly large role to experts and professionals in policy development, and treat political actors as inconvenient barriers to efficient, effective policy design rather than as democratically elected representatives of the people. With the explosion of information over the past few decades and its growing role in government decision-making, concern has been raised about the growing power of experts to shape the thinking of elected representatives, and their lack of accountability. Critics of the network participatory approach, in turn, express concern that elevating networks as the main driver of policy-making relegates governments to an overly passive role of implementing policy stances developed outside the formal government policy system. Theories of 'groupthink' have also cast doubt on assumptions fundamental to the network participatory approach, suggesting that group pressure to conform will produce uncritical thinking in policy networks and in society as a whole.

BLENDING THE RATIONAL AND PARTICIPATORY APPROACHES

The divide between the rational comprehensive and network participatory understandings of policy is far from absolute. High-performing public officials succeed in balancing these competing imperatives on a daily basis in their professional practice, while scholars and practitioners from various disciplines and fields have advanced reconciliation between the rational and participatory approaches by developing various integrated and blended models.

A thorough review of this literature is not possible here, but a few key thinkers deserve brief mention. Foremost among them is Nobel laureate Herbert Simon, whose work ranged across multiple disciplines from economics and psychology to computer science and drew upon Freud, Lasswell and others, as well as his own study of human (particularly administrative) behaviour. Simon tried to seek an accommodation between the assumptions of economic rationality about perfect information and optimising behaviour, and the realities of 'bounded' rationality, which include limits on time, access to information, and capacity to process information, as well as subterranean currents of emotion and desire. His work influenced countless intellectual contributions to the fields of public policy, public administration, and organisational behaviour over the past half-century, including collaborative work by Simon and March (1958) and theories of sub-optimal decision-making by Cyert and March (1963).

In the spirit of Simon, Charles Lindblom (1968) suggests that most policy development occurs via practical shortcuts to comprehensive rationality and piecemeal methods; his incrementalist approach to applied problem-solving and decision-making is not only descriptively accurate, but also carries some normative value. Lindblom carefully studied the phenomena of political negotiation and judgment, and argued for the superiority of democratic decision-making over synoptic planning as decision-making mechanisms, while also acknowledging the systematic biases that characterise markets. He reminds policy analysts that good policy depends ultimately on good politics, but does not therefore dismiss the potential contributions of policy workers.

If policy advice can be used to help policy-makers overcome their cognitive impairments, as described by thinkers such as Lindblom and Simon, then it can play a small but important role in salutary social change. Such impairments stem not only from rationality's limits but also from the power of social convergence to entrench dysfunctional ideas and the temptation for elites to embrace ideas that protect their own advantages. Therefore, both rationality, in its many, varied forms, and participatory networks need to be understood before policy processes themselves can be understood and improved.

The 'garbage can' theory is another attempt at a more realistic model of decision-making behaviour. Cohen et al (1972) described decision opportunities as garbage cans in which three elements or streams – problems, solutions and participants – slosh around and occasionally mix. The model is distinctive in that it portrays solutions and problems moving independently rather than sequentially, with solutions looking for problems as much as problems are seeking solutions. Linkages of various kinds are discerned by participants working to connect up problems with solutions, thus leading to policy proposals and choices in which instruments are linked to purposes. Understanding policy development as a network-driven phenomenon is a natural next step.

John Kingdon's (1995) 'window of opportunity' framework describes how the garbage can's problem and solution streams come together to generate policy decisions. Although Kingdon's framework is intended as a descriptive model of the way policy agendas are set, it also provides professional guidance on producing value-added policy analysis and advice. Kingdon brings together the techniques of applied problem-solving (the problem stream) with an understanding of and engagement with public concerns and attendant political risks (the politics stream), with an eye also to the work being generated in policy networks of interest groups and researchers (the policy stream). This view stresses the potential for policy to be influenced by public opinion and wider economic, social and environmental pressures, as much as by government's deliberations and decisions.

Parsons (1995:295) notes the contribution of Dror (1964) and Etzioni (1967), whose views of decision-makers drew on rational analysis, while also acknowledging the creative value of intuition, hunches, feelings and impressions. Dror's model attempted to provide a model of decision-making that was both descriptive and prescriptive, with a view to improving the quality of policy work. By contrast, Etzioni's model bridges the divide by softening the assumptions of rationality, while promoting the benefits of a long-term strategic perspective on policy, again with both descriptive and prescriptive components.

Baumgartner and Jones (2002) borrowed the concept of 'punctuated equilibrium' from the fields of evolutionary biology and computer science to provide a metaphor to describe policy change. The authors suggest that policy tends to remain relatively stable over long periods, with only incremental changes, until the perceptual and cognitive errors embedded in those policies accumulate to cause sudden shifts in public and elite understanding of problems. These 'punctuations' alter the balance of power between groups representing entrenched interests and those seeking to fight them. The theory suggests that it is the entry of new participants to a debate, and the multiple interactions among groups and policy subsystems, that result in strong pressures for change which cannot be resisted. The theory also emphasises the role of the media in cycles of punctuated equilibria, as media portrayals can contribute to the instability of images and institutions.

Baumgartner and Jones' theory blends ideas about policy rationality with an understanding of counter-rational forces and the balance of power between key actors and institutions; it is one of the few genuinely predictive theories available. The authors tested the explanatory power of their ideas in several policy areas. Their findings support both a network-based approach to policy-making, focused on the power of shifting and self-reinforcing combinations of actors and institutions to trigger policy change, and a rationality-based approach, which acknowledges the complexity of policy issues and therefore the need for policy subsystems to be dominated by issue experts.

The rationality v network participation debates are far from over. Theories and models developed to date have drawn significant contributions from all branches of social science, and have served to illuminate many important dimensions of and factors in the policy world: from policy stability to tinkering to revolutionary reforms, from political horse-trading to community-led action, taking in the full range of actors and institutions from interest groups to bureaucrats to political elites, expert elites, elite cadres of government advisers, and the public at large.

The role of the state itself as an 'actor' of sorts, or an independent variable in models of social change has been revived and explored by other scholars. The menu of orthodox policy-analysis tools has subsequently expanded to include stakeholder analysis and public engagement, research contracting, systematic literature reviews, bargaining, and negotiation.

BICYCLES, TRICYCLES, QUAD BIKES: THE ANTI-MODEL MODEL

A core message of this book is that competition between images of policy work – rational v participatory, positivist v post-positivist, politically charged v independent, realistic v idealistic, state-centred v public-centred – cannot be resolved by any single theory or model of the policy-making system, no matter how intricate. Policy-making in practice nearly always involves multiple systems, each operating on its own terms. Policy decisions and actions are the products of these systems interacting with each other, sometimes purposefully and sometimes randomly.

Chance often intervenes, too, as for example when New Zealand's Dairy and Clean Streams Accord policy was hatched in an impromptu meeting between the chairman of the country's largest dairy co-operative and a powerful regional government official in the Air New Zealand Koru Lounge at Auckland Airport (Tyson 2004). The results of policy-making processes are rarely predictable in advance and often difficult to explain even in hindsight.

We provide two small examples of how things can go wrong with the 'inside game'. Multiple forces, from internal coalition strife to external stakeholders, the media, or unforeseen events, may propel government into a panic cycle (figure 1.6). Panic-driven policy-making may, in turn, trigger an unproductive crisis management response (figure 1.7), which feeds the vicious cycle. These models describe reality, warts and all, and provide a sharp contrast to most of the descriptive policy cycle literature.

Figures 1.6 and 1.7 show that making policy 'on the fly' not only

Figure 1.6 The panic loop

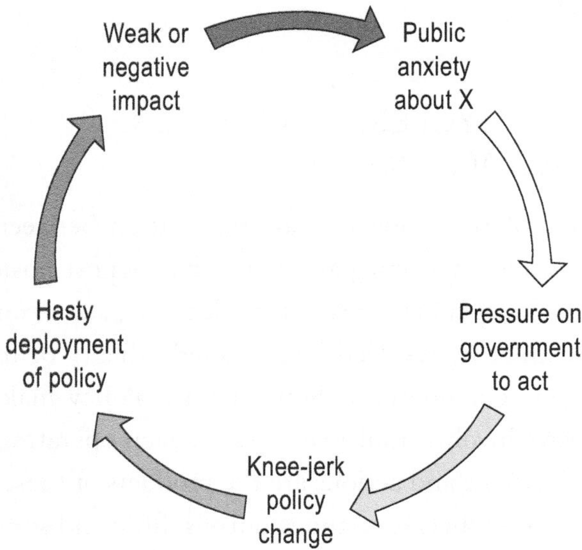

squanders opportunities for policy learning and innovation, but also carries big, downstream political risks.

Any reliable, usable model of policy-making needs to adapt to nearly constant changes, as policy-making processes adjust to meet ever-new demands and circumstances. Models should be reviewed regularly, and, if necessary, reprogrammed, upgraded, or replaced. They should feature built-in adaptability.

Perhaps what policy practitioners and theorists really need in this age of personalised, 'i'-prefixed smart-gadgets is a portable, multimedia, internet-enabled smart-model supported by a constant flow of new downloadable software applications to match every possible policy-making situation.

Dreams of technology aside, what this boils down to is the need for a more ad hoc and impromptu approach to policy models, whereby scholars and practitioners sketch the various policy pathways that they observe most often, and focus on understanding them, rather than try-

Figure 1.7 The crisis management loop

ing to design a single, universal model that explains everything from a declaration of war to a change in formulas for paying country doctors.

CONCLUSION

Policy analysis and advising are important sources of checks and balances in the Westminster constitutional tradition as well as a multi- and inter-disciplinary approach for bringing information, knowledge, wisdom, and experience to bear on public decisions. This pragmatic, opportunistic profile makes policy analysis a difficult field to model and theorise, but models abound nonetheless. Those sketched in this chapter have provided some important milestones in the development of the field; however, no single model or theory can capture the richness and complexity of the real policy-making world. In lieu of a single, grand model, ad hoc models of policy can be useful to both policy scholars and practitioners operating in a dynamic policy-making environment.

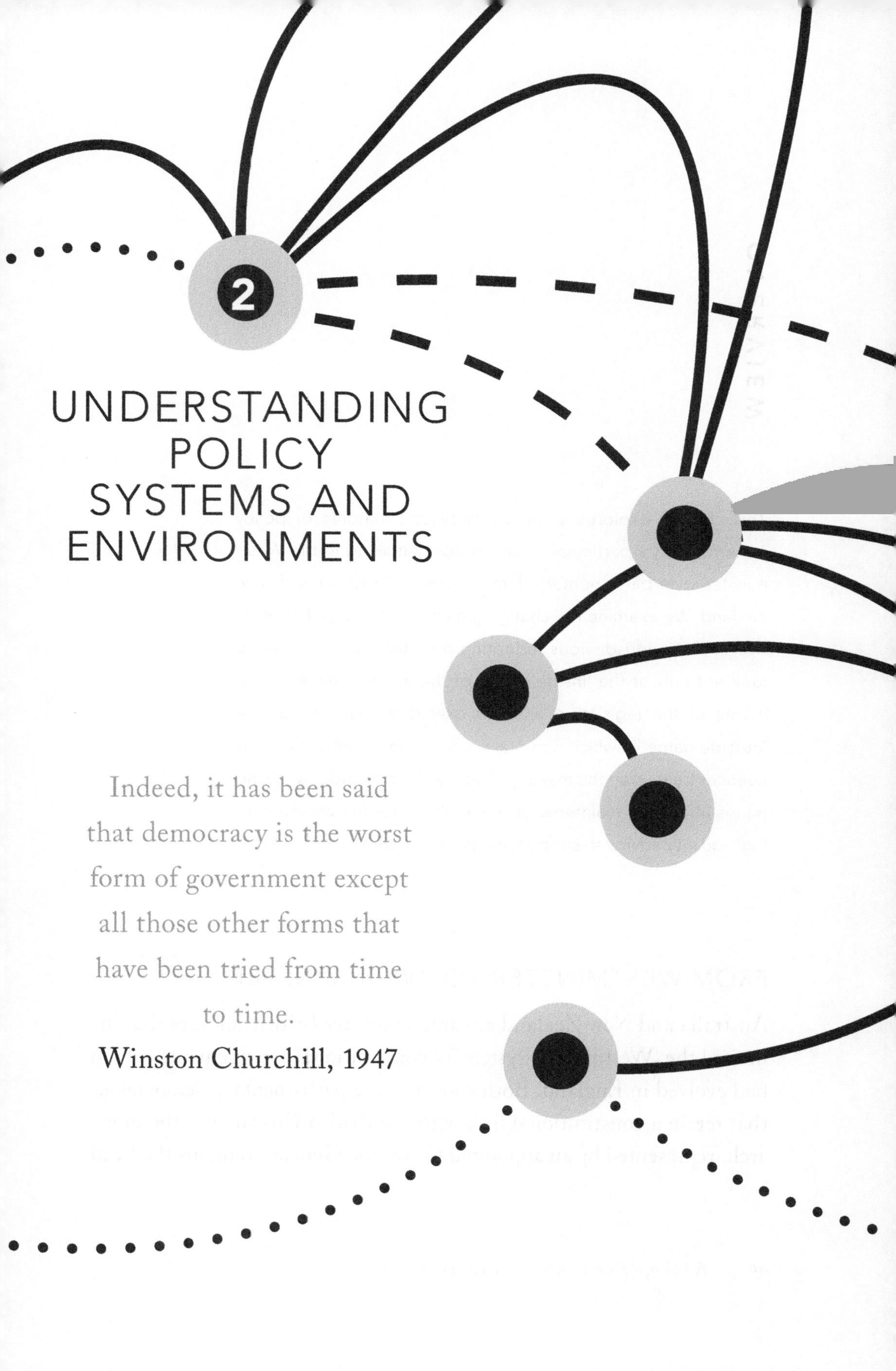

2

UNDERSTANDING POLICY SYSTEMS AND ENVIRONMENTS

Indeed, it has been said that democracy is the worst form of government except all those other forms that have been tried from time to time.

Winston Churchill, 1947

This chapter explores some characteristic features of policy systems, with a particular focus on policy-making in the Westminster-style parliamentary democracies of Australia and New Zealand. We examine the changing environment of policy practice in these jurisdictions, adopting a systems perspective to look not only at the 'inside game' of the institutional arrangements of the legislature and the executive, but also at the 'outside game' in which non-state actors and environmental influences bear upon the making of policy. We conclude by raising issues about the maintenance of capability for the provision of high-quality advice to support the policy system.

FROM WESTMINSTER TO 'WASHMINSTER'

Australia and New Zealand are among former British colonies that inherited the 'Westminster system' of constitutional arrangements, which had evolved in England. Both countries are parliamentary democracies that retain a constitutional link with the British Crown, and the monarch, represented by an appointed Governor-General, remains the head of state. This is a largely ceremonial role, but the authority of the parliaments of both countries to enact laws remains contingent upon the royal assent.

However, the convention, which is rarely if ever broken, is that the head of state acts on advice from the government. New Zealand is a unitary state; whereas the Commonwealth of Australia is a federation of states and territories, each with its own parliament in addition to the federal parliament, adding layers of complexity to the process by which policy is developed and promulgated. New Zealand has a unicameral parliament, having abolished its upper house some fifty years ago, while the Australian parliaments are bicameral, with the exception of that of Queensland.

Administrations and constitutions come in many shapes and sizes; some radical simplification is needed if we are to generalise at all about the kinds of constraints they represent on the provision of policy advice. There are two predominant global models of the inside game of policy development: the 'Westminster system' of the United Kingdom, and the 'Washington system' of the USA. The interaction between the authorising political power and the policy advisory systems is the area that especially interests us here.

Although there is some disagreement as to the defining features of a Westminster-style system, as distinct from those that are merely typical (such as bicameral parliaments), most analyses concur in treating certain features as essential: the sovereignty of parliament; ministerial accountability to parliament; concentration of power in the cabinet; an officially recognised opposition; and – the crucial criterion for our purposes – a professional, non-partisan public service (Patapan, Wanna & Weller 2005). This last item traditionally means that policy advice is given to ministers by career public servants, who are committed to providing successive governments of whatever political stripe with 'frank and fearless' advice that is based on disinterested analysis of the facts, free of ideological bias, and unfettered by short-term political imperatives.

The Westminster model of policy advising has been challenged and modified over many years, as the professional bureaucracies compete with other increasingly diverse sources of policy advice. In particular the rise of overtly political advisory influences, such as ministerial 'minders', has called into question the viability of an apolitical expert advisory service; and the career model of policy work is challenged by the rise of political appointments to advisory roles, within or alongside the public service.

Policy advisory systems in Australia and New Zealand have been changing fundamentally in response to various internal and external influences, and giving advice to ministers and governments has become more contested there as elsewhere. In Australia especially, independent 'think tanks' and consultancy firms have a growing role in providing advice to ministers on policy matters. At the same time concerns have been expressed about the quality and capability of the public-sector advisory system and its ability to contribute public value to decision-makers and citizens.

There is a perception that the Westminster policy advisory model has been mutating to produce 'Washminster' systems – hybrid offspring of the Westminster and Washington models, increasingly resembling the more politicised advisory arrangements that prevail in the USA. The term has been used particularly about Australia, which has a system of federal and state and territory governments, like the USA and Canada. Both developed strongly bipartisan systems, with Labour parties resembling their British counterpart (and roughly equivalent to the Democrats in the US scheme); the other end of the political spectrum has been represented by the Liberal and National Parties in Australia and the National Party in New Zealand in recent times.

The value that the Westminster system attaches to a formal opposition, recognised as a government-in-waiting, is premised on a two-party system, which the Australian preferential voting system continues to deliver. The introduction of a proportional representation system in New Zealand in 1996, however, has brought a number of smaller parties into parliament and has delivered successive coalition governments. So far there has always been one dominant opposition party, which on some issues has acted in concert with smaller opposition parties.

The Westminster policy systems in Australia and New Zealand have changed in many ways in recent years in response to various pressures influencing policy-making the world over. Some of these pressures for change derive from globalisation itself, which has removed some of the discretion governments once had to adopt policy settings that were not aligned to those in other countries. Open economies can constrain the policy choices open to any government.

For example, inconsistencies of policies across jurisdictions have been cited as undermining Australian competitiveness. There is general agreement that Australia is over-governed, but no clear consensus as to the appropriate alternative. Twomey and Withers (2007) have suggested that a two-tier structure would enable federalism to reach its full potential in the six C's: check on power, choice, customisation of policies, competition, creativity, and co-operation.

The 'wicked' issues that increasingly challenge policy makers are no respecters of borders or sovereignty. For example, global warming demands a comprehensive and expensive response from every country. On the plus side, globalisation means that a substantial international evidence base is becoming available to guide policy analysis.

The international homogeneity brought about by globalisation is provoking a countervailing response in some countries, in the form of pressure for more differentiation at regional and local levels, sometimes called 'glocalisation'. In the context of policy development, it fosters consultation, participation and co-production in search of locally specific solutions to local issues. It thus encourages governments to look beyond their internal resources for policy ideas, challenging the closed institutional basis of policy development through reliance on professional bureaucracies.

Joined-up government

Policy problems have also changed, growing harder to resolve. As the policy agenda shifts from simple problems to complex multi-sectoral and social and environmental issues, government agencies have been asked to work together across organisational boundaries, in search of consistency and critical mass. Various initiatives have sought to improve the collective governmental response, such as work in Australia by the Management Advisory Committee (MAC 2004) and the New Zealand State Service Commission's 'no wrong door' philosophy regarding its dealings with the public.

The trend toward whole-of-government responses to policy challenges raises co-ordination issues. These are more pronounced in Australia because the federal system involves multiple levels of government, and there are major differences in policy development practices between the various states and between federal and state levels of government. A strengthening of central agencies has been necessary to provide linkages between government and the private and community sectors, to establish public–private partnerships, and to facilitate the contracting out of service delivery. In New Zealand and Australia state organisations have sometimes responded adversely to this trend toward whole-of-government co-ordination in the policy development environment. Sometimes internal competition between government agencies for a leadership role in a policy area results in high transaction costs as efforts and resources are spread thinly across several agencies whose agendas are not well aligned.

Consultation and co-operation with non-government actors

Advisers and decision-makers have come to appreciate the benefits of input from stakeholders and peak organisations into policy development, especially in dealing with the public. However, individual citizens and groups have needed to improve their understanding of policy processes to participate effectively in the development of policy affecting them.

In Australia and New Zealand consultation and engagement with citizens in the policy process has become increasingly common. Citizen engagement seeks to avoid implementation failure, when governments unleash policy changes only to find the community lacks ownership of either problems or solutions. There is concern, however, that extensive public participation in policy-making reduces the ability of elected representatives to provide leadership, and incurs high transaction costs; and doubt has been cast on the idea that consensus can be procured by extending the range of participants in the policy development system.

Governments are increasingly going beyond fulfilling consultation requirements into working with external partners on policy development in deeper forms of engagement that accord a more active role to outside parties. The theory of collaborative advantage (Huxham 2003) proposes that better outcomes can be achieved by facilitating networked collaboration between the public, private and community sectors, rather than relying upon internal resources. Australia has had more experience than New Zealand of collaborating with and contracting out policy work to the private and community sectors. Shortly after the Australian Labor Party won the 2007 federal election, Prime Minister Kevin Rudd announced an intention to draw more heavily on the private and community sectors in policy development, and to broaden the experience base of public servants.

Policy, politics and advice

The intersection of policy and politics gives rise to complexity in public policy work, particularly when electoral advantage is an implicit criterion alongside the others in evaluating policy options. Some languages use the same word for policy and politics, and practice in certain cultures reflects this verbal and conceptual convergence. A distinction between politics and policy, however, is deeply embedded in Anglophone culture and institutions, and specifically in the Westminster ideal of an apolitical public service. It is a subtle distinction at times, and one that requires a 'fine balance between determining what might be the "political" context for particular policy advice and introducing partisan elements' (Weller & Stevens 1998:584)

These changes in the environment for policy advising create both opportunities for and threats to the traditional public-sector advisory system. Australian governments appear to be migrating toward a Washington-style model, in which public-sector advisers several layers down the system are politically appointed, and change with each change of government. At both state and Commonwealth levels in Australia, it is common for some senior government appointments to change with a new government, while this practice is much less common in New Zealand.

New Zealand's MMP system involves post-election agreements and policy developments need to be negotiated issue by issue, which involves a great deal of brokering across party lines. While an independent and apolitical public service is maintained, ministerial advisers as well as politicians have become increasingly involved in this deal-making process. While developing cross-party support is essential for a government to function in the MMP environment, it is inappropriate for a public servant to assume this role in a Westminster-style advisory system.

Public servants need an acute awareness of political considerations, such as the collective policy priorities of the government of the day, the expressed interests of the relevant minister, and the views of stakeholders who could threaten the policy's successful implementation. They also need to know where the boundary lies between legitimate political concerns and the no-fly zone of party political interests.

Partisan politics are strictly off limits for public officials, at least in principle. In practice, however, it can be difficult to distinguish between appropriate and inappropriate demands. For example, officials and ministers should know the difference between writing the factual, analytical, and argumentative portions of a minister's speech and applying the spin. But is the boundary between the two always clear in any particular sentence or paragraph? Not necessarily.

Similarly, officials have a genuine obligation to engage with community leaders who can shed light on a policy problem and help ensure the final policy's operational success. But they should not be required to do so just because particular community leaders are close to the minister or the party in power. Are the two kinds of community influence easy to distinguish? Not always, and therefore 'stakeholder analysis' easily slides into partisan considerations.

Officials may be tempted to shield their ministers from unwanted policy proposals. But ministers themselves need to make the final judgments to resist or co-operate with such proposals, armed with all the relevant information that the officials can provide; second-guessing ultimately reduces the decision-making power of those elected to serve. Officials who adopt the role of the decision-maker's proxy can interfere with a healthy process of political debate and negotiation. Knowing what to filter for the minister and when requires tremendous maturity on the part of public servants, as well as clear judgment and the courage of their convictions. No wonder the Westminster ideals are continually under pressure.

Indeed, we have sensed a growing strain of resigned acceptance that the traditional Westminster ideals cannot long survive. Formulae such as 'frank and fearless' advice are sometimes treated as quaint relics of a bygone era, particularly in and around the Australian public service, where hard-nosed political realism is *de rigueur*.

The growth of special or 'ministerial' advisers in Australia has altered the scene – either aggravating or alleviating these political dilemmas for public servants, depending on local practices and perceptions. The number of ministerial staffers is substantial in Australia (in 2006, 469, relative to 78 in the United Kingdom, 201 in Canada and 51 in New Zealand (Tiernan 2007:26)), and many of them have political ambitions. They are a new and important player in the policy game and can often play a gatekeeper role (Anderson in Colebatch (2006)). A particular tension arises as public-service advisers work with and alongside ministerial advisers, sometimes impeding the ability of public service advisers to offer 'frank and fearless' advice. At times analysis and politics appear to be on a veritable collision course, with the former interested in clarifying issues, and the latter preferring to obscure them and to pursue immediate political advantage irrespective of probable outcomes in the longer term.

The 'children overboard' episode in Australia (Weller 2002) is a vivid demonstration that ministerial advisers were willing to misrepresent events for the short-term political advantage of their minister. In *Power without Responsibility*, Anne Tiernan charts the rise of ministerial minders over the past thirty years, noting their growing numbers, seniority and status, suggesting that ministerial staff are 'out of control' and pose risks for ministers, the public service and Australia's system of governance. The introduction of a code of conduct for ministerial advisers working in the Commonwealth has been a response to some of these concerns.

There is another view on the matter, which is that Ministers need support and advice and ministerial advisers can play a very valuable role in a Westminster system. They can insulate public servants from political demands and allow them to focus on providing apolitical professional advice. When there is a good understanding of roles and respect among the parties, public service advisers and ministerial advisers can and do work together effectively, providing ministers with professional and political advice to inform policy choices. The nature and magnitude of the issue varies across jurisdictions and New Zealand experiences are different from those at Commonwealth and state levels in Australia. Eichbaum and Shaw 2008 suggest the need for a more nuanced examination and discussion of the relationships between ministers, public servants and ministerial advisers.

Michael Keating's (1996:66) model of the 'essential partnership' aptly describes the proper division of labour between public servants and political advisers:

> Public servants should contribute a depth of analysis,
> sustained coverage of issues over long periods of time, an
> understanding of how realities of implementation need to
> influence policy design and a corporate memory. Ministerial
> staffers' particular contributions will be fast footwork, capacity
> for trouble-shooting, immediate access to the Ministers and a
> good knowledge about the political, media and parliamentary
> environments.

If so inclined, ministerial staff could take the political heat off their public service counterparts, and create a buffer between public servants and ministerial politics, rather than dragging everyone into the party-political game. In practice, the nature of these relationships depends heavily on the styles, beliefs, and personalities of all involved, including ministers themselves.

Scott Prasser (2006) in an article on 'Providing Advice to Government in Australia' describes some of the difficulties that beset a bureaucracy providing 'cold' (rational) advice in a climate where 'hot' (political, emotive) advice is what politicians think they need (table 2.1).

Table 2.1 Comparing rational (cold) and political (hot) advice

Rational (cold) advice	Political (hot) advice
Information based	Relies on fragmented information, gossip
Research used	Opinion / ideologically based
Independent / neutral and problem solving	Partisan / biased and about winning
Long term	Short term
Proactive and anticipatory	Reactive / crisis driven
Strategic and wide range / systemic	Single issues
Idealistic	Pragmatic
Public interest focus	Electoral gain oriented
Open processes	Secret / deal making
Objective clarity	Ambiguity / overlapping goals
Seek / propose best solution	Consensus solution

SOURCE Prasser (2006)

Prasser also analyses the influences that can make policy go astray. Many of them derive from the political environment, such as dominant ideologies, which are hard to shift even when the evidence does not support them, and party and organisational tensions and politics.

What about the reverse of the politicisation problem – excessive independence on the part of policy advisers? Tempting as it may be at times, public servants should not try to divine the public interest entirely by their own lights, or take policy-making into their own hands. Policy analysts, advisers, designers, and implementation planners always need to take account of political conditions, including the views of the government of the day and the known views of operationally relevant stakeholder groups. Fortunately, this message appears to be well understood much of the time.

As Keating (1996:114) observed about Australia: 'I don't see that most public servants are constantly tortured souls, if I can put it that way, having to decide between what they think is in the public interest and what the government philosophy is.' Although Keating's observations hold in New Zealand too, a few more 'tortured souls' may be found on the eastern side of the Tasman Sea because of the apparently greater robustness of the 'free and frank' ideal there, and its inevitable tendency to clash occasionally with what ministers want.

How do public officials cope with the challenge of balancing independence and responsiveness? Keating suggests that they cope by understanding that there are multiple legitimate points of view on what constitutes the public interest. The government's framework is one particular way of seeing the public interest and one way of pursuing it, but not necessarily the only one. The government's position should always be tested rigorously, and advice should be based on the results of that testing; but once the government has taken a decision, good practice norms require public servants to back off. No nagging, no sulking is allowed.

Gary Hawke (1993:64) has observed that the more difficult balancing act may be between short- and long-term concerns or, as he expresses it, 'between producing what the minister wants now, investing staff time in ensuring that a project is well defined and properly managed to produce what the minister wants in the reasonably near future, and thinking about the issues which will be prominent in a year or so'. Hawke endorses the need for policy advice agencies to consider issues that a future government will need to be informed about, and notes the sometimes delicate trade-off between 'preparation for the future' and 'minimisation of political embarrassment' stemming from potential requests for official information. The future-oriented developmental work is sometimes harder to justify in departmental budgets, and is therefore always vulnerable from a resource perspective.

PUBLIC SECTOR POLICY SKILLS

While the public sector employs many people with technical skills and expertise, public-sector advisory work is largely done by generalists with good research, problem-solving and communication skills. When policy advisers decide how to progress policy work on a specific issue, they draw on knowledge, skills and capabilities more often associated with art, science and craft. Aspects of science are involved as advisers bring together information and evidence and apply specific methods – such as modelling or cost–benefit analysis – to project the outcomes of different policy proposals and make judgments regarding their merits. The highly specific features of some issues and the requirements of clients and stakeholder groups also require analysts to develop softer skills and capabilities, involving judgment rather than technical analysis.

Increasing public participation in policy development is putting pressure on policy officials to build their facilitation skills. As policy-makers increasingly recognise the need to engage with a broad range of actors and institutions outside the formal government policy cycle, the roles of policy advisers and analysts are changing to accommodate this recognition.

Policy advisers at any level need a good understanding of the environment in which policy is developed, including the relationships between policy advisers, decision-makers, and stakeholder groups. Analysts and advisers also need a good appreciation of the rationale behind the policy stances taken by key actors in the authorising environment.

Skilled policy developers hone their craft and develop the insights necessary to combine analysis with judgment in designing policies, managing policy agendas, and helping governments develop effective policies and programs.

The art, science, and craft of public service policy work fills a vital niche in Westminster-derived constitutional monarchies such as Australia and New Zealand, serving to provide checks and balances against short-term, partisan imperatives and poorly conceived policies. When the system is working as intended, advice delivered by the public service differs from all other competing sources of advice in its freedom from vested interest, its greater reliance on professional disciplines, its transparency and its continuity between governments. Unlike other advice providers, it could be said that public officials are expected to be biased toward the well-being of all citizens, not just the loudest or most powerful or most politically salient; biased toward sound reasoning and evidence; and biased toward the collectively determined priorities of the government of the day, but with an ear always cocked for issues awaiting future governments. These duties are sometimes rolled into the shorthand term 'impartiality', but it fails to capture the rich subtleties of the role.

A SYSTEMS PERSPECTIVE

In this section we introduce the systems perspective that we see as necessary for approaching complex problems or those where there is uncertainty about causes and effects, so a wide net must be cast to capture all the influences that should be taken into account. In later chapters we describe a range of useful tools and methods to assist in producing policy advice that is 'fit for purpose' in addressing different kinds of problems.

The systems perspective is not new to policy writing, nor is it a general theory that seeks to replace other useful approaches. Its purpose is to reach beyond some of the limitations of those policy models that restrict the scope of inquiry into a problem, limit the actors engaged in the search for solutions, or tilt the proposed solution toward government-led policy action.

A systems approach to policy analysis and advisory work focuses on the dynamic interactions between actors, institutions and influences, rather than upon static structures. And it looks beyond the 'inside game' of the institutional arrangements of the legislature and the executive, to the 'outside game' in which non-state actors and environmental influences bear upon the making of policy.

This is not to offer a complete, monolithic model of 'the system', in either a descriptive or a normative sense; it is simply acknowledging that the business of policy-making is affected by and influences multiple interacting systems beyond the institutional boundaries of governmental systems. No single model or approach accounts for this complex of systems sufficiently for either theoretical or practical purposes. Our response is to draw upon multiple models and approaches to policy work, acknowledging their usefulness and their limitations, in search of an accurate perspective and a thorough understanding.

Policy analysis and advising for ministers and elected officials are undertaken most obviously by public servants in government ministries and departments. Policy work is also done by many other people in the public and private sectors who make contributions to policy analysis and advisory work. These individuals, organisations and institutions will rarely have such direct involvement in offering governments ways to address issues of public concern.

Government policy-making institutions establish and perpetuate formal systems and processes to order and manage the development and tendering of policy advice. They operate at all levels, starting relatively low – drafting responses to correspondence from the public ('ministerials') is a routine task for many a junior policy adviser. Departmental officers also research and draft responses to questions for oral answer in the House; and there is a highly formalised process by which cabinet papers – substantial policy proposals from departments or ministries – are drafted and submitted for the cabinet's consideration. These institutional systems are adjusted incrementally to suit the changing management environment, and the preferences and priorities of successive governments, but they are relatively stable.

Their method of working is largely predictable: the options for solving the problem to hand are determined, and their costs and benefits compared systematically, in order to recommend the one that promises the greatest benefit. This assumption is reflected in various models of or heuristics for policy advising, many of which refer to 'the policy cycle' as if it were a fixed, predictable, self-contained entity.

'Cycle' models, as described in the previous chapter, treat policy development as authoritative decision-making by a process with prescribed steps. This view of the policy-making process is sound enough as an account of the routine process of decision-making, in which the policy analyst is cast as an objective technician, charged with imposing a rational, selective framework on problems and potential solutions. Stakeholders are involved only as sources of information, or as a sounding board for solutions developed within the government advisory system. There may be some provision for consultation during the policy development process, but often more with a view to informing stakeholders about existing options and enlisting their support than to mutual engagement in developing and analysing policy options.

The linear, top-down approach suits public-sector agencies, where policy design is in practice a process, with an institutional framework, and advisers have specific clients in the form of their managers and a political decision-maker. But they are also expressly employees or 'servants' of 'the public', and a wider 'outside game' therefore demands recognition. When Weimer and Vining (2004:27), for example, define policy analysis as 'client-oriented advice relevant to public decisions and informed by social values', the last component acknowledges the context from which policy derives value and legitimacy.

Many authors have commented on the changing policy environment and suggested that its greater complexity in these environments demands new models and skills (Bochel & Duncan 2007; Briggs 2005; Howard 2005; Roberts 2000; Scott 2003, 2005, 2008; Tiernan, Wanna & Edwards 2009).

We argue for understanding the policy environment still more broadly – not only including the citizenry from which it derives its mandate, but taking in the whole context, local and international, economic, political, geographical, ideological. This means that policy analysis has to look beyond the 'inside game' involving advisers and their immediate clients, and recognise the multifarious changing influences, local and global, that shape the environment in which the need for policy arises. Policy must consult the 'outside game' not only to retain legitimacy, but also in order to respond innovatively and effectively to policy challenges. This is not an argument for vast increases in expenditure on policy analysis to ensure that no stone has been left unturned, but rather for taking the time to determine all the major influences at work, in order to get an unbiased picture of the situation and possible alternative approaches to a solution.

The inside game is not hermetically self-contained. Its boundaries with the wider world are porous, and their actors and influences interpenetrate extensively. The institutionally-bounded inside game of generalist policy professionals has itself changed significantly, as the policy environment has become more contestable, especially since the public-sector management reforms of the 1980s and 1990s. Many more government and other agencies now provide input into advice, introducing more perspectives, and creating a need for co-ordination and coherence. And increasingly the government policy institutions are tapping into sources of expertise and knowledge entirely outside of the public sector; public agencies contract out a good deal of specialised advisory work, and buy in expert advice from diverse sources.

The outside game: network, world or universe

A systems perspective takes in the larger, messier influences of the outside game upon policy, which are much less amenable to capture by tidy institutional processes for linear decision-making than the inside game. Looking through a much wider lens, various theorists (Considine 2005; Easton 1965; Howlett & Ramesh 2003) have proposed a policy *world* or even *universe*, in which very broad groupings of actors and institutions operate, identified as 'state', 'international' and 'societal' in Howlett and Ramesh's approach. They interact dynamically, exchanging information and exerting influence, in order to advance their various interests, creating a turbulent environment.

This kind of perspective differs from the narrower view not only in its reach, but also in its conceptual foundation. Considine (2005) suggests a radical re-definition of policy as the work done by groups of policy actors who use the available public institutions to articulate the things they value. Actors and institutions conceived this way include not just individuals and groups, but also their rules, norms, principles and ideas. This thinking reaches outside the formal government advisory system and challenges the more instrumental view of public policy as serial problem-solving to understand it as something more like navigating a complex, rapidly-changing map.

The outside game is complicated by growing expectations from the public that policy processes should be more participatory and inclusive of 'the community'. The concept of community, imprecise as it is, is also changing relationships between state democracies, market capitalism and civil society, leading to consultation mechanisms and partnerships of various types (Adams & Hess 2001).

This more inclusive view of the policy system puts the spotlight on the way democratic governments exercise the power and authority granted to them by citizens to impose taxes and decide how to spend them, and maintain their citizens' confidence. It throws a different light on the authorising environment from which policy derives its legitimacy. The simpler linear view traces the influence of power from the public as electors to the government, then from the government as elected representatives back to the public via the agency of the policy system. But the more participatory conception of democracy resists this linearity, involving public input into policy at various points in the 'policy cycle' by means of consultative processes.

This trend has diminished opportunities for public servants to drive the policy design agenda, to play the role of 'objective technician'; while it has expanded the policy world or universe – the range of considerations analysts and advisers must consult, and the relationships they must negotiate.

Taking a broader view of the role of societal actors in policy development means acknowledging the forces of societal change and the fact of globalisation, which has posed tough new problems for the makers of public policy. Concerns about terrorism and global warming, for example, are shaping domestic policy in many countries; and trade and defence agreements and international conventions have their domestic policy implications, as do relations with international organisations.

Borders have become increasingly porous to financial dealings and economic influences. Societal change and globalisation converge in the emergence of intractable or 'wicked' issues, which often cross jurisdictional boundaries and on which there is no consensus as to definitions, never mind solutions, and often no clear mandate to act. Such issues challenge conventional public policy systems, in respect of the legitimacy and also the effectiveness of their responses.

A comprehensive systems approach to policy development, then, should look to both legitimacy and efficacy, attending to both inside imperatives and the enormous, turbulent realities of the 'outside game'. This will mean taking in the interaction of state and non-state actors, and integrating applied problem-solving with an understanding of public concerns and political risks.

It will mean staying plugged in to media sources and to the knowledge and understandings being generated in policy 'networks' and 'communities'; it will mean awareness of economic, social and environmental pressures, as well as domestic and international political imperatives.

MODELLING THE POLICY SYSTEM

No linear or cyclical model will capture the complex and volatile realities of the policy world, or their implications for policy formation. In practice, policy tasks are encountered as collections of imperatives, some deriving from the outside, some from the inside game, in various combinations and proportions, with varying degrees of urgency, sensitivity and tractability. Any attempt to model the whole as a single system is likely to yield something too elaborate and too subject to qualification and variation to be of much practical use.

Attempts to theorise or describe the policy universe typically come with diagrams, maps, or other graphic representations of its components, contours and processes. They are usually least satisfactory when they claim to represent the entire policy universe, more successful when they depict only particular aspects of it. It is preferable to exploit the strengths of various descriptions and theories to deal with the complexity.

In chapter 1 we looked at various multi-stage models such as those of Bardach (2009) and Althaus, Bridgman and Davis (2007). They offer approaches to problem-solving and decision-making, with a focus

Figure 2.1   Policy roles and styles

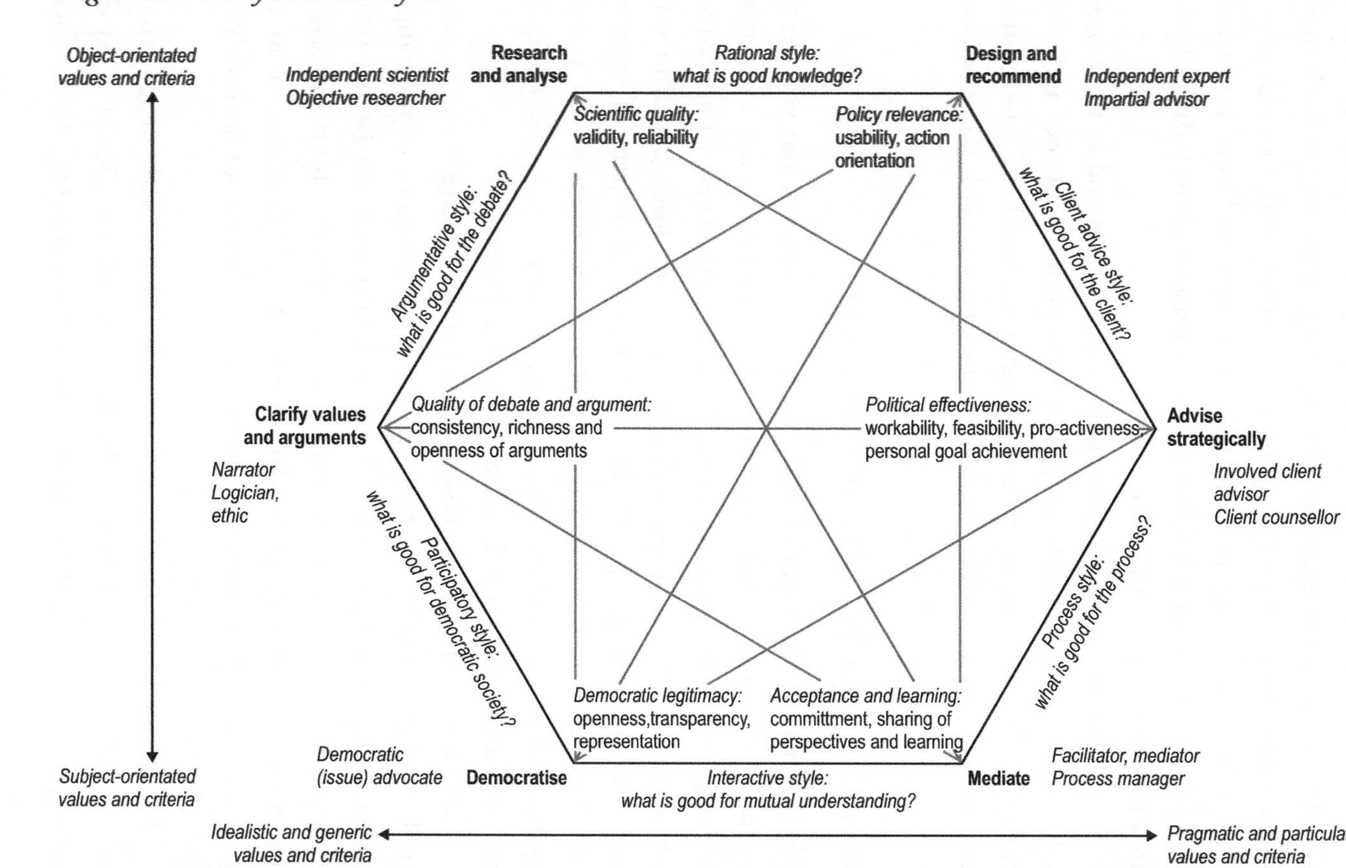

SOURCE Mayer, van Daalen and Bots (2004)

on the generalisable intellectual activity involved in policy processes. There are, however, models that take a more practical, less abstract view of the work of policy practitioners, and are thus better equipped to recognise the complexities of the outside game and of policy responses to its contingencies.

Mayer, van Daalen and Bots (2004) have developed a mapping of policy roles, based on an analysis of actual policy work in the Netherlands, which takes into account the multiplicity of methods and ways of working and the roles of various actors and institutions in the policy system. The Mayer et al framework sought to strengthen and legitimise the profession and its value for the public decision-making process. It was developed to '(re)structure the discipline of policy analysis into a single conceptual model', but it also has a very practical dimension resulting from its foundation in detailed observation of real practice, despite its avoidance of prescription. The framework serves three purposes – understanding policy analysis as a discipline, contributing to the design of new policy analysis methods and projects, and providing guidance for evaluating such projects and methods.

The Mayer et al framework is based on six 'archetypal policy activities'. Other elements, such as policy 'styles' for various purposes and contexts, and underlying values and criteria, have been layered on these activities (figure 2.1).

The model distinguishes between object- and subject-oriented criteria and values on one axis and between idealistic, generic values and pragmatic, particular ones on the other. In the model these variables are linked to the roles and tasks to be undertaken by policy analysts and the selection of particular policy tools and methods. It is multi-dimensional, showing the dynamic relationships between the various elements of the policy analysis process and the role of the analyst undertaking it. The framework helps to determine which steps are relevant to the particular policy analysis being undertaken. It is flexible and versatile, and encourages the analyst to use the framework to design processes customised to the task at hand.

The Mayer et al framework may confer competitive value on advice (Scott 2005), because it encourages innovation and creativity. It has responded to the evolving and maturing of the field of policy analysis, and offers potential for further development. However, its complexity makes it difficult to understand and apply consistently.

Both the Bardach and Mayer et al models can be useful to advisers and analysts. The complexity of the Mayer et al framework requires a sophisticated understanding so may suit more seasoned practitioners, while Bardach's checklist approach can be a useful starting point. Both models recognise the need for a tailored approach to policy work, but Mayer et al acknowledge citizens and key stakeholders as clients and key actors in policy advisory work. The models can be combined – it is possible to fit many of the roles undertaken by Bardach into the top part of the Dutch hexagon.

POLICY SCENARIOS

In lieu of a single, grand model of policy-making, we present here some common scenarios of policy development in Australia and New Zealand. They are not comprehensive, universally applicable, or definitive, but they highlight the many routes that influences on policy development can follow, and they show the interpenetration of the outside and inside games. They illustrate the need for a systems perspective on complex issues.

Although each policy-making event is unique in its details, certain recognisable patterns can be observed emerging repeatedly out of the mass of particulars. Figures 2.2 to 2.4 depict familiar policy development scenarios pieced together from our observations. The sketches that follow represent recurring sequences of events that fall out somewhat predictably in certain circumstances.

Take the 'Crisis and reaction' scenario from figure 2.2. Although governments come to power with carefully planned and negotiated policy agendas, unpredictable events often overtake them. Earthquakes, cyclones, terrorist attacks, epidemics, scientific breakthroughs, and financial windfalls or collapses remind us that both disasters and opportunities can bring crisis. When the outside world breaks in on the policy-making world suddenly and dramatically, rapid response and adaptation are required. Policy responses are made in the heat of the moment.

Such events call for multiple measures to manage the situation, reduce confusion, minimise damage, remedy harm, and take steps to prevent a recurrence if possible, or to prepare effectively for inevitable recurrence. Short-term measures will necessarily be rolled out in haste, but if government moves into the 'Learning from experience' scenario in figure 2.2, the problems that inevitably arise from hasty program interventions can be analysed in real time and remedied. Governments that adapt well to crises and adjust their responses on the basis of early feedback are more likely to succeed in managing the situation, reassuring the affected populations, and minimising both real and political damage. Governments that plunge ahead with ill-conceived or poorly implemented responses may find themselves in a downward spiral of failure known as a policy fiasco (the US federal government response to Hurricane Katrina comes to mind).

Governments that botch the reaction to a crisis can expect opposition parties to capitalise on their failure, plunging them into a round of 'Ritual combat' politics (figure 2.2) and drawing valuable attention and resources away from addressing the crisis itself. The slightest whiff of policy failure is sure to bring a stampede of opposition denunciations and media exposés. Ritual combat politics of varying intensities accompany all of the policy scenarios and play a vital role in keeping govern-

Figure 2.2 Policy scenarios 1

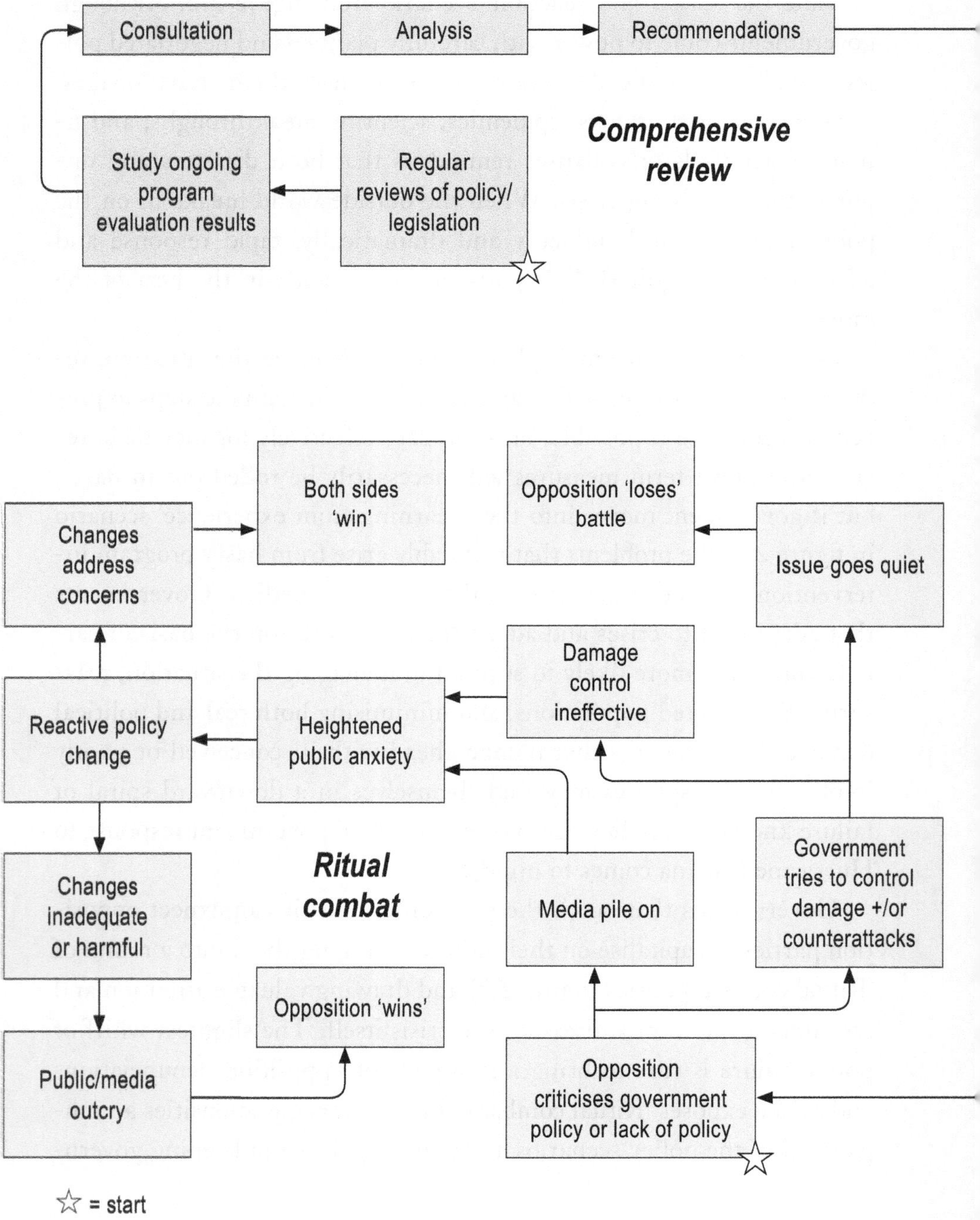

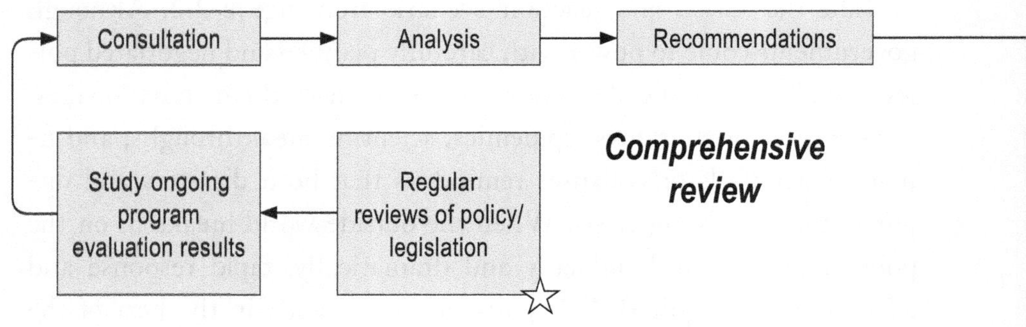

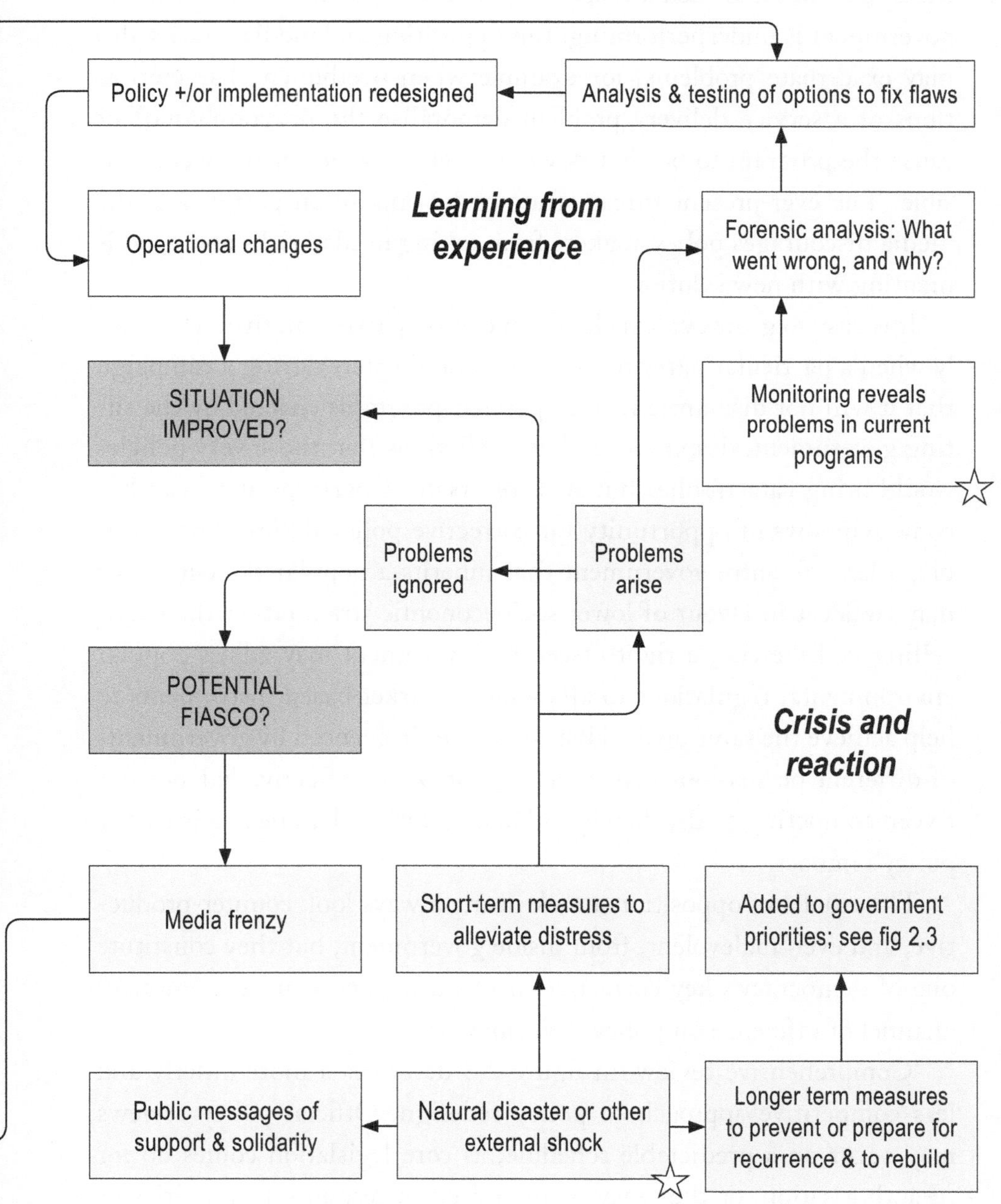

Policy +/or implementation redesigned
Analysis & testing of options to fix flaws
Learning from experience
Operational changes
Forensic analysis: What went wrong, and why?
SITUATION IMPROVED?
Monitoring reveals problems in current programs
Problems ignored
Problems arise
POTENTIAL FIASCO?
Crisis and reaction
Media frenzy
Short-term measures to alleviate distress
Added to government priorities; see fig 2.3
Public messages of support & solidarity
Natural disaster or other external shock
Longer term measures to prevent or prepare for recurrence & to rebuild

ments alert. When the system is working well, combined pressure from the opposition and media helps bring needed attention to areas where government is underperforming. But opposition and media attacks also may exacerbate problems, for example when overblown characterisations of a service delivery problem demoralise the program's staff or cause the program to be shut down altogether when repairs were possible. The ever-present threat of attack by opposition parties and the media discourages policy-makers from taking needed risks and experimenting with new solutions.

It is easy to grow cynical about opposition parties' motives, especially when a particular party reassures potential voters during a campaign that it will not dismantle various popular programs enacted by the sitting government, despite its earlier predictions that those very policies would bring catastrophe. But such reversals of party position can become windows of opportunity for corrective policy design. For example, a left-of-centre government that inherits a popular tax-cut policy may tweak it in favour of lower socioeconomic strata rather than cancelling it. Likewise, a right-of-centre government may adjust popular environmental regulations to allow more market-based instruments to help achieve the same goals. Hybrid policies influenced by governments of different persuasions can sometimes strike an effective balance between competing goals, thereby enhancing rather than neutralising the policy's impact.

The rituals of opposition attack nearly always look counter-productive, and even malevolent, from inside government, but they constitute one of democracy's key corrective mechanisms and can be a powerful channel of influence on policy development.

'Comprehensive review' in figure 2.2 describes a more orderly and less competitive approach to policy redesign. Official policy reviews may occur on a predictable schedule, as core legislation comes up for re-authorisation, or they may be organised in response to inquiries or censure of various types. Official reviews allow assessors to step back and scrutinise the performance of programs, probe their logic, gather evidence about their effectiveness, and recommend changes to improve performance. Depending on the interest shown by stakeholders, opposition parties and the media, such reviews may proceed in relative peace, or they may be subjected to the most intimate 24/7 scrutiny. Either way, the opportunities to learn from evaluation findings and from the monitoring of experience in implementation agencies are valuable sources of policy learning.

Other avenues for policy development and reform include pressure from key figures inside or outside government who take on the role of 'Policy Entrepreneurship', independent bodies such as Royal Commissions that are charged with responsibility for making 'Policy at arm's length', or policy analysts and advisers who provide early warning systems of issues in 'Anticipation' mode (figure 2.3).

In the latter case, advisers function as eyes and ears for ministers, alerting them to changes in the policy environment and foreseeing problems and opportunities so that advance action can be taken and solutions devised. By contrast, policy entrepreneurs tend to be committed to advancing a particular policy or program idea, and they set about to mobilise resources and support for their preferred intervention.

Royal Commissions are one vehicle for arm's-length policy analysis, but they are sometimes viewed with suspicion as plots to bury rather than address policy issues. Governments may indeed use independent policy processes cynically, to avoid the political risks of either decisive action or open refusal to act, but they usually pay a price in reputation. A better use for Royal Commissions is to explore creative solutions to policy issues that have become mired in partisanship.

Policy analysts and advisers cannot control government's motives for reviewing policy, but they can take each exercise seriously and generate the kinds of analytical findings that cannot easily be ignored. The ex-

Figure 2.3 Policy scenarios 2

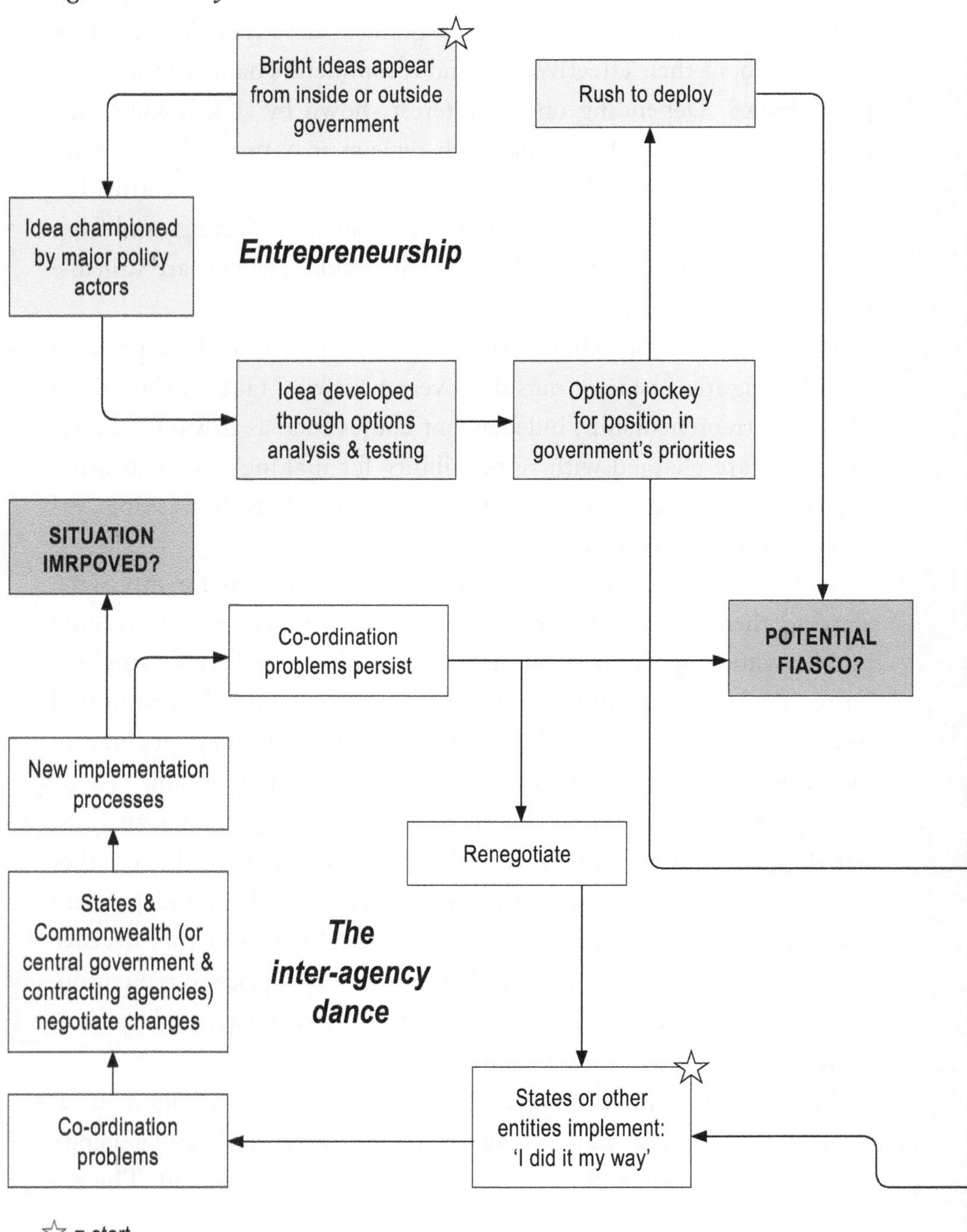

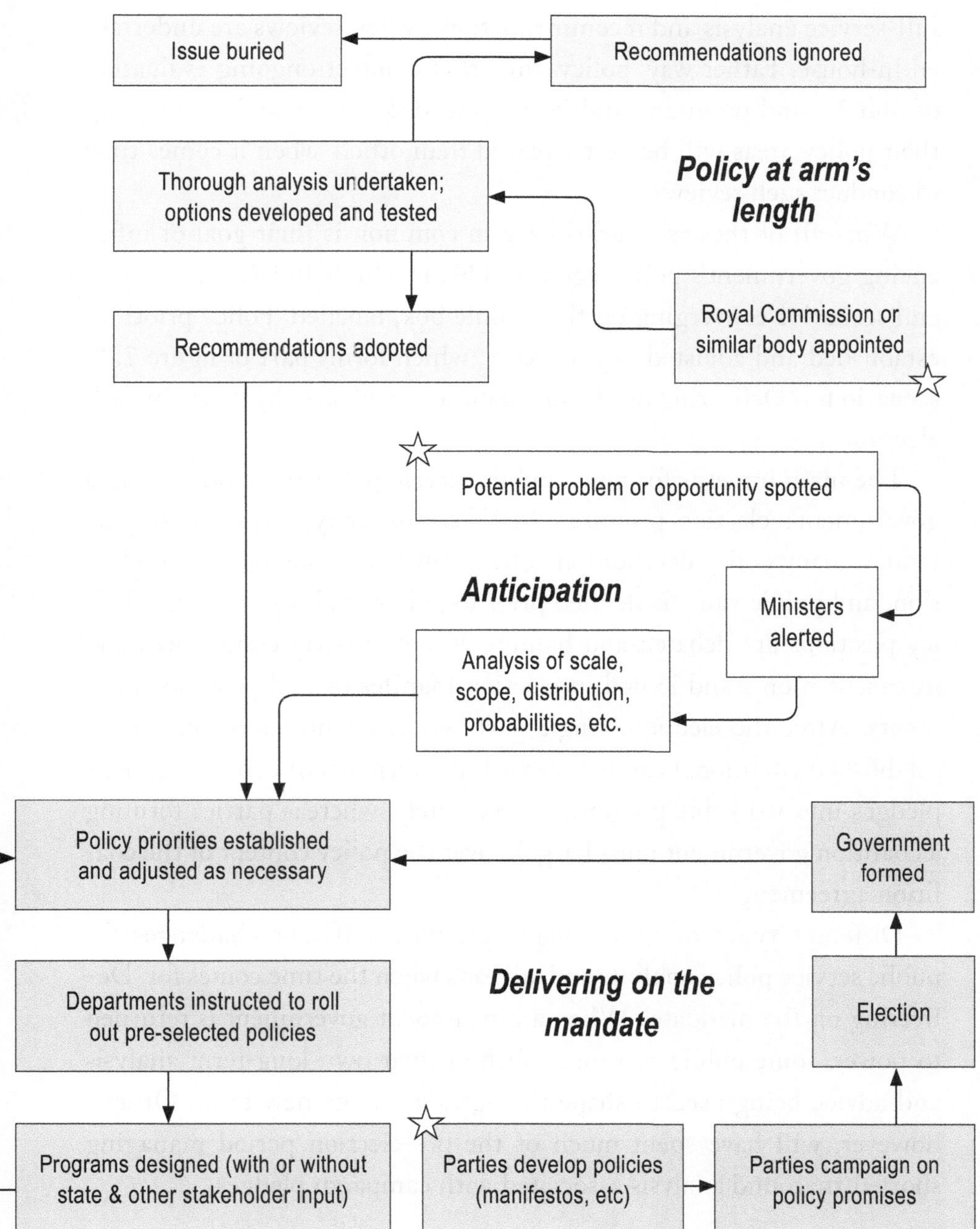

Issue buried
Recommendations ignored
Policy at arm's length
Thorough analysis undertaken; options developed and tested
Royal Commission or similar body appointed
Recommendations adopted
Potential problem or opportunity spotted
Anticipation
Ministers alerted
Analysis of scale, scope, distribution, probabilities, etc.
Policy priorities established and adjusted as necessary
Government formed
Departments instructed to roll out pre-selected policies
Delivering on the mandate
Election
Programs designed (with or without state & other stakeholder input)
Parties develop policies (manifestos, etc)
Parties campaign on policy promises

pected role of public servants in this scenario varies from co-operation with outside assessors, when independent reviews are undertaken, to full-service analysis and recommendations, when reviews are undertaken in-house. Either way, policy units that conduct ongoing evaluation of policies and programs and keep up to date on research concerning their policy areas will be better placed than others when it comes time to conduct such reviews.

What all of these scenarios have in common is their goal of influencing government's policy agenda. This is why figure 2.3 shows several scenarios converging on the middle box, labelled 'Policy priorities established and adjusted as necessary', which forms part of figure 2.3's scenario for 'Delivering on the mandate' as established by voters in each election.

The main impetus for much public service policy work flows from a government's election promises. In Westminster-type systems in particular, many policy decisions are effectively taken long before the election, and public value is defined prior to policy analysis or design. Policy positions are debated and hammered out at party conferences and in caucus rooms and issued in election manifestos and position statements. After the election, single-party governments (and some well-established coalitions) can get on with the business of converting their pledges into workable programs immediately, whereas parties forming a coalition government must bargain over the policy content of the coalition agreement.

Different types of governments generate different challenges for public service policy analysts and advisers when the time comes for 'Delivering on the mandate'. When an incumbent government is returned to power, some public servants will find their own long-term analysis and advice being used to shape the agenda for the new term. Others, however, will have spent much of the pre-election period managing short-turnaround analysis associated with campaign pledges.

Newly elected governments invariably make some changes to the public service, although more so in Australia than New Zealand. Some new ministers will reorganise departments to promote their programs and suit their governing style, often only gradually building trust with senior advisers. During this period of adjustment, it is not uncommon for some public servants to feel sidelined. Required to implement policy preferences that were shaped by the new government while in opposition, they may feel that they are being relegated to lowly roles as implementation planners or even risk absorbers, while their high-level advice is being ignored. Coalition governments further complicate the picture, sometimes requiring public servants to serve multiple masters. For example, creative constitutional arrangements in recent years have included ministers outside cabinet and minor parties with oversight roles in particular policy areas. In such novel settings, public servants can feel that they are working for multiple masters with different agendas and at risk of being drawn inappropriately into party-political issues. New Zealand's experience thus far with MMP has produced some unstable coalitions, which have brought corresponding policy instability.

Regardless of incumbency, it is often said that policy analysis in the 'Mandate' pathway operates in practice as an ex post justification for decisions that have been taken on the basis of insufficient information in party caucuses, in cabinet, or on the whim of the minister. But this does not render rigorous analysis redundant; ex post analysis and advice can be useful if it elicits the risk and success factors associated with the chosen policy idea, and provides policy design options accordingly. If good, risk-aware advice is offered and rejected, or not offered at all, then the implementation of the manifesto will proceed in ignorance, with a greater risk of failure. Even when advice goes unused, professional advisers need to be on the record with their advice on major issues on which they were expected to have expert views.

The interface of policy/implementation designers with operational agencies is also of utmost importance to governance and may proceed along several scenarios. Figure 2.3 describes one such scenario, 'The inter-agency dance', in which implementation becomes a perpetual negotiation between policy and delivery agencies, which in a federal system often means between different levels of government.

In federal systems such as Australia's, the realities of inter-governmental tension and competition continually shape policy via negotiation, compromise, and occasional stalemate between levels of government. A 'vicious cycle' may develop when negotiating processes feed institutional conflict rather than resolving or channelling it productively, which usually results in inefficiency, unhappy staff, and unhappy clients. But when negotiation brings the parties to a better-informed, shared understanding of what is to be accomplished and how, the vicious cycle is broken and outcomes may be the better for the involvement of multiple levels of government. The same inter-agency patterns of policy shaping may apply in non-federal or unitary systems such as New Zealand's, for example when services are delivered by non-governmental agencies on the basis of negotiated contracts.

Many policy scientists look forward to the day when research will exert a consistently powerful influence over policy-making, but that day has not yet come. Research that is disseminated effectively sometimes influences public and stakeholder views, thereby indirectly shaping policy. Some research results are taken up by advocacy groups and used to bolster their arguments, providing another vector of indirect influence. Thus, research matters, but it is rarely the predominant influence in policy-making. Figure 2.4 describes one scenario in which research aids policy learning ('Learning through research'), and another in which research is used as a smokescreen for ignoring a particularly controversial or intractable policy issue.

Figure 2.4 uses the cheeky expression 'Self help' to describe policy development around governance structures and state sector reforms.

This is the most obvious point of overlap between policy and public management concerns, where scenarios invariably begin with an impassioned effort to raise standards of public service delivery across departments but quickly encounter various obstacles to change, including inertia itself. As noted in figure 2.4, however, even though the policy impacts of state sector reform are rarely dramatic, they often have subtle but important impacts on daily practice.

Finally, 'Goading the private sector' refers to a vector of policy influence in which government refrains from intervening directly but pressures other actors, such as businesses, to take action to address particular public problems. Such pressure may take the form of threats to regulate an industry, for example, which often creates sufficient incentives for industries to develop their own self-regulatory schemes.

Figures 2.2 through 2.4 only scratch the surface of the many policy development processes familiar to observers of the Australian and New Zealand scenes. Other scenarios could be drawn depicting influences on policy development that originate from beyond national boundaries. Many international organisations are important for Australia and New Zealand, as fertile sources of policy ideas and as potential sources of policy compulsion. Northwestern University, for example, maintains a library of international governmental organisations with more than 180 listings. Agreements overseen by the World Trade Organization constrain domestic economic policy choices, and many United Nations treaties and covenants commit signatory nations to particular policy directions.

In a 'glocalising' world, top-down pressure from international organisations is often matched by bottom-up pressure from local stakeholders. This ranges from lobbying by producer boards, business councils, or peak social organisations to grass-roots protests and community campaigns. Such efforts may result in policy paralysis, for example when an

Figure 2.4   Policy scenarios 3

Experts study
& debate

Difficult issue needs
research & development

Time goes by

Death by research

Attention wanes

Results ignored
& forgotten

Waste of
resources

Policy decisions
remain uninformed

Lost opportunity

Some methods
adopted readily
at first

Enthusiasm &
discipline wanes

Some methods
ignored

Self help

Efforts to
disseminate good
practice around
departments

Residue of good
effects persists

New good
practice methods
found

Central agencies continually
searching for aids to good
governance

= start

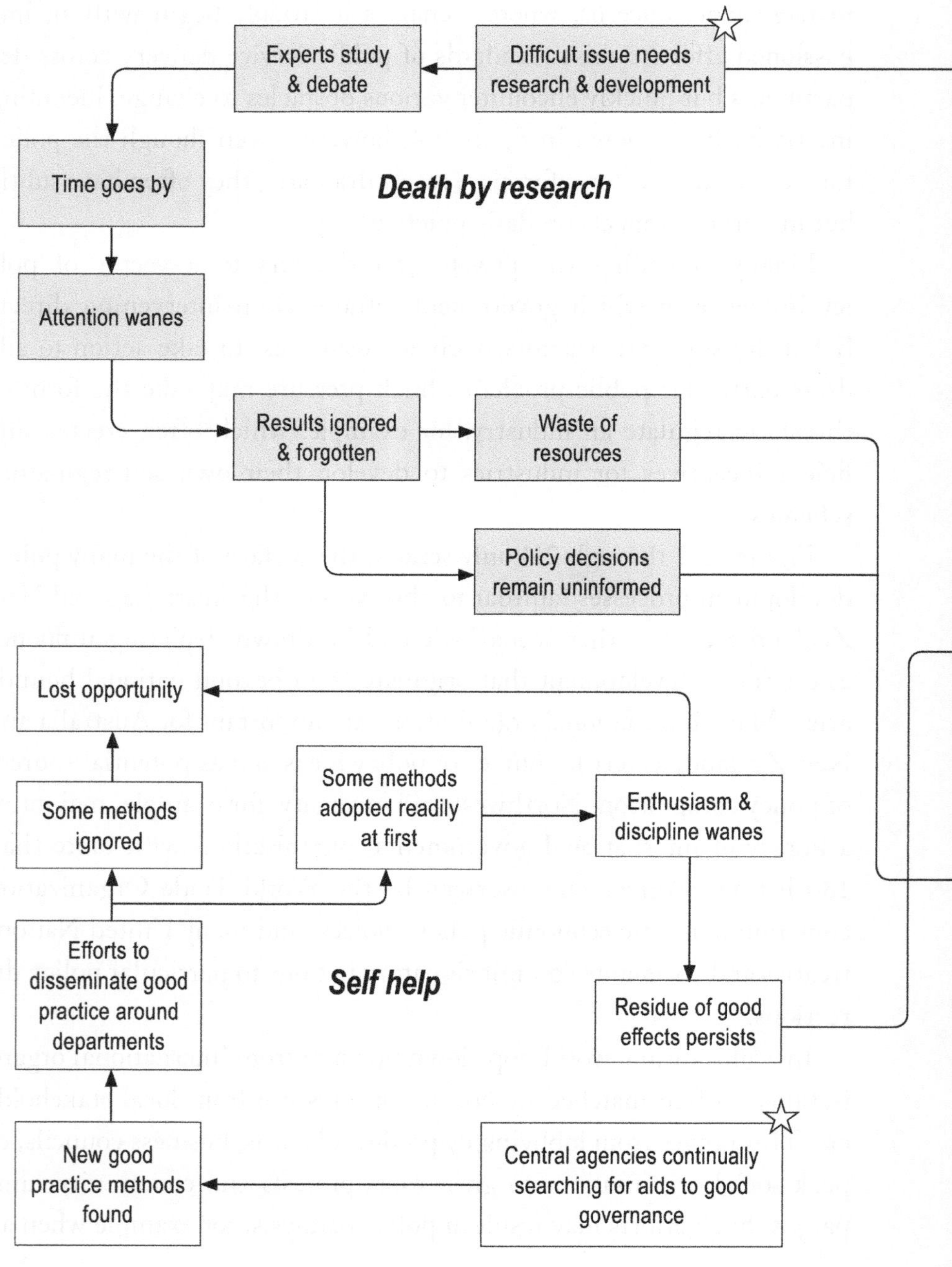

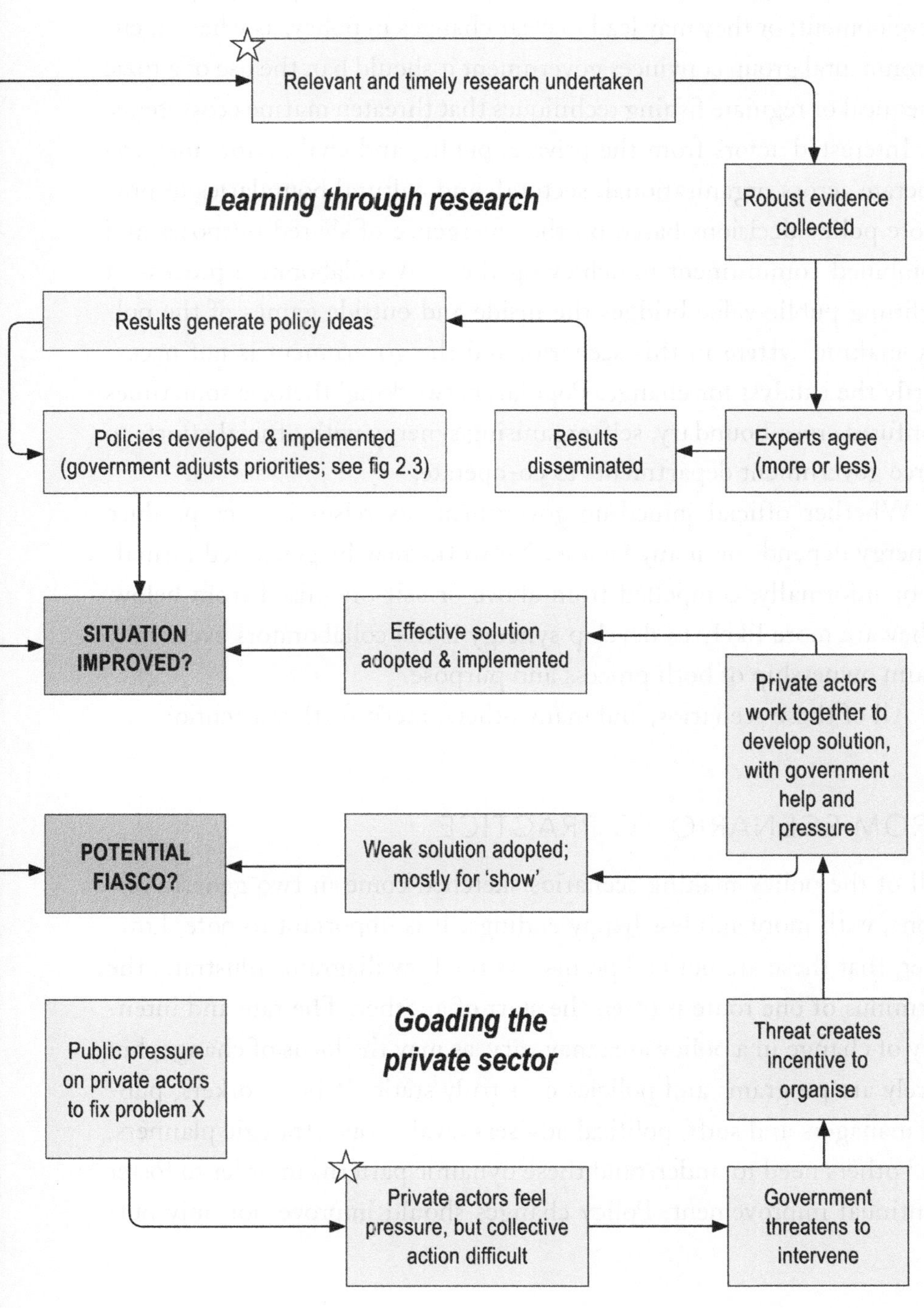

Relevant and timely research undertaken
Learning through research
Robust evidence collected
Results generate policy ideas
Policies developed & implemented (government adjusts priorities; see fig 2.3)
Results disseminated
Experts agree (more or less)
SITUATION IMPROVED?
Effective solution adopted & implemented
Private actors work together to develop solution, with government help and pressure
POTENTIAL FIASCO?
Weak solution adopted; mostly for 'show'
Goading the private sector
Threat creates incentive to organise
Public pressure on private actors to fix problem X
Private actors feel pressure, but collective action difficult
Government threatens to intervene

environmental group succeeds in delaying but not stopping a planned development; or they may lead to clear changes in policy, as when an environmental group convinces government it should ban the use of a toxic chemical or regulate fishing techniques that threaten marine ecosystems.

Interested actors from the private, public, and civil sectors may co-operate across organisational, sectoral, and cultural boundaries to promote policy decisions based on the emergence of shared purposes and combined commitment to achieving them. A collaborative process of defining public value bridges the inside and outside games of the policy-making system in this scenario, and the government is not necessarily the catalyst for change. Popular 'networking' rhetoric sometimes confuses cross-boundary, self-organising synergy with official efforts to force government departments to co-operate.

Whether official joined-up-government exercises in fact produce synergy depends on many factors. Networks may be generated formally or informally, compelled from above or self-organised from below. They are more likely to develop synergy if the collaborators eventually claim ownership of both process and purpose.

All of these scenarios, and many others, merit further attention.

FROM SCENARIO TO PRACTICE

All of the policy-making scenarios sketched come in two generic versions, with more and less happy endings. It is important to note, however, that these are not end points. As the flow diagrams illustrate, the terminus of one route is often the start of another. The rate and intensity of change in a policy area may vary, as may the locus of change, but rarely are programs and policies ever truly static. Policy workers, public managers and staff, political advisers, evaluators, strategic planners, and others need to understand these dynamic patterns in order to foster continual improvement. Policy changes should improve not only outcomes for people at a specified point in the future, but also the capability of the whole system to learn and improve.

Awareness of the likely routes along which policy-making tends to proceed can help practitioners reconcile and incorporate the imperatives of the inside and outside games, and channel policy-making energies toward the best possible results.

The arrows, paths and channels of various models can be used to chart the flow of policies' precursors or constituents: authority, influence, ideas, theories, information, opinion, pressure, feedback, instructions, and demands. But there remains the task of weighing and analysing them, and crafting policy proposals on the basis of the results.

The virtual architecture of cyberspace provides a metaphor for the elusive character of the systems or worlds or sectors upon which policy draws. These worlds do not correspond directly with actual places, institutions, or even networks of entities, or with the connections between them. They behave like the virtual domains and sites of the World Wide Web, and bear similarly fluid relations to each other. On the web, top level domain labels such as .edu(.ac) or .com or .govt suffixes provide useful general information about a website's source and context, but restrict neither access to it nor the flow of information into and out of it from other domains. And any website can include hyperlinks and thus potential linkages in other domains. The same permeability and fuzzy borders characterise the worlds, or domains if you like, of policy-making. Strict boundaries cannot be drawn between them, and the interconnections among them have the potential to enrich the world in which real-world policy issues are addressed.

QUALITY AND VALUE IN POLICY WORK

Assessing quality in policy advice raises conceptual and practical difficulties. The quality of policy work is difficult to define and assess because it is at once art, science and craft and proceeds in a complex and uncertain environment. It is also value-based and must confront competing views about the nature of problems and the outcomes resulting from different courses of action. The contribution of a policy analyst is to design options and to link them to alternative values and impacts – and to produce projected outcomes of the consequences of different policy options and choices. Good quality policy work does this well and it is not necessarily a negative reflection on the quality of policy work that a client or interest group is unhappy with the advice.

An article published by Dr Allan Behm and his colleagues (Behm et al 2000) explored value-adding policy analysis and advice, using intensive interviews with current and former ministers and senior officials. The research linked the issue of quality and capability in policy advice to notions of leadership. The study showed that public servants had good core transactional policy skills – and delivered factually correct, well-informed policy products. But also observed were a lack of 'transformational' policy skills, which look beyond immediate facts and obvious conclusions. The interviews suggested that some public servants lacked vision, creativity, political awareness, risk sensitivity and a holistic understanding of government's aspirations. Table 2.2 identifies the transactional and transformational skills associated with providing value-adding policy analysis and advising.

The Australian Public Service Commission has responded by fostering a more strategic approach to policy development – using programs to promote strategic thinking and develop technical skills, such as environmental scanning, modelling, scenarios and futures research. There is also an emphasis on cultural change to foster more collaborative ways of working with citizens and stakeholders, and to develop options involving partnerships across the public, private and community sectors.

Table 2.2 Value–creating model of effective policy services

<table>
<tr><td>RESPONSIVE, TRANSACTIONAL, STATIC, CORE COMPETENCY FACTORS</td></tr>
<tr><td>1 Foundation values</td></tr>
<tr><td>Timeliness; achievability; factual correctness; honesty and integrity of advice; credibility of adviser; non-partisan loyalty to government; fearlessness of adviser.</td></tr>
<tr><td>2 Critical values</td></tr>
<tr><td>Understanding of government's policies and priorities; consultation across the functional program; sensitivity to the customer's priorities; responsiveness.

Relevance; practicality and focus; clarity and comprehensiveness; exercisable options; accessibility of the service provider; dedication – 'someone who cares'; speed in error recovery.</td></tr>
<tr><td>STRATEGIC, TRANSFORMATIONAL, PROACTIVE, VALUE-CREATING FACTORS</td></tr>
<tr><td>3 Transforming values</td></tr>
<tr><td>Political awareness; consultation across entire organisation; risk sensitivity; iterative dialogue through 'feedback loops'; responsibility (stand up and be counted); timing; proactive; all sources; consistency; concise, succinct and simple; alert to best thinking.</td></tr>
<tr><td>4 Defining values</td></tr>
<tr><td>Whole of government; creative and innovative; political instinct; vision; partnership between customer and service provider; pride in sharing the outcome; willingness to market government policies.</td></tr>
</table>

SOURCE Behm et al (2000)

MAINTAINING POLICY CAPABILITY

Ministers and state-sector agencies in many Westminster-type governments, including New Zealand and Australia, have expressed concern about declining policy capacity and capability in the public sector: limited hard evidence has been presented on the nature of these capability gaps or deficits.

In a paper published in 1996, a study by Guy Peters for the Canadian Centre for Public Management Development, entitled 'The Policy Capacity of Government' reported 'a widespread perception that the policy capacity of governments has eroded since the mid-1970s', citing factors such as increased public advocacy and advice from the public sector, globalisation, fiscal constraints, intractable cross-cutting issues, competing sources of policy advice, increased expectation of citizen involvement, concerns for citizens' rights, and diversity and responsiveness in service delivery.

Peters drew attention to extensive change in the public service policy environment: in the roles of senior public service advisers, the emphasis on policy relative to management responsibilities, and the complexity of policy. He also noted a loss of experienced analysts. Such recurring concerns about public sector policy capability are raising fundamental issues about how to assess and ensure the quality of analysis and advice.

There are strong echoes of these observations in authoritative commentaries in Australia and New Zealand. These discussions have led to renewed efforts to define the attributes of high-quality policy advice and to establish principles to assess and guide policy practice.

CONCLUSION

In this chapter we have described the changing environment in which politically neutral policy advisers operate: the increasing complexity for them in terms of politicisation of advisory services, competition for access to decision makers, demands for co-ordination to address wicked issues both within the state apparatus and with non-government actors in the policy universe. We have commented on well-known models of the policy process that are useful in different contexts. We have argued for a systems perspective on complex policy issues, to alert policy practitioners to the important influences on policy development, from both inside and outside the formal policy system. This perspective redresses the tendency in other policy models to unduly emphasise government interventions, which may diminish the potentially valuable contribution from others.

Against this background we raised difficult issues of defining and assessing quality in policy work and the capabilities required by individuals, organisations and the sector as a whole. These matters are at the heart of subsequent chapters and essential to any strategy for lifting the performance of the policy advisory system.

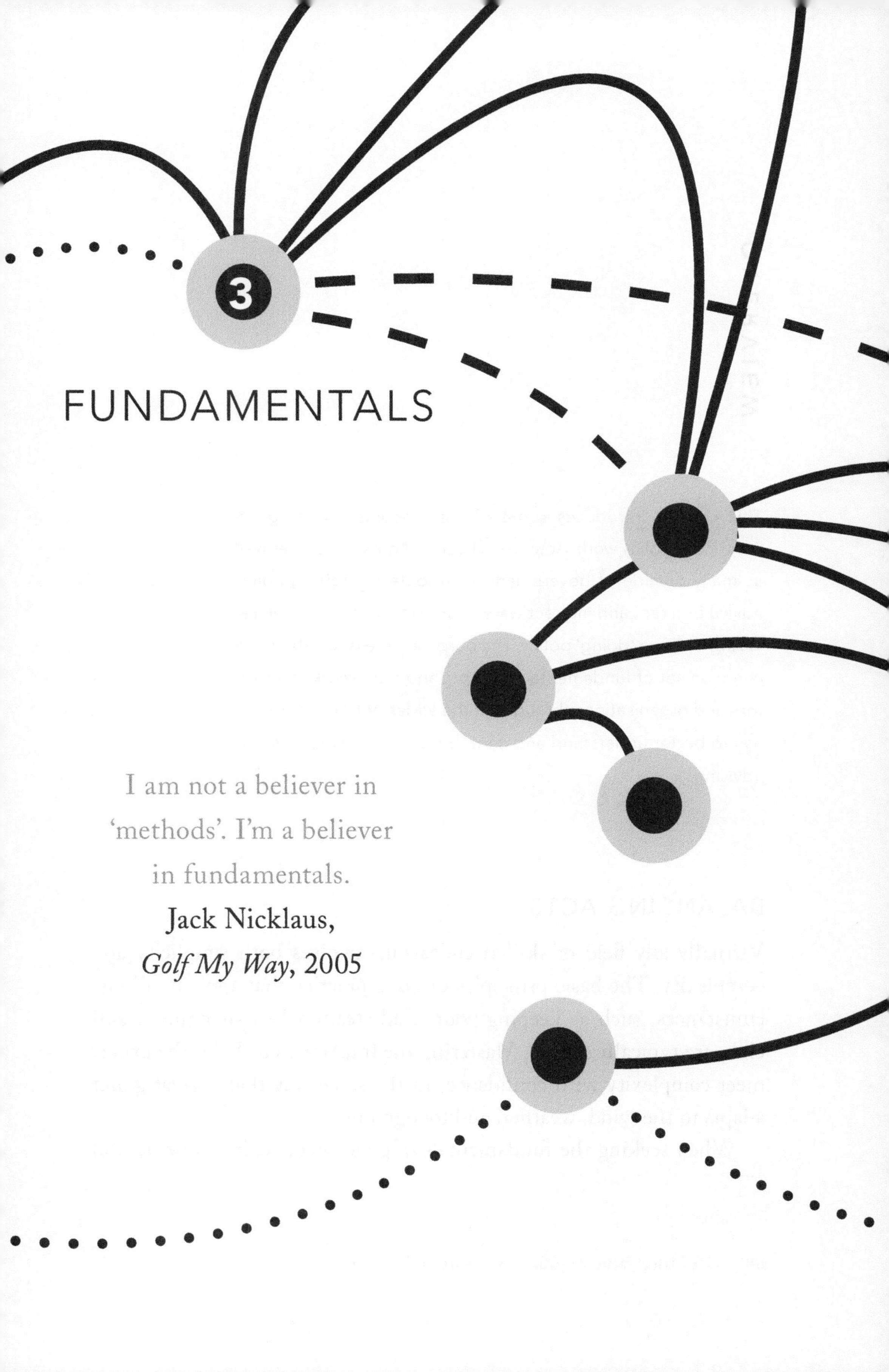

3 FUNDAMENTALS

I am not a believer in
'methods'. I'm a believer
in fundamentals.
Jack Nicklaus,
Golf My Way, 2005

This chapter introduces some of the fundamentals of good practice in policy work. Actors in all parts of government, as well as many outside of government, contribute to crafting policy advice in direct and indirect ways; many do so without even realising they are 'doing' policy. The purpose here is to establish a common set of fundamental concepts and frameworks that actors and organisations throughout the wider policy system can use to better understand and contribute to policy analysis and advising.

BALANCING ACTS

Virtually any field of skilled endeavour involves both simplicity and complexity. The basic principles of good practice that apply in all circumstances, such as keeping your head steady when swinging a golf club, are typically simple. Mastering the fundamentals helps the expert meet complexity with confidence, in the same way that a great golfer adapts to the wind, weather, and topography.

When seeking the fundamentals of good practice, it can be helpful to work backwards from the ultimate purpose – the final product to be created or the final goal to be achieved. In golf, it all comes down to impact with the ball (Nicklaus 2005). In policy work, the final target is policy advice that adds value to the work of decision-makers. And what is good public policy? Expanding on the conception of public policy presented in chapter 1, when governments adopt appropriate roles and apply effective instruments to the pursuit of desired results, we call that good public policy. People will differ over the meanings of 'appropriate', 'effective', and 'desired', but the basic principles hold regardless of how these disputes are resolved.

In order to enable good policy-making, analysts and advisers need to manage the continually evolving demands of the policy system described in the previous chapter, but they cannot do so in either the public or private sectors without the support of their managers and organisations. Government departments and other organisations that seek to advise decision-makers need to strike a balance between short-term and long-term considerations, research and action, rigour and relevance, breadth and focus, national and local needs, interest groups and the broader public interest, ideals and the art of the possible, and insider and outsider games.

A useful way to think about such balancing acts comes from Aristotle, who conceived virtue and excellence as an ability to find the proper mean between extremes of deficiency and excess. According to Aristotle, the virtue of courage is the mean between cowardice (too much fear) and foolhardiness (too little fear), and temperance finds the right balance between drunkenness (too much consumption) and abstinence (no consumption). Means vary from situation to situation. Thus, anger may be an extreme emotion, but it is appropriate in the face of deep injustice. The human being of excellent temperament knows when and where to express anger or compassion, and how much.

Likewise, the seasoned policy adviser knows, from training and experience, how far to push a policy proposal and when to back off, how broadly to explore an issue and when to cut from research to recommendations, when to seek guidance from the client and when to exert more independent thinking. The means in these examples can be moving targets, for they vary from government to government, and by organisation, setting, and circumstances. The best advisers learn how to read these variables and the risks associated with them. They continually find the dynamic equilibrium in each situation, and their organisations support them to develop and apply this faculty. In policy work, means and extremes correspond with the three elements of the definition of policy we offered earlier – roles, instruments, and results. Understanding these basic dimensions provides the fundamentals for good practice in policy analysis and advising. The rest of this chapter explores each in more depth.

ROLES FOR GOVERNMENT AND NON-STATE ACTORS

Exercising state power can produce either benefit or harm. Good public policy-making processes recognise this fact and ensure that government's substantial powers to persuade and coerce are applied appropriately.

Advice that is flawed in its orientation to roles of government tends to be either state-centric or state-phobic; it either views government intervention as the first, best solution to every problem or seeks to reduce government's role at every turn. Policy advice that clings to either extreme treats the public and private sectors as competitors for power and resources, rather than potential allies or partners. It overlooks the many ways in which governments, community organisations, voluntary social agencies, families, clubs, small businesses, large corporations, trade unions, and many other organisations can and do work synergistically to achieve publicly valued purposes.

Value-adding policy advice avoids ideological capture and finds the sweet spot between state-centric and state-phobic extremes. It stays open to creative institutional arrangements, including hybrid public–private innovations, while also paying attention to the boundaries established by civil liberties. It notes rules of thumb about when government intervention is more and less likely to produce net benefit within economic theories of market and government failure, and applies these appropriately, with due respect for circumstances. It learns from experience about what works, and tailors institutional roles to fit the needs of each time, place, and policy issue. Good policy advice begins not with a pre-determined preference for more or less government, but with a thorough scoping of realities on the ground and an open mind.

When should government get involved, and how?

Most Australians and New Zealanders feel comfortable with the idea of government arresting suspected murderers and punishing those who are proven guilty in a fair trial. Most also feel comfortable with government extending assistance to people who cannot work, negotiating trade arrangements with foreign countries, operating schools and hospitals, building and maintaining highways, and testing drinking water for impurities. In contrast, most Australians and New Zealanders probably would not feel comfortable with a government legislating mandatory attendance at the ballet, setting the price of shoes, or conducting monthly inspections of all private homes to search for illegal drugs. Why the distinctions?

Liberal democracies such as Australia and New Zealand embrace the general idea that government exists to serve the citizens who elect it and fund it with their taxes, and that certain limits should be placed on government's intrusion into citizens' lives. Although political parties tend to disagree, often vociferously, about exactly where the limits of government should lie, it is hard to find anyone who seriously disagrees with the principle itself. In public policy, limits on government activity are often defined on grounds of either economic theory or civil liberties. The term 'civil liberties' refers to those freedoms that protect citizens from abusive state power. They follow from the concept of human rights and may be enumerated, as in the United Nations' Universal Declaration of Human Rights or in a national Bill of Rights contained in either a constitution or statute (New Zealand uses the statutory form), or they may be an implicit component of a country's governance institutions (as in Australia, where debate about the need for a formal bill of rights or human rights charter is perennial). Either way, certain rights and liberties, such as right to a jury trial, right to equal protection under the law, and freedom of speech and assembly, are generally considered non-negotiable under most circumstances in liberal democracies.

When one person's actions interfere with another person's acknowledged or perceived rights and liberties, this usually constitutes *prima facie* justification for government to intervene. By the same token, when proposed public policies threaten to violate anyone's rights and freedoms, the civil rights framework signals that government is breaching its boundaries and needs to be reined in. Thus, a fundamental requirement of good policy development is to work within the boundaries of human rights and civil liberties, unless questions need to be raised about how those rights and liberties have been determined or interpreted, in which case such questions should be raised and addressed through due processes.

Economic theory has developed a narrower track for thinking about the appropriate role of the state vis-à-vis markets in producing and distributing the things that people want from society. The economics framework proceeds in two steps: (1) identifying situations in which markets are likely to fail to generate optimal outcomes, thus opening up the possibility that government should intervene (that is, market failure); and (2) identifying situations in which government intervention is likely to cause additional problems, raising doubts about the desirability of government intervention (that is, government failure). In both cases, the operative criterion of interest is efficiency rather than protection of rights or liberties.

Market failure

Market failure occurs when one or more of the characteristics of perfectly operating markets – which include large numbers of buyers and sellers, equal access to information needed for rational decisions, and prices that capture all relevant costs – is missing, leading to less than optimal allocation of resources, or inefficiency. The presence of market failure is sometimes taken as preliminary evidence that government ought to intervene to generate better results, but other factors also need to be considered. The type of market failure involved and the setting of the problem provide clues as to the appropriate role for government to play in each case.

Negative externalities are probably the best known and most widely used of the market failure frameworks in public policy. Take the straightforward case of particulate pollution from smoky wood heaters, leading to respiratory health problems. This has become a significant issue in many parts of Australia and New Zealand in the winter months, especially where temperature inversions cause smoke to be trapped in valleys. The New South Wales government estimates that 40 per cent of winter pollution in the Sydney metropolitan area is attributable to wood heaters. Both Tasmania and South Australia operate 'Smokewatch' programs to encourage responsible use of the devices and monitor pollution patterns.

Air pollution is a paradigmatic negative externality in microeconomics, meaning a cost of production that is borne by one or more third parties rather than by the producers or consumers of the product. Because the cost of this negative externality – air pollution – is not included in the selling price of the relevant good or service, that good or service tends to be overproduced and overconsumed. Emissions from wood-burning heaters impose environmental and health costs on everyone in their vicinity. If those environmental and health costs were included in the manufacturer's production costs, they would be passed on to consumers. The price of the heaters would increase accordingly, demand would decrease, and emissions would be curtailed. When third parties absorb the environmental and health costs that constitute emissions externalities, they in effect subsidise the producers and consumers of wood heaters, which artificially inflates both demand and supply and leads to a non-optimal market equilibrium.

In theory, this type of obvious market failure should be easily remedied by internalising the externality. Internalisation could mean adding the environmental and health costs of wood heaters to their costs of production and thus to their purchase price, through a levy on wood heaters, for example, or a requirement to install scrubbers in the devices. Alternatively, private contracts could be drawn up between wood-burner users and those harmed by emissions to arrange compensation for the latter. This is how a market failure diagnosis helps determine possible roles for government intervention.

In practice, however, internalising externalities can be difficult because many externalities are difficult to measure due to the harms being indirect, diffuse, and intertwined with other factors. For example, how many cases of respiratory illness are due to smoke pollution alone, rather than, or in addition to, other causes? How much of this pollution can be blamed on wood heaters and how much on planned forestry burnings? What portion of treatment costs should be attributed to smoke pollution, and wood heaters as a particular source of smoke? What contributions do woodburner-generated greenhouse gases make to global climate change, and how should the economic impacts of climate change be calculated? What share of total costs is attributable to wood heaters? What about other environmental impacts including those of chopping down trees to fuel the devices? What about damage to amenity values, for example from smog caused by wood heaters and other forms of wood burning? How high should a levy or compensation contract be set to fairly reflect the true harms?

These are only some of the questions to be answered before the negative externalities generated by wood heaters can be calculated and then internalised. In cases such as this, it is useful to identify market failures, where they are present, early in the analysis. In addition, it is nearly always useful to explore the motivations of those perpetuating the market failures and the various obstacles to change before designing a role for government intervention. Some externalities, to continue with that example, are easy to remove technically – such as requiring pollution scrubbers to be installed in the exhaust systems of wood heaters – but they may be hard to achieve economically and politically because of high monetary costs or inconvenience. In other cases, the obstacles are behavioural – people have to be convinced to change their habits. A thorough analysis of the policy problem should include all of these background features of the story, so that options can be designed to take advantage of easy solutions and address the obstacles to change.

Negative externalities associated with wood heaters are a small example of the market failure framework at work. Identifying a problem as a market failure helps advisers understand the incentives (both economic and non-economic) maintaining a problem. It can boost analytical power because specific policy instruments are designed to address specific forms of market failure. Thus, framing a policy problem as a particular type of market failure readily produces a preliminary list of possible policy options and helps jump-start the creative process, as described later in this chapter.

It is important to note that market failure concepts need not apply only to the financial and economic dimensions of policy issues. For ex-

Table 3.1 Market failure frameworks for problem understanding

Category	Description	Example
Natural monopoly	A single firm can produce a good or service more cheaply than any other market arrangement, often because economies of scale are present. Competition is impractical and inefficient.	• Cable TV • Electric lines • Government bureaus (sometimes) • Industry-based export marketing (for example Fonterra in New Zealand)
Negative externality	Consumption or production generates costs (monetary or otherwise) for people other than the producers or consumers because the market price of the good does not capture all of its costs. In other words, a third party suffers but receives no benefit.	• Air pollution generated by steel production • Alcohol- or drug-induced violence • Animal welfare problems in farming
Positive externality	Consumption or production generates benefits (monetary or otherwise) for people other than the producers or consumers because the market price of the good does not capture all of its benefits. In other words, a third party gains but does not have to pay.	• Education • Home maintenance (benefits to neighbours)
Information asymmetry	Rational, utility-maximising choices require good information. Some parties to a transaction (for example, buyers or sellers) may possess less information about the goods being exchanged than the other party, which interferes with rational choice.	• Consumer safety • Movie content (hence, the need for ratings) • Readability of contracts • Professional credentials of service providers
Preference-related problems	Some goods may qualify as 'merit goods', meaning that society determines that people should consume them for their own benefit, even if they don't want them. (The focus on the consumer's own welfare distinguishes merit goods from goods with positive externalities enjoyed by others.) Society considers some preferences out of bounds ('demerit goods') and some groups unfit to make rational choices regarding their own welfare. These frameworks provide rationales for paternalistic intervention.	*Merit goods* • high culture • compulsory education *Irrational groups* • addicts • young people • senile elderly *Illegitimate preferences (demerit goods)* • prostitution • pornography

NOTES

1 The problem of excessive transaction costs is not usually included as a classical market failure, but we think it fits.

2 This is another non-standard item on the list, but one that is especially apt in 2009.

Category	Description	Example
Public goods	In these cases, it is difficult to identify who benefits from the good and most people won't pay for it voluntarily. Competitive markets will not produce the good because of the difficulties of identifying users and charging for it. Pure public goods exhibit both: • non-rivalrous consumption (one person's partaking of the good does not reduce another person's access), • non-excludability (excluding someone from consuming the good is impossible, impractical, or illegal). These features open the door to free riding, when someone enjoys more than their fair share of a benefit or less than their fair share of a burden. For example, parents who do not help with fundraising at their children's school benefit (indirectly, through their children) from the efforts of parents who do help. Non-union employees in a workplace may benefit from the dues paid by union members because collective bargaining lifts everyone's salary.	Note variations: *Pure public goods* • national defence • street lights *Toll goods* (non-rival in the absence of congestion but excludable) • roads and bridges • wilderness areas *Common property goods* (non-excludable but rival) • pasture land • fisheries • deep-sea minerals
Thin markets or market dominance	Thin markets consist of few sellers and/or few buyers who can manipulate prices. When one or more firms become 'too big to fail' or 'too strategic to fail', they exert disproportionate influence over the whole market.	• Oligopolies • Cartels • Mega-banks • National airlines
Transaction (or co-ordination) costs[1]	The costs of using markets to obtain some goods and services may be excessive; these include costs associated with search and information, bargaining, keeping trade secrets, and policing and enforcement of contracts. In such cases, institutions such as firms may arise to provide these goods and services internally, rather than relying on networks of independent contractors.	• Brokerage fees and commissions • Appraisal fees • Time spent finding the best service provider • Time spent drawing up a contract and monitoring it
Panic[2]	Rumours can destroy market rationality swiftly and cause both consumers and producers to act in ways that damage their own welfare as well as putting whole systems at risk. Once begun, panics are virtually impossible to control.	• Stock market crashes • Banking crises
Barriers to co-ordination and collaboration	Firms may benefit from co-ordinated activity, but because the benefits will be spread across co-operating firms, no single firm has enough incentive to organise the initiative.	• Supply networks • Codes of practice • Industry trade associations (common remedy)

SOURCE Adapted from Weimer and Vining (2004).

ample, we can speak roughly of demand for and supply of non-monetisable goods such as public legitimacy, community solidarity, or social diversity, and explore the market-like factors that govern their consumption and production. Table 3.1 lists the main categories of market failure, with examples showing that market failure frameworks apply not only to economic policy but virtually across the board to social, environmental, cultural, and infrastructural policy.

Other grounds for government intervention

Some of what governments do has nothing to do with market failure, of course. Foreign policy, for example, looks after relations with other countries. Economists might classify global peace and international economic stability as pure public goods, a type of market failure, but this rather banal observation provides little guidance to developing foreign policy. It stretches the market failure concept too far. Other conceptual systems are needed to frame foreign policy analysis.

Some government activities arise from what might be called network failures, or the inability of individuals and groups with complementary interests to find each other and co-ordinate their activities for mutual benefit. Matching workers with jobs, helping immigrants settle in their new communities, engaging in trade negotiations, jollying industries along toward self-regulation, and overseeing the purchases of failed banks: these are all examples of policies driven by the need for high-level co-ordination to help keep social and economic systems operating effectively. Government may, in some of these cases, meet that need through direct action or facilitation.

Welfare state programs also evade the market failure net. Even when markets are working at peak efficiency, they are likely to generate a distribution of income and opportunities that is perceived as inequitable according to mainstream norms. Because markets are not expected to generate adequate incomes for all participants, issues such as poverty

Table 3.2 Distribution failures

Category	Description	Example
Inequality of opportunity	Societies that distribute income largely via the market must ensure that labour markets operate fairly and everyone has access to education and training to develop their talents. Income should reflect relevant variables such as the value of skills (as determined by the market) and the effort expended, but should not reflect irrelevancies such as race, sex, age, or background.	• Discrimination • Variation in public school quality
Inequality of outcomes	Societies may find the results of market-based income distribution unacceptable and seek to make adjustments to satisfy various definitions of equity.	• Poverty • Deprivation • Radical economic inequalities leading to social inequalities
Inequality of access	Democracy suffers when rich citizens have greater voice than poor citizens.	• Pressure group inequalities • Elitism by elected representatives and officials
Violation of basic rights	The Universal Declaration of Human Rights describes the bottom line for governments with respect to protecting their citizens' essential liberties.	

and deprivation are not classed as market failures despite their deep roots in the economic system. The job of reducing social inequities therefore tends to fall largely to governments (with significant, but uneven help from the voluntary sector) through various instruments of the welfare state, including direct cash payments to the unemployed and disabled, tax benefits for low-income households, in-kind assistance in the form of housing and social services, and various formulae for reducing financial disparities between schools, health districts, and other institutions. Concerns about equity are common drivers of social policy development, though social policy players differ in their views and concepts of equity. Efficiency also figures prominently in discussions of the welfare state, but as a secondary consideration related to minimising waste and delivering services efficiently, not as a primary reason for government intervention.

In such policy areas, making social distribution more equitable is not just one among many objectives; it is the main act, the central purpose, the chief source of legitimacy for government's role. For this reason, it could be argued that these issues form their own category of problem frameworks focused on failures of social distribution, as catalogued in table 3.2, rather than market failures or government failures.

Government failure

Market failures and social distribution problems lurk around every corner, and analysts should avoid the temptation of thinking that once a market or social distribution failure is identified, the appropriate role for government has been sussed. At least two further steps need to follow.

First, analysts need to explore the possibility that government intervention to correct market failures will produce government failure instead, thus requiring further analysis to determine the lesser of the two evils. In the case of taxing wood heaters, for example, government may be influenced unduly by rent-seeking interest groups that represent producers of gas-burning stoves, a cleaner alternative to wood fuel and a direct competitor. The influence of the gas-burner lobby may cause government to set the levy on wood heaters too high, conferring unfair market advantages on makers of gas-fuelled devices and inducing an inefficient allocation of resources in the heating market. Analysts should stay alert to these problems and look for ways to tweak government policies to reduce the probability and magnitude of government failure.

Secondly, analysts need to consider whether government failure may be the source of the original policy problem. Where government is already deeply involved in a policy area, poor outcomes may be due to systematic failures of public provision rather than market failure. For example, age-old complaints about the lack of customer orientation and poor service at publicly owned and operated post offices and motor vehicle registration agencies are often attributed to the lack of competition for providing these services (that is, government-imposed monopoly, which combines market and government failure) and the alleged inwardness of bureaucratically operated organisations. Once an analyst frames the problem this way, natural remedies include changing the role of government fundamentally by privatising the service, as many countries have done with their postal services, or contracting out the service, which theoretically generates competition among bidders. Alternatively, policy might introduce various performance-management initiatives designed to counteract bureaucracy's alleged weaknesses and improve outcomes, thus changing the way a government department does business rather than changing the role of government altogether.

Table 3.3 identifies key types of government failure. Features of market failure, distribution problems, and government failure can be identified in nearly every policy issue. It is rare to find a solution to a problem that can evade all three sources of disappointment. Oscillation between market failure and government failure is also an ever-present danger. Governments may intervene to correct a government failure, but in the process, create new problems resulting from other kinds of government failure, which creates pressure for government to restore market control, which leads predictably to market failure, and round and round we go. Movement in either direction may exacerbate social inequalities as well.

An important goal of policy analysis is to anticipate these cycles of market and government failure and channel them constructively by designing policies that employ the best features of market-based and

Table 3.3 Government failure frameworks

Category	Description	Example
Direct democracy problems	Voting provides only an imperfect mechanism for aggregating individual preferences. Therefore, neither direct referenda nor representative elections provide complete and precise information about what a society desires. • Paradox of voting • Intensity and bundling of preferences • Tyranny of the majority	Electoral 'mandates' are rare.
Narrow interests	Decisions made by elected representatives suffer various defects related to re-election pressures, tensions between serving one's constituency and serving the public interest, and the tendency to pay more attention to noisier groups.	• Rent seeking • Difficulties in targeting • Short time horizons • Posturing
Bureaucratic supply problems	Economic theory predicts that government agencies will slip easily into inefficiency because they do not face the competitive pressures of the marketplace. Efficiency is often harder to measure (valuation of output), harder to monitor (agency loss), and harder to achieve (inflexibility, lack of competition, etc) in the public sector than in the private sector.	• X-inefficiency • 'Discretionary budgets' • Monopoly service delivery
Principal–agent problems	Although principals of organisations (owners, bosses, or political masters) rely on agents to pursue the organisation's agenda, the activities of the agents will not always align perfectly with the principals' intentions. This mismatch reduces the organisation's effectiveness and imposes costs for screening agents, monitoring their behaviour, and cajoling / coercing better performance.	• Bureau capture • Ministers' wariness about the public service
Moral hazard	When government cushions individuals or firms from the consequences of their risky behaviours, it may cause individuals to be less cautious and take more risks. This is a standard side effect of insurance.	• Corporate bail-outs • Laws requiring no-fault auto insurance • Mountain rescue • Government deposit guarantees

Category	Description	Example
Co-ordination and collaboration problems	Lack of incentive by individual departments to co-operate leads to under-provision of joined-up activities within the public sector and across the private and public sectors. This is the public sector equivalent of positive externalities that go unrealised due to incentive problems.	• Missing projects
Short time frames and narrow horizons	In a highly competitive democratic framework, there are few political incentives for policymakers to pursue long-term solutions to problems. They will be out of office before the credit for success is attributed. Likewise, there are few political incentives for policymakers to pursue global solutions to problems because beneficiaries of these policies in other countries cannot vote for them.	
Transparency problems	Governments can carry out their business in secret if citizens don't pressure them for transparency. When voters do not know what government is doing, it becomes more difficult to exercise informed democratic judgments. Secrecy also nurtures corruption and self-interested decision-making.	

source Adapted from Weimer and Vining (2004).

bureaucratic mechanisms. This requires crafting roles for government and other actors that generate net benefits over harms, and net successes over failures, while also protecting the vulnerable. When none of the forms of failure can be overcome completely, policy work aims to find the least disagreeable option among many, rather than the panacea.

Basic choice problems

Some issues do not require elaborate problem frameworks or deep inquiries into the appropriate role for government. Consider a local council that needs to choose between three possible sites for a new swimming pool, each with advantages and disadvantages. This choice is a relatively simple matter of projecting costs and benefits for various potential sites and comparing them. Advisers charged with making recommendations on the pool's location need not delve into the positive externalities associated with swimming pools or the question of whether swimming pools qualify as public, private, or quasi-public goods. The task at hand is more about maximising a set of objectives associated with the location of the facility and less about framing and solving a specific problem.

Operational policy problems

Operational policy issues involve second-order problems, which hover below the radar of the failure frameworks but can still make or break outcomes.

Take the question of how to deliver vaccines in a flu pandemic, for example. The problem is one of capacity relative to surging demand, with the usual delivery sites – primary care surgeries – likely to be overwhelmed. The search for alternative delivery sites requires a keen understanding of both the health care delivery system, including the distribution and availability of the workforce, and people's daily movements (particularly of those people most vulnerable to flu). This may qualify as a complex operational and logistical policy problem, and one for which the features of the problem – capacity relative to overwhelming projected demand – need to be well understood, but failure frameworks are unlikely to be very helpful in doing so.

Non-state actors

State-centric bias is a serious occupational hazard for anyone working in government who contributes to policy development. Government is a highly complex institution, and public servants have to spend huge amounts of time and energy learning how it functions. Many public servants are also heavily invested in making existing government programs perform as well as possible. People who choose to work in the public sector typically believe in the power of government to improve citizens' well-being. For all of these reasons, no one should be surprised when public service policy advisers reveal a conscious or unconscious preference for public intervention. It is natural for public servants to see government as the first line of defence against social, economic, and environmental problems and the first responder to any opportunities for improving well-being.

Optimal policy development, however, requires policy advisers to overcome their state-centric biases and entertain a wider range of roles for both state and non-state actors, including non-intervention when appropriate. Government departments have always co-operated in various ways with business organisations, trade unions, community groups, voluntary social service organisations, churches and clubs; and many of these relationships have become more formalised in recent years through partnerships, memoranda of understanding, and contractual arrangements. Good policy advice stays alert to these possibilities by continually asking not only whether and how government should be involved in addressing particular problems and opportunities, but also who else might contribute and how institutional roles can be made to harmonise.

Types of roles

Governments may play several different roles within a single policy option. For example, health care financing and delivery arrangements commonly involve both state and non-state organisations assuming roles as funders, purchasers, or providers of services as well as regulation and ownership roles.

Other variables may be required to describe the linkages and interfaces between various roles of public and private sector actors and institutions. For example, does the public health system determine eligibility and access criteria on behalf of the population, or can individuals select their own services directly, or select from a choice of purchasing agents? Even if policy advice is being delivered to a government, it is important to weigh up whether government is best positioned to take on the necessary roles, either on its own or in partnership with other sectors. Increasingly governments are looking to form partnerships with the private and NGO sectors; therefore it is important to see what each sector is particularly good at, and policy analysis should explore and evaluate alternative roles for both state and non-state actors.

Understanding problems and opportunities

The legitimacy of government involvement in an issue often turns on the nature of the problem or opportunity motivating attention to the issue. The more an analyst learns about the nature of the underlying policy problem or opportunity, the better placed they will be to understand how government might interact effectively with other institutions to improve outcomes. Throughout all phases of a policy project, analysts must assemble and review what they know about the economic, social, technical, cultural, and other important forces causing or perpetuating the policy problem. Where gaps are found, they should look for additional information. Systems mapping approaches discussed in chapter 4 can help with this fundamental task.

Thorough problem analysis is plain good sense, because it saves us from working hard to solve the wrong problem. Take, for example, the case of an industry group seeking government training subsidies to ensure an adequate workforce to keep up with demand for its product. Policy officials need to verify the facts and causal connections before adopting the industry group's prefabricated definition of the problem (that is, worker shortages due to lack of training in industry X). Such shortages may be temporary, highly localised, or imagined, in which case the problem definition will prove to be mistaken. If the mistaken problem definition is used in policy analysis, resources will be wasted developing options to address the wrong problem, and a potentially unnecessary or counter-productive role for government may be validated.

The best policy response to a temporary, localised, or imaginary worker shortage may be a watching brief, in case the problem corrects itself, or a policy of facilitating worker mobility across localities. Even if long-term, system-wide worker shortages in fact exist in a particular industry, they may be caused by wage differentials, working conditions, or public perceptions of the work, rather than lack of training, in which case policy responses may need to be deflected from training. Immigration rules may need to be reviewed as well.

Indeed, a closer look at this will reveal that 'lack of training' is not a problem definition at all, but a policy solution (that is, more training) dressed up as a problem. Such a pseudo-problem definition skews the whole analysis toward a narrow range of training-related options and obstructs the analyst's view of other possible solutions to the worker shortage (assuming it is real). Good-practice policy analysis should avoid the temptation to accept someone else's problem definition without scrutiny, do the research needed to expose other causes of the problem, and recognise the old trick of disguising a solution as a problem.

Because a missed opportunity may be classified as a type of problem, we will often use the term 'problem' to encompass both elements and avoid having to repeat the clunky phrase, 'problems and opportunities'. Strict libertarians and others committed to shrinking government may argue that public policies should address only certain, carefully circumscribed types of problems and leave the opportunities for private parties to pursue, but that view does not fit our approach, which shuns ideological approaches to role-of-government questions across the board. Some problems and opportunities surely are inappropriate objects of government attention, but most of these determinations cannot be made strictly on principle. Close, careful study of each issue and its context is required.

Population and issue-based policy frameworks

Sometimes more tailored policy frameworks are developed to help analysts and advisers deal with policy developments relating to specific population groups or sectors, or particular kinds of policy issues. These frameworks provide guidance to policy agencies whose particular areas of responsibility affect the populations or concern the issues in question.

In New Zealand, for example, the Ministry of Pacific Island Affairs adapted a generic policy framework with overlays to incorporate important Pacific cultural values, to help policy agencies reflect these values in policies affecting Pacific people. The Ministry of Women's Affairs, which promotes gender analysis throughout the New Zealand public sector, has similarly invested in developing a Gender Analysis Framework for use by other agencies to assess the gender implications of policy proposals of all kinds.

Te Puni Kōkiri (the Ministry of Maori Development) has developed a Māori Potential Framework, which encourages Māori to build and capitalise on their 'collective resources, knowledge, skills and leadership capability'. This framework differs from more conventional approaches in its affirmative focus on potential, capability, and contribution, rather than deficits, excesses, harms, or problems. The Ministry is also working to develop a Treaty Framework, to frame policy issues and options with implications for the Crown and Māori under the Treaty of Waitangi.

Strategic conversation

Avoiding state-centricity and state-phobia may require wholly different approaches to policy development than are typically found in government departments. Sometimes what is needed is a joint thrashing out of issues by members of key institutions, both public and private, and the people with the greatest stake in the outcomes. This process may include jointly framing the problem (or opportunity), jointly identifying public purposes, and jointly undertaking options exploration and analysis — a process collectively known as strategic conversation, or sometimes, policy co-production. Such conversations may occur at the local or regional level or under the aegis of national summits and blue-ribbon panels charged with breaking through political stalemates and finding fresh approaches to heavily entangled problems.

INSTRUMENTS: LINKING POLICY OPTIONS TO PROBLEMS AND OPPORTUNITIES

It is often said that governments should do the right things (using the best instruments) and do them well (with effective implementation). Value-adding advice supports both goals with a steady flow of information, a keen eye for promising ideas, and the exercise of reasoned judgment in sorting and assessing options.

Defective policy advice regarding instruments and courses of action occupies the extremes of a continuum from boundless enthusiasm to stubborn resistance. Very few policy officials in our acquaintance fit either stereotype perfectly, but many will go too far toward one end of this continuum or the other from time to time.

Stubborn resisters develop strong attachments to current policy. They may excel at spotting small opportunities for improvement and often enjoy tinkering, but they typically refuse to envision big alternatives to the status quo. They detest changes of government. At the other pole, boundless enthusiasts can be identified by their wholehearted and uncritical embrace of every new policy idea that comes along. They are the fashion slaves of the policy world, adopting and promoting whatever ideas have been endorsed by the international policy elite as being à la mode. Occasionally, a boundless enthusiast will latch on to a single proposal and push it hard at every opportunity. When this happens, they morph into axe-grinders. Both extremes of resistance and boundless enthusiasm flow from a deficiency of critical judgment and a failure to appreciate the particular needs of each policy situation.

Good policy analysis avoids these traps by searching widely for new ideas while also studying local circumstances carefully before making recommendations. It learns from direct experience, intelligence gathered on the ground, dialogue with citizens and stakeholders, and available research findings about what is likely to work, for whom, and under what conditions. It looks for promising home-grown ideas as well as the best ideas emerging from the academic and professional literatures. It neither dismisses nor accepts the superiority of current policy, out of hand.

In order to develop well-designed, appropriate policy instruments and implement them effectively, advisers need to understand as fully as possible the problem or opportunity to be addressed and the factors contributing to it in the larger social, economic, cultural, and physical environment. If government intervention is justified on the basis of market failure in the form of negative externalities, for example, policy mechanisms need to be devised to either internalise the externality, via levies or private contracts, for example, or control the associated harm, perhaps with command and control regulations or agreements with industries to self-regulate. Good policy advice presents decision-makers with genuinely promising options that suit the situation at hand and show real potential for addressing the policy problem effectively. There is no magic number for how many options an adviser should supply, but all options included in a piece of advice need to be worth considering. Advisers should avoid rigging up 'straw man' options to make the favoured option look good in comparison; the best options will look their best when compared with authentic, worthwhile alternatives.

Not infrequently, analysts may find only one policy option that deserves serious attention. If so, they should explain the reasons for the selected option's superiority, catalogue the rejected options and their flaws briefly, and then proceed to a choice of design features for the selected option. Value-adding policy advice categorically rejects the so-called TINA (there is no alternative) principle and its implied justification for mono-option advice. There are always alternatives, although they will sometimes reside at the level of design and operational details rather than high-level direction setting or choice of instrument. No matter how tightly a minister, local council, or governing board may constrain the options menu, there are always opportunities for creativity in design and implementation planning.

Devising policy options is core business for officials in many areas of government, who must learn how to pitch options at the appropriate level. Consider the three domains of policy introduced in chapter 1. In the responsive policy domain, where governments have pre-selected both policy purposes and instruments, options must take the form of variations on a set theme. If government has pledged to adopt an emissions trading scheme (ETS), for example, then options development should focus on offering alternative designs for an emissions trading scheme, all of which would achieve government's objectives of complying with Kyoto Protocol targets and aligning with international carbon markets. In the operational policy domain, options must be drawn more narrowly and will tend to focus more on implementation processes – such as defining consistent accounting practices within an ETS. In the relatively wide-open spaces of the direction-setting domain, both instruments and purposes are negotiable and wholly new ideas are welcomed – such as alternatives to the emissions trading paradigm for reducing greenhouse gases.

Problem frameworks redux

We are continually surprised at how often policy options included in an analysis appear disconnected from the policy problem itself. Per-

Table 3.4 Matching policy instruments to problem definition frameworks

Policy instrument	Problem definition to which it responds	Examples
Taxes and fees	Negative externality	• Cigarette tax, petrol tax, congestion charges in central business district
Subsidies via grants or tax credits	Positive externality	• Research and development tax credits, state funding for universities
Rules and regulations	Negative externality, public good, preference-related problems, inequality of opportunity, rights violations	• Age restrictions on cigarettes and alcohol, driving laws, auto emissions standards
Enforcement of basic rights	Rights violations	• Equal opportunity legislation • Bill of Rights laws
Direct purchasing or provision of goods and services	Natural monopoly, public good, preference-related problems, transaction costs, inequality of outcomes	• Social services, hospital care, police, fire, military
Direct provision of information	Natural monopoly, public goods	• Census data, vital statistics, travel warnings
Public education campaigns	Information asymmetry, negative externalities, preference-related problems	• Anti-smoking, anti-drug, anti-drink-driving, safe sex, family violence awareness, etc campaigns
Safety net transfers	Public goods, inequalities of opportunity and outcomes	• Unemployment benefits, student allowances, Accident Compensation Corporation in NZ
Corporate bail-outs	Negative externality, market dominance (banks that are 'too big to fail'; companies that are too strategic to fail)	• Air New Zealand
Government guarantees	Positive externality, panic	• Banking deposit insurance • Export guarantees • Farm payouts
Ombudsman services	Negative externality, unequal representation (voice), inequalities of opportunity and outcomes	• Industry-specific and general ombudsmen, parliamentary commissioners

Policy instrument	Problem definition to which it responds	Examples
Creation of tradable property rights	Negative externality, public good	• Fishing quotas • Emissions trading schemes under Kyoto Protocol • Radio spectrum auctions and secondary markets
Monitoring and surveillance	Information asymmetries, public good	• Intelligence services • Closed-circuit TV on city streets
Labelling	Information asymmetries, negative externality	• Health warnings • Travel warnings • Nutrition and GM labels
Licensing and certification	Information asymmetries, negative externality	• Driving licenses • Medical licences • Marriage licenses
Privatisation	Bureaucratic failures, principal–agent problems	• Railroads • Postal services • Banks and insurance
Threat of regulation facilitating voluntary action by private sector	Negative externality	• Voluntary agreements • Codes of practice
Public–private partnership	Co-ordination failure, public good	• Roading • Infrastructure
Advice, encouragement, support to facilitate voluntary action by private sector	Positive externality, negative externality, co-ordination failure	• Co-regulation • Industry-led regulation
Community partnership	Co-ordination failure, third-sector problems, narrow interests	• Memoranda of understanding • Community development facilitation and support
Organisation of participatory and deliberative activities	Representation problems, direct democracy problems, narrow interests	• Citizen juries • Citizen forums
Public management reform and restructuring	Bureaucratic supply problems, principal–agent problems, lack of transparency	• Competition in services
Policy-making process reforms	Transparency problems, representation problems, direct democracy problems, narrow interests	• Freedom of information laws • Anti-corruption initiatives • Changes to electoral systems (for example MMP in NZ)

haps this results from policy teams segmenting their work too sharply, charging one set of analysts with problem scoping duties and another set with options development. In these cases, the final product may be a carefully researched and insightful description of the problem accompanied by a thorough cataloguing of policies that have been used elsewhere and proposed by others, but with no analysis of whether the options address the known causes and effects of the problem at hand. Off-the-shelf policy options may appear relevant at first glance, but they nearly always require substantial tailoring in order to fit the needs of a particular time, place, and people. Sometimes they do not fit at all.

Good options follow naturally from a sound understanding of the problem – such as instruments for internalising an externality or directly supplying information to correct an information asymmetry. Some advisers lose sight of this fundamental principle, however, and fall into the trap of reaching for off-the-shelf options when time is short, or confining the search for options to current debates. Others fall into the trap of including only government interventions as options, rather than broadening their understanding of roles for other, non-state actors and considering how government policy can facilitate activity by other players to address the problem.

Linking options to problems is easiest when the market and government failure frameworks apply. The analyst in these situations can generate a list of relevant instruments readily by matching types of market, government, or distributive failure with their cognate policy remedies. Table 3.4 provides a sample of how this works, based on similar exercises presented by Weimer and Vining (1999), Ledbury et al (2006), and Birkland (2006). Think of table 3.4 as an options menu or options library in progress. Readers will want to add to it from their own experience and insights.

Policy problems and opportunities that do not lend themselves to framing through a market failure, social distribution, or government failure lens cannot benefit fully from table 3.4. Still, the adviser searching for options can use lists of typical government activities to stimulate ideas. Table 3.4 can be used in this way, as can 'Things Governments Do', the appendix to Bardach's guide.

When policy issues can be framed using market failure, social distribution, and government failure frameworks, table 3.4 becomes useful in several ways. If the analysis has proceeded according to the usual Bardachian sequence, which starts with problem definition, then the problem definition can be used to find particular problem frameworks in the middle column. These frameworks can be matched against relevant policy instruments in the first column. Alternatively, the analyst who is compelled to start with a solution can work backwards to the problem, and then identify additional options to supplement the original solution.

Backing into problem definition

As an example of this technique, take the case of recycling, which may be the most popular and widely practised pro-environmental activity of our time. Because recycling is so widely accepted, few people step back to ask what problem it is seeking to address. Any policy analyst asked to develop strategies for expanding recycling volumes should ask the question: What is the problem for which this program is the anointed solution?

In the case of recycling, its popularity may be due to the fact that it addresses several problems simultaneously, some of which are illustrated in figure 3.1. When materials are recycled rather than thrown in the rubbish, pressure on landfills eases, pollution caused by improper waste disposal is reduced, fewer virgin materials have to be harvested, and citizens' commitment to protecting the environment may be reinforced (that is, their apathy diminished) as a result of developing a new daily,

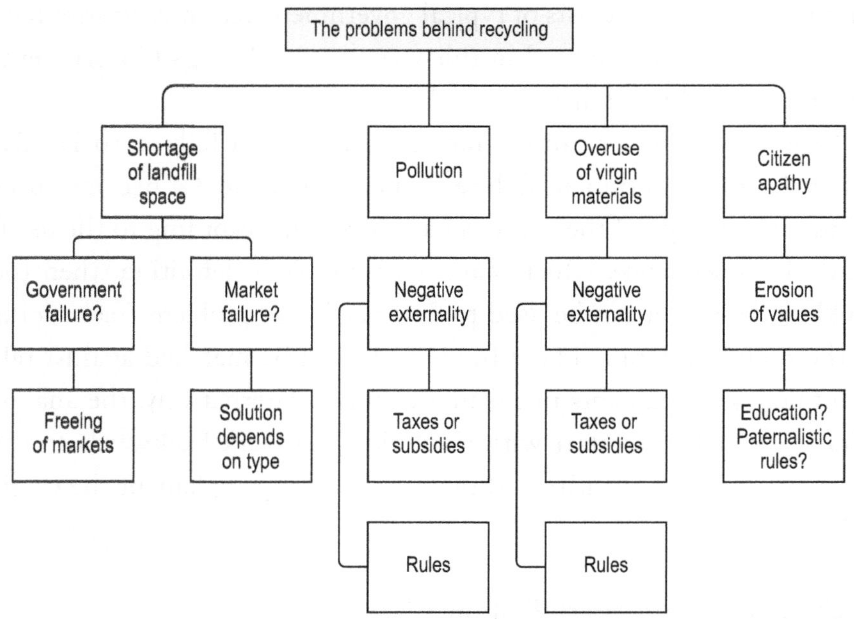

pro-environment habit. Figure 3.1 classifies each of these problems according to the usual problem frameworks discussed above, except for the last one, which requires the addition of a new problem category associated with citizen apathy.

Revealing the multi-centred nature of the background problem may be interesting in itself, but the reason for conducting this exercise is to produce sound policy recommendations. If the advisers do not understand the problems for which recycling is the chosen solution, their advice may fail to address those problems.

The exercise illustrated in figure 3.1 offers two avenues for generating recommendations. Firstly, advisers may use the results to craft modifications to current recycling policies to make them more effective in addressing the identified problems, for example by promoting recycling of some materials more than others based on different materials' relative impacts on the environment. Secondly, advisers may generate new policy proposals using table 3.4 and the problem frameworks identified in figure 3.1. Some of these additional policy ideas surely would encourage more recycling, but others would promote alternative solutions to the identified problems as well. Selected alternatives, once vetted, could be recommended alongside the enhancements to recycling to generate even better results.

Following are some of the ideas that flow from figure 3.1, in random order. Many of the listed options are familiar because they have been implemented in various jurisdictions.

- Placing per-household fees on waste disposal (host fees, etc)
- Regulating landfills
- Placing fees on use of virgin materials
- Subsidising recycling more generously
- Offering deposit refunds on containers and other materials
- Mandating recycling
- Pricing waste disposal on a unit basis (with recycling free of charge)
- Running public education campaigns to inform people about the benefits of reducing packaging material, reusing items, and recycling
- Rewarding households for low rubbish volumes and related outcomes (either materially or with feel-good rewards)
- Sponsoring contests to stir competition and innovation around low-waste behaviours
- Sponsoring fairs to promote products made from recycled materials
- Banning or placing a levy on excessive packaging
- Facilitating industry-led regulation of packaging and/or waste disposal practices

- Requiring labels indicating use of virgin materials in selected products
- Mandating government procurement of supplies made from recycled materials.

All of these options follow directly from an understanding of the policy problem, and therefore qualify as genuine options until further analysis can be conducted to weed out the less promising ideas.

Sources of policy options

Fashions come and go in policymaking as they do in every other field, pushing policy analysts and advisers to stay current and embrace the latest ideas. Pressure to conform may come from several directions at once, including academic and professional networks, organisational imperatives, and stakeholder groups.

Provision of free and frank advice requires both familiarity with, and detachment from, the latest policy fashions. Policy developers working in all domains need to recognise the latest policy ideas and understand the arguments for and against them, while maintaining the critical capacity to distinguish between fads and genuine innovations. They need to cultivate the skills to judge popular policies and assess a policy's relevance to their own jurisdiction. They also need to keep exploring alternatives and maintain their own creative capacity to devise wholly new approaches.

Policy advisers can avoid becoming fashion slaves by cultivating multiple sources of policy ideas and options. Such sources may include, among others:

- Bright ideas and favoured programs of ministers, board members, or other bosses
- Programs that have been tried, evaluated, and proven effective in other jurisdictions (with the caveat that things may work differently in different places and times)

- Ideas circulating in professional policy networks
- Home-grown ideas developed in local communities
- Innovations proposed by academics
- Programs endorsed by international organisations
- New ideas emerging from think-tanks and interest groups
- The adviser's own knowledge and experience of the policy area
- Problem frameworks and related solutions discussed above (see table 3.4)
- Generic lists of 'things governments do'
- Analogies with options used in other policy areas
- Updates on historical approaches to a perennial problem
- Stories told by citizens on the ground, especially those directly affected by the policy problem.

Innovative policy options sometimes flow from theoretical analysis. To take one of many possible examples, the growing field of behavioural economics offers the principle of 'liberal paternalism' to guide construction of policy options. Coined by Cass Sunstein and Richard Thaler (2009), the term 'liberal paternalism' sounds like an oxymoron, but represents a paradigm-busting merger between two central insights about human nature and power: (1) the liberal idea that people should not be coerced strictly for their own good, which explains liberal restraints on social engineering projects; and (2) the paternalistic idea that people sometimes want to be coerced, or at least strongly pressured, for their own good, which explains why personal trainers at the neighbourhood gym always have plenty of clients.

In the context of problem gambling, the principles of liberal paternalism have led some jurisdictions to adopt a policy known as voluntary exclusion or self-exclusion, in which casinos, clubs, hotels, and other gambling venues operate the voluntary equivalent of a blacklist. Customers who acknowledge that they have a gambling problem can choose, in a moment of lucidity and self-control, to place their names on the list of people to be excluded from these venues. This ensures that in future moments of weaker self-control, the problem gambler can rely on an external authority to say 'no'. Customers who join the voluntary blacklist are essentially granting authority to the casino to act on behalf of their own rational and authentic long-term interests in order to override their own irrational and addiction-clouded, short-term impulses.

Self-exclusion programs operate widely throughout Australia, with features of the programs varying from state to state. For example, casino programs are controlled by legislation in all states, but clubs and hotels in Victoria, ACT, and Queensland operate their programs under voluntary codes of practice. The duration of exclusions, number of venues that can be chosen, and revocation mechanisms also vary between states. Enforcing the voluntary bans has proven difficult in many cases, leading to lawsuits by problem gamblers who were allowed entry when they should not have been. Although venues can be fined for not detecting and removing people on the voluntary ban list, the courts have not required casinos to reimburse losses incurred by self-excluded problem gamblers.

The principle of liberal paternalism also guides the use of 'opt-out' rather than 'opt-in' features in national savings schemes. New Zealand's Kiwisaver program, for example, is not a mandatory savings scheme, but all new employees are automatically enrolled in the scheme and must actively disenrol if they do not wish to participate. This simple default mechanism is designed to overcome negative inertia, which prevents many people from joining existing savings programs because of the inconvenience associated with setting up an account, while also exploiting positive inertia, which causes people to continue saving once they have started because of the inconvenience associated with disenrolling. The theory is that once participants begin to see their savings accumulate, they will feel good about saving and pay less notice to the discomforts of lower take-home pay. Default enrolment gives people a taste of savings behaviour in the hope that they will continue saving either because they like it or because they can't be bothered to withdraw. It thereby addresses certain mild forms of irrationality such as short-sightedness, procrastination, and aversion to delayed gratification.

Experts generally agree that opt-out mechanisms increase participation, making policies with such mechanisms strong performers. Arguments against programs such as Kiwisaver tend to focus either on qualms about paternalism of any stripe (liberal or not) or on the practical challenges of ensuring performance by the financial companies doing the investing. New Zealand writer Janet Frame (1961) got the former in one when she quipped, '"For your own good" is a persuasive argument that will eventually make a man agree to his own destruction'. Some critics of Kiwisaver-type programs argue that the default enrolment mechanism interferes with consumer decision-making by imposing unnecessary transaction costs (that is, time required to disenrol) on the exercise of free choice. They argue that some people would be better off not saving, or saving in other ways. In other words, critics argue that the paternalistic elements of these programs trump the liberal elements and that people should be trusted to make their own savings plans without undue interference. The counterargument points out that default enrolment increases the welfare of many more people than it disadvantages by helping people save who otherwise would not. The central trade-off appears to be between higher rates of participation and higher barriers to consumer sovereignty – both of which are expected to result from default enrolment.

To the extent that the principle of liberal paternalism, and the options it produces, qualify as emerging policy fashions, advisers should treat them with caution, because their novelty makes them alluring, but they are, as yet, untested. As with all options, regardless of source, widely applicable ideas such as voluntary exclusion and opt-out mechanisms need to be thoroughly examined in the context of local needs and constraints before recommending them.

RESULTS: KNOWING WHERE WE WANT TO GO

A policy option is a hypothesis about how an instrument of government activity (or inactivity) is expected to achieve a result that serves a declared purpose. It combines instrumentality with intent, mechanism with mission. Policy options need to be assessed before advice can be crafted: this is the most fundamental of fundamentals, and the next chapter covers it in depth. But what standards should be used for assessment? This section addresses that question.

Policy should articulate desired results clearly in the form of policy goals. Defective advice about goals may take many different forms: articulating only those goals that make current policy or the favoured policy option look good, mirroring the adviser's personal values, skewing policy goals toward key stakeholders' interests, listing reams and reams of goals in order to keep every stakeholder happy, advancing vague and inoffensive goals that sound nice but are essentially meaningless, or failing to identify any public purposes at all. All of these bad practices collect at one or the other end of a spectrum, from waffling to tilting. They are a menace to good policy advice, because all policy recommendations sink or swim on the strength of their ability to achieve clearly signalled purposes. If such purposes are missing, misconstrued, or watered down to platitudes, then the recommendations designed to achieve those purposes cannot hold.

Good policy advice in this sphere balances between waffling and tilting. It provides a reasonable number of plainly articulated, unambiguous statements of purpose (goals) that can focus and guide policy choice without dictating conclusions. These are connected to specific measures, wherever possible, to clarify what is meant by them.

Effectiveness and efficiency are the most common standards for judging policy, followed by fairness and equity. Good policies should be effective in achieving results and do so efficiently, meaning with minimal expenditure relative to benefits achieved. Good policies should also be implemented using fair processes; and their costs and benefits should be distributed equitably. Some policy options aim to maximise other values as well, such as client choice or community solidarity. Finally, options should be assessed according to standards of feasibility: can the option be implemented within likely resource and capability constraints?

When key players within the policy system disagree about what effectiveness, efficiency, fairness, equity, and even feasibility mean in the context of a particular policy question, advisers need to take their bearings from key stakeholders, clients, and predominant social norms. For example, a policy analysis can incorporate primary and secondary standards for judging options. Primary standards would be based on the values and interests of the client, which means the government of the day in public service policy advising, along with any widely agreed standards. Secondary standards would be based on other, competing values and interests and may be expressed as risks or potential side effects to be monitored.

Effectiveness

This is the pre-eminent standard for judging policy options, partly because it captures much of what people care about in terms of policy's impacts on their lives, and partly because it seems to provide an objective measure against which policy proposals can be assessed. Effectiveness refers to a policy's ability to produce desired results in the form of direct or indirect benefits for citizens. In order to count as a bona fide policy result, the result needs to have been caused by policy rather than other factors, such as international economic trends.

This is known as the problem of attribution – or the problem of determining how much of a particular outcome should be attributed to policy interventions and how much to other factors. To what extent can government claim credit for an increasing rate of economic growth? To what extent should government be blamed for a rising crime rate? The attribution problem dogs results-based public policy and management initiatives everywhere at both the ex ante and ex post phases.

The field of program evaluation specialises in ex post measurement and assessment of effectiveness, always seeking improved methods for overcoming the attribution problem and learning how, why, and when policy 'works' to generate desirable results for citizens. The problem of attribution causes the most trouble at the front end of policy work, or the ex ante stage of assessment (predicting effectiveness before decisions have been taken). Ex post evaluation should employ the same measures of effectiveness used to compare and judge policy options at the ex ante stage. This allows policy advisers to check the accuracy of their projections and learn from successes and failures.

At least as challenging as the problem of attribution is the problem of whose definition of effectiveness should be granted priority. The client's views carry a lot of weight, of course, but responsible policy advice will stretch beyond the client's outlook if it appears narrow or mistaken. The practice of searching broadly for standards of assessment must strike a mean between recklessness and excessive caution. When the client needs to know (regardless of whether the client wants to know) how a policy option would be likely to perform against the standards favoured by other stakeholders, then advisers need to deliver this information and analysis.

Some desired results are wholly intangible and, therefore, impossible to measure directly, if at all. New Zealand's iconic 'nuclear-free' policy and the Australian government's apology to its Indigenous people are classic examples. In the case of the nuclear-free pronouncement, the purpose is to express a collective moral position and invite other global citizens to adopt a similar position. It seeks to keep alive a counter-establishment vision of foreign relations and international balance-of-power politics in which nuclear weapons have no place, an alternative to the status quo acceptance of a nuclear world. In the case of the Australian apology, which took the form of a parliamentary motion and a much-watched formal address by the Prime Minister, the purpose was to affirm the ideal of universal human dignity, heal relations among Australians of Aboriginal and non-Aboriginal descent, and establish a foundation of mutual respect in Aboriginal policy development going forward.

How would an evaluator measure the results of these policies ex ante or ex post? On the one hand, the evaluation question can be seen as irrelevant because the public purpose being served in each case is largely expressive rather than causative. As long as these two policies express the consensus or super-majority views of New Zealanders and Australians, they should be considered successful. No 'results' are required. On the other hand, some would argue that the side effects of the nuclear-free policy have included damage to some of New Zealand's most important international relationships. If such damage outweighs the value of moral expression, then the policy may need to be reconsidered, but if not, then some international tensions may be considered the price of standing up for one's principles. An expected side effect of the Australian apology has been an opening for lawsuits brought by victims of 'laws and policies of successive Parliaments and governments that have inflicted profound grief, suffering and loss on these our fellow Australians' (quoting from the text of the parliamentary motion), but people disagree about whether such lawsuits and the compensation being sought represent progress or excess. To date, the balance of New

Zealand opinion remains strongly in favour of the nuclear-free position, and the motion of apology in the Australian Parliament received unanimous support.

Attention to unintended side effects is a fundamental tenet of good policy practice. Not all policy results are intended. For example, it has been noted that restricting advertising of junk food to reduce obesity might enable producers of these products to lower the prices of unhealthy snacks, thus attracting more sales rather than fewer. In this case, the unintended effect of the policy threatens to undermine the intended results. In other cases, a policy may achieve its main aim but also generate side effects, that is, subsidiary or secondary results. Adoption of an emissions trading scheme to reduce greenhouse gases, for example, would likely shift employment away from the oil and gas industries toward renewable energy industries in the long run. Is this a desirable side effect? Side effects may be good, bad, or indifferent.

Statements of effectiveness or desired results may take several broad forms:

- Solving a problem (for example, reducing carbon emissions, ending the war in Iraq, keeping the unemployed out of poverty)
- Managing a problem (for example, cleaning up after a natural disaster, helping drug addicts reduce their drug use and maintain functionality)
- Jollying someone else along to solve or manage a problem (for example, keeping bank credit flowing after the economic meltdown of 2008–09)
- Mitigating harms (for example, reducing mortality and injury associated with car crashes, slowing the spread of blood-borne diseases among injecting drug users)
- Multiplying or expanding benefits (for example, encouraging eligible beneficiaries of a program to enrol)

- Cultivating opportunities (for example, building on big events such as the 2000 Sydney Olympics and the 2011 Rugby World Cup to boost follow-up tourism)
- Meeting possible threats (for example, preparing for large-scale terrorist acts and/or natural disasters).

In addition, to be deemed successful, policies must produce desired results economically, or at minimal cost, relative to benefits generated; and do so fairly, with equitable distribution of benefits and costs.

Results determine whether or not government power has been exercised effectively and whether the selected course of action has achieved its purposes. Words such as result, impact, effect, and outcome are often used interchangeably. Regardless of terminology, the fundamental concept remains the same: the likely effectiveness of policies should be thoroughly assessed before making recommendations.

Efficiency and costs

This assessment standard simply adds a cost component to effectiveness to reflect the goal of maximising value for money.

Cost–benefit analysis is the theoretical paradigm for analysing efficiency. It can be very useful in analysing bricks-and-mortar options and other issues in which costs and benefits are clearly identified and easy to express in dollar terms. The analyst proceeds by listing all of the costs and benefits associated with each policy option, calculating their dollar value (discounted for future value, where appropriate), adding up the columns, and comparing the final scores of each option to choose a 'winner'.

Sometimes the best option will have the largest total net benefit value; at other times, it will be chosen based on the ratio of benefits to costs. In cases where benefits are difficult to monetise, cost-effectiveness analysis can be used instead of cost–benefit analysis to compare natural units of outcomes per dollar or dollars required to produce each natural unit of outcome (for example, tonnes of carbon removed from the atmosphere or number of child abuse cases prevented).

Costs may be an important criterion on their own. Cost to government is often a key driver of policy decisions, but short-term costs can seem more important than long-term ones and agencies will often see shifting costs to individuals or to other agencies as beneficial.

Equity and fairness: a hard case

Efficiency and effectiveness are well-known and well-understood standards for judging options, thanks in part to careful study of both phenomena by economists. Effectiveness standards have a lovely, common-sense quality about them as they often follow directly from the problem definition as its mirror image. For example, if the problem is air pollution from wood heaters, then the obvious standard for comparing policy options must be less air pollution generated by these devices. If the problem is an explosion in mortgage foreclosures leading to homelessness, then one standard for comparing policy options must be reduction in homeless cases caused by mortgage foreclosure. (NB: this is subtly different from a reduction in mortgage foreclosures themselves, which may not affect homelessness if the policy tends to serve the least vulnerable mortgage-holders, most of whom would not be at risk of homelessness.)

By contrast, equity and fairness standards tend to be less intuitive and more prone to ideological disputes. Some policies exist largely for the purpose of counteracting the inequalities of income and opportunity that efficient markets tend to generate. In these cases, equity operates as a problem framework rather than as one more criterion in a list. In other cases, policies that aim first and foremost at effectiveness will include equity as a side goal or constraint to be traded off against effectiveness if necessary. Likewise, fairness, which is used here to refer to the processes through which a policy is implemented, usually operates as an important side constraint. Equity standards judge the content of a policy (for example, eligibility criteria for subsidised housing – do they take sufficient account of need?), whereas fairness standards focus on due process (for example, processing of applications for subsidised housing – are all applications given equal attention?).

When assessing distributive impacts, the distinction between horizontal and vertical equity is often helpful. The principle of vertical equity focuses on reducing disparities. It requires people who are situated differently to be treated differently so that the gap between them narrows. All targeted resource allocation policies, including public assistance benefits and affirmative action programs, aim for vertical equity and should be assessed against vertical-equity criteria. Other policies of all kinds may have important and unintended side effects for vertical distribution, for example when a decrease in the Reserve Bank interest rate lowers the average incomes of retirees, many of whom live off the interest on their savings.

The key distributive principle in vertical equity is generally proportionality; resources are to be targeted proportionally to the relevant differences between people. Relevant differences typically relate to need, because needier individuals or groups are thought to be situated differently for the sake of vertical equity. They receive more of certain types of government assistance in rough proportion to their greater needs. Occasionally, relevant differences between individuals or groups take the form of social standing, as with claims linked to indigeneity. Lifetime social contribution and achievement are the relevant differences on New Year's Day when the honours lists are announced. Talent and potential are the relevant differences when it comes to distributing Olympic training subsidies. Ability to pay is the relevant difference at income tax time in a progressive tax system.

Need-based vertical equity programs often attract controversy. In particular, affirmative action and other distributive programs based on ethnicity regularly come under attack for using ethnicity as an imprecise, hard-to-define, and potentially divisive proxy for need. Opponents in these debates sometimes argue over the strength of the empirical link between ethnicity and disadvantage; but even where the empirical links are undeniable, Australians and New Zealanders often express a preference for using income or other direct measures of deprivation, rather than ethnicity, as the relevant characteristic for purposes of distribution.

Some benefits and burdens are traditionally distributed on strictly equal grounds: jury duty; passports; voting privileges/obligations (one person, one vote); free, compulsory education; and the right to legal representation are examples. Constitutional democracies do not give some people more votes or less jury duty than others to compensate them for deprivations in other areas of life or to reward achievements. Nor do they deprive citizens of legal protection when they break the law, which is why prison inmates are not allowed to beat up other prison inmates as they please. The principle guiding all of these policies is horizontal equity, which requires people who are situated similarly to be treated exactly alike. In many cases of horizontal equity, the relevant characteristic is citizenship – all citizens are thought to be situated similarly, regardless of ethnicity, income, sex, or talent, when certain fundamental goods and burdens are being distributed.

Policies may have intended or unintended distributive impacts in either or both the vertical and horizontal equity dimensions, and analysts should stay alert to these.

Other values

Results determine whether or not government power has been exercised effectively with respect to a targeted purpose, but they do not speak to the appropriateness of government action. The aforementioned hypothetical policy of mandating ballet attendance may be highly effective in boosting audience numbers (a targeted purpose), but this does not make it a good policy.

The Latin phrase, *fiat justitia ruat caelum* – commonly translated as 'let justice be done though the heavens may fall' – provides a counterweight to results-based policy-making and a potent reminder that there are some things more important than results. If the abolition of slavery had caused widespread economic disaster, would it still have been the right thing to do? Theories of human rights say yes, *fiat justitia ruat caelum*.

Criteria for assessment

Good policy advice needs to articulate its desired results clearly and forthrightly so that policy options can be judged against them. The specific indicators used to measure the achievement of purposes are known as criteria.

The word 'criteria' means standards or tests, and in this context refers to the specific measures used in a policy analysis to test for effectiveness, efficiency, fairness, equity, feasibility, and other relevant values. For example, criteria of effectiveness for an emissions trading scheme would include changes in levels of carbon emissions and overall greenhouse gases in the atmosphere. Value-adding policy advice needs to specify the criteria being used to judge policy options in order to avoid recommendations with unacknowledged or unrecognised biases. Because measurable criteria depend heavily on available data, good practice in this area of policy advice requires thorough knowledge of data sources.

This component of policy analysis – criteria – adds value to policy advice by reminding both analysts and decision-makers that policy choice does not involve only a choice among options. In many cases, it also involves a choice among values or objectives, thus requiring advisers to articulate the possible values at stake, even when some of them clash. Take the relatively tame example of whether or not to charge customers per unit of water used within a local authority. This decision pits efficiency against equity and short-term expenditures against long-term savings. Charging per unit of water brings clear efficiencies in terms of covering the true costs of maintaining reservoirs, pipes, pumping stations, and so on, as well as encouraging water conservation. However, it may put additional budgetary strains on some low-income households, especially those with higher water needs because of large families or medical conditions; and requires a large initial expenditure to install water meters. Which of these values should prevail? The policy-maker will decide, and the adviser can add value to the decision-making process by clarifying the nature of the choices between values as well as the instrumental options.

Criteria for assessment in the above example might include upfront costs of installing meters, ongoing costs of billing and chasing missed payments, percentage of total costs that could be recovered by charging, projected impact on water conservation, and projected impact on high-need, low-income households. Using specific measures as criteria is nearly always a good idea if they can be developed to clearly reflect relevant underlying values.

Values that take the form of intangible ideals, such as expressing a moral stance (for example, nuclear-free New Zealand) or pursuing reconciliation between peoples (for example Australia's apology to the 'stolen generations'), may be difficult to measure directly. Other values will take the more concrete, measurable form of material consequences such as higher income, greater educational attainment, more balanced trade flows, or fewer terrorist acts. Criteria should capture both types of values (see figure 3.2) and include both intended and unintended outcomes (that is, side effects). Whether they are representing ideals or consequences, core goals or side effects, the central purpose of criteria is to provide targets against which policy ideas can be tested before they are included in advice to government.

Advisers should ask the following questions when developing crite-

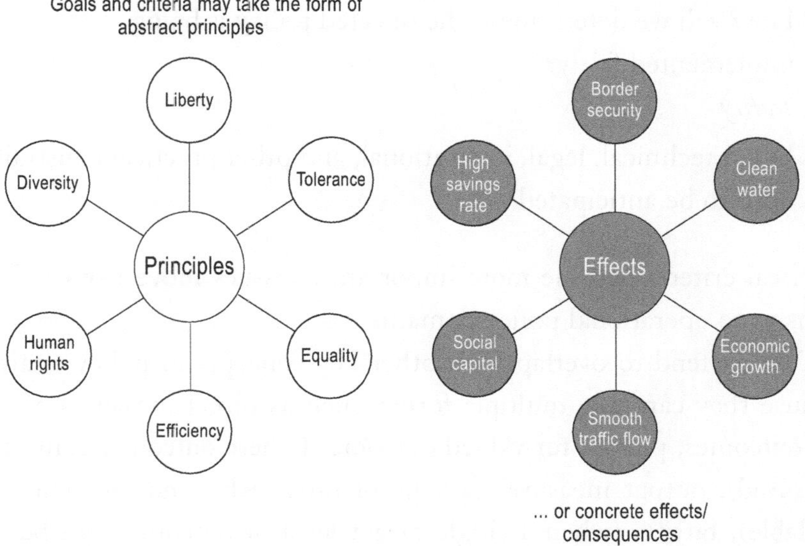

ria for policy analysis. Each dot point may require one or more separate criteria, but advisers should beware of very long lists of criteria, which can make the analysis unwieldy.

Effectiveness

- What is to be accomplished in this policy area, and how will we know if the selected policy has succeeded?
- What possible side effects need to be anticipated?

Efficiency and value for money

- What are the costs of each policy option and how do these relate to expected benefits?

Equity and fairness

- How should the impacts, side effects, costs, and benefits of the selected policy be distributed among individuals, groups, geographical areas, industries, etc? How will we judge if they are distributed equitably?

- How will we determine if vulnerable groups are further disadvantaged by the selected policy?
- How will we determine if the selected policy is being implemented fairly?

Practicality

- What technical, legal, institutional, and other practical constraints need to be anticipated?

Practical criteria become more important as issues move from the responsive to operational policy domains.

Criteria tend to overlap with other key concepts in policy analysis because they can take multiple forms, such as direct measures of valued outcomes, proxies for valued outcomes (where outcomes cannot be measured), output measures (a type of proxy when no outcomes are available), targets (when a single target level of outcomes can be defined), and performance indicators. In table 3.5, for example, both seizures of dangerous goods and complaints to the human rights commissioner look more like outputs than outcomes, but they are the best criteria available in each case because outcomes cannot be directly observed.

Security, bio- or otherwise, is a classic challenge for criteria selectors because measuring real improvements in security requires accurate information about underlying threats. What proportion of potential threats were in fact thwarted or prevented by policy? Answering this question requires both an accurate numerator (actual threats known to have been discovered and stopped) and an accurate denominator (potential and unknown threats). The latter is nearly impossible to measure, almost by definition: if advisers could count unknown threats, the threats would no longer qualify as unknown. Likewise, deterrence is an important policy goal in the crime and security portfolios, but it defies observation and, therefore, measurement, for precisely these reasons. We can never know exactly what crimes would have been committed in the absence of deterrence, and therefore, cannot know what has been deterred. In hard cases such as these, analytical criteria may need to take the form of outputs (services rendered) rather than outcomes (results achieved).

Table 3.5 Examples of criteria

Value	Criterion
Educational achievement	Change in student test scores (+)
Biosecurity	Seizures (number or volume) of dangerous goods (+)
Health status	Quality-adjusted life years gained (+)
Freedom	Choices available (+)
Tolerance	Complaints to human rights commissioner (–)
Economic growth	GDP per capita (+)

Some criteria may deserve more weight than others because they represent a widely held view or because they represent the government of the day's priorities. Criteria can be arrayed in order of importance within a policy report, or the analyst can assign numerical weights to the criteria if a final scoring tally is intended.

Where do criteria come from?

Analysts may present too many or too few criteria. Too many criteria make it virtually impossible to complete an analysis, whereas too few criteria tend to omit important values from the decision. There is no standard optimal number of criteria. Analysts should trim their lists as far as possible without sacrificing any important perspectives.

Key sources of criteria include:

* goals and objectives of the client, whether or not that is the government of the day

- relevant stakeholders (whose values and interests may clash)
- under-represented groups in the population
- groups particularly vulnerable to the policies in question
- meta-values of the society, such as one finds in the constitution or expressed in characteristic norms of the society.

Analysts may need to engage in consultation around criteria to ensure that diverse views and values have been considered. Public service policy officials are best able to engage in this type of detached and inclusive approach to criteria writing because they do not represent any particular subset of society's interests. At the same time, policy officials working within government must strike a balance between an inclusive approach to criteria and a clear understanding of the government of the day's values, purposes, and priorities.

EVIDENCE

Across all three components of good policy, policy developers should seek the best possible evidence to inform policy recommendations. It is unfortunate that Bardach makes 'assembling evidence' its own step in the eightfold path, because it needs to occur at every stage of a robust policy analysis process no matter what grand approach is used.

In policy circles, the term 'evidence' often seems to be a sort of nickname for empirical research findings. The OED online defines evidence much more broadly as 'something serving as a proof' or 'the grounds for belief', which include 'testimony or facts tending to prove or disprove a conclusion'. Thus, where relevant research has not been undertaken, advisers can still generate evidence-informed policy advice by assembling relevant facts, testimony (including results of consultations with experts, stakeholders, and citizens), and common-sense arguments that constitute grounds for supporting or rejecting particular policy options. It is good to remember that public engagement activities are not just about building support for an eventual policy decision. They provide avenues for gathering valuable evidence – on-the-ground intelligence about real problems and promising solutions.

RECOMMENDATIONS

The central purpose of policy analysis is to inform policy advice, the final product of policy work. Policy advice may be presented formally or informally, in written or oral formats, and with varying degrees of confidence or caution.

Not all policy advice concludes with endorsement of a particular course of action. When trade-offs among criteria need to be made, policy advice often leaves the final analysis to the decision-maker. Recommendations then take a contingent or 'if-then' form in which the adviser says to decision makers: 'Choose option A if you care most about value X. Choose option C if you care most about value Y'. Occasionally, none of the available policy options survive the analysis, in which case advisers usually counsel to make no change and stay with the status quo until better options can be discovered or developed.

Although most recommendations are delivered to specific users of the advice, such as ministers, boards of directors, local councils, or op-ed writers, there is always potential for policy advice to inform the larger public debate on an issue. It is sometimes through this 'back-door' channel that advice has its greatest impact.

CONCLUSION

Mastering the fundamentals is key to becoming an expert in virtually any field, including policy analysis and advice. Good public policy is that which uses the legitimate powers of government (often in partnership with other institutions) to establish well-designed policy instruments that will serve valid public purposes. Value-adding policy advice enlightens decision-makers as they face the challenge of delivering good policy outcomes to citizens. It avoids the ideological traps of state-centricity or state-phobia and the stereotypical extremes of boundless enthusiasm for new policy ideas or stubborn resistance to policy change. It provides clear, focused goals against which policy options can be assessed.

Value-adding policy advice carves out appropriate roles not only for government but also for non-state actors, and identifies policy instruments capable of addressing the problems and opportunities being experienced on the ground. It neither waffles nor grinds an axe. It always asks hard questions about the likely effectiveness, efficiency, and equity of policy as well as giving attention to other criteria that are of concern to the ministers or other client for advice.

The fundamentals of good practice described here do not form any orderly sequence of tasks. They can be addressed in whatever order suits the analyst, as long as all are covered eventually. The next chapter explores three complementary methods for putting these fundamentals into play.

PUTTING THE FUNDAMENTALS INTO PLAY

4

Advice is generally judged by results, not by intentions.

Cicero, 106–43 BC,
Letters to Atticus

Which policy will achieve the desired purposes? Answering this question is the *raison d'être* of policy analysis and the foundation of good policy advice. It is the most fundamental of the fundamental building blocks of good practice. Unfortunately, it is also the most difficult of puzzles because it requires policy teams to predict how a multitude of different variables will interact to produce benefits and harms. This chapter introduces three approaches for scrutinising policy options and assessing their capacity to deliver.

THREE APPROACHES

The fundamental principles of value-adding policy advice and the balances to be struck between extremes of practice, as discussed in the previous chapter, should guide policy work at every juncture, but those who would influence or create policy advice need practical tools and methods for putting these fundamentals into play. At the start of a policy project, shovels are sometimes needed to clear a path through mountains of information and torches to penetrate the dark places where no information exists. As the project proceeds, compasses are needed to prevent analysts from wandering off into irrelevancies and distortions. Although no tool or method is ever perfect, and some can be overused, it is hard to progress toward value-adding advice without the discipline of method.

David Weimer (1998:114) urges policy analysts to 'avoid self-deception' when they construct recommendations for decision-makers. Self-deception is a good term for this fundamental trap, because it recognises the fact that many analysts and advisers – particularly those working in the public service, but others, too – want to provide unbiased, impartial, well-informed advice, and try hard to do so. When they fail, the failure is rarely due to deliberate efforts to mislead. It may result from professional and organisational biases in favour of particular types of intervention, such as engineers who like to address problems by building things and social workers who believe strongly in case management. Members of professions and organisations often do not recognise their shared views as biases. Failures of impartiality also may result from external pressures to play favourites among interest groups. Biases may be built into an organisation's mission for purposes of counter-balancing dominant social biases – as in the case of a ministry focused on the needs of a particular population group or any one of a thousand NGOs.

Good tools and methods, applied appropriately, can reduce bias and improve thoroughness and incisiveness. The three broad approaches to assessing policy options described in this chapter are composed of different sets of tools and methods to be applied in different analytical settings. They are not perfect substitutes for each other, but neither are they mutually exclusive alternatives. In many cases, the best policy advice will be produced when all three approaches are woven together, if time and resources allow.

THE OUTCOMES MATRIX

The outcomes matrix is a device for systematically comparing policy options on the basis of their predicted impacts and displaying the results of the comparison. Whether it is called an outcomes matrix (Bardach), a goals/alternatives matrix (Weimer), or a multi-criteria decision-analysis matrix (a term used in operations research), the central purpose of the matrix is to aid policy choice by helping decision-makers understand how different options would be likely to perform against different indicators of value.

The matrix has three main components. The selected policy options to be compared (component 1) and the selected criteria for assessing those options (component 2) are set out in the shell of the matrix – the column and row headings. The projected outcomes of the options as measured against the criteria (component 3) are recorded in the interior cells. These projected outcomes may be expressed quantitatively or qualitatively, depending on the availability of data. The value added by the matrix depends upon the honesty and accuracy of the outcome projections. Policy advisers want decision-makers to choose the options with the greatest probability of producing positive net results, but this is impossible if the projections are wrongly estimated.

Setting up a matrix shell takes no time at all once the criteria and options have been decided. The hard work in the set-up stage occurs in the process of identifying, packaging, and articulating criteria and options, as discussed in the previous chapter. Consider again the previous chapter's example of a local council that needs to choose between three possible sites for a new swimming pool. The best choice may not be obvious, but the problem itself can be structured relatively easily using an outcomes matrix such as the one shown in table 4.1.

Matrices can be adjusted to reflect various features of an issue. Take the ANZSOG teaching case of the *Australian Competition and Consumer Commission (ACCC) v Video Ezy*. In this case, the ACCC had

		Options	
Criteria	Site A	Site B	Site C
Proximity to users / convenience			
Construction costs			
Parking access			
Opportunity costs for land			
Environmental impact			
Neighbourhood support			

been tasked with monitoring and penalising price exploitation by businesses before the introduction of a new Goods and Services Tax (GST) in 2000. Because GST was replacing an array of existing taxes, which varied across different types of business inputs and outputs, it was not always clear what net impact GST would have on the final price of any particular good or service. This atmosphere of confusion created an opportunity for unscrupulous businesses to raise their prices without attracting attention, because the odds were good that consumers would attribute any price rises to GST, and businesses would not have to shoulder the blame. When the Video Ezy movie rental chain raised its overnight video hire charge from $6 to $7 shortly before the GST rollout, the ACCC suspected exploitation and set about negotiating a return to the original price and an apology to customers. Video Ezy held their ground, maintaining that the price increase was justified and had nothing to do with GST.

Negotiations broke down, and the ACCC was left with two choices. It could crack down hard on Video Ezy, thereby sending a signal to

Table 4.2 Matrix of policy options for the ACCC

| | Options | |
Criteria	Prosecute	Do not prosecute
Probability of Video Ezy lowering price		
Deterrent effect on other possible price exploiters	If successful … If unsuccessful …	
Effect on ACCC's organisational reputation	If successful … If unsuccessful …	
Effect on ACCC's overall relationship to business community		
Cost		

other businesses to play by the rules. If successful, this approach would help cement the ACCC's reputation as a serious watchdog, but if the court found in favour of Video Ezy, the loopholes in the price exploitation law would be exposed and the ACCC might be seen as unreasonable and ineffective. Alternatively, the ACCC could avoid the risk of a failed prosecution by focusing on its educational activities and softening enforcement. It could also wait for a more open-and-shut case of price exploitation to come along before prosecuting. In this situation, much hinges on the probability of a court deciding in the ACCC's favour.

The ANZSOG case asks readers to put themselves in the shoes of the ACCC chairman and choose a course of action. An outcomes matrix, such as the one shown in table 4.2, helps structure the decision.

As illustrated, the criteria for the *ACCC v Video Ezy* case are complicated by the need to consider two different scenarios under the first option – successful or unsuccessful prosecution. In addition, the criteria include organisational management concerns (mainly the effect on the ACCC's reputation and relationships) as well as direct program results. Policy and management decisions often shade into each other in this way, and often require similar analytical inputs.

Projecting outcomes

Once options and criteria have been agreed and slotted into the matrix, all the analyst needs do is fill the blank cells, estimating the probable impacts of each option regarding each criterion. In other words, they need to predict the future under each option and then judge the relative value of that future as defined by the criteria. Such a procedure, which Bardach calls 'outcomes projection', sounds simple in the abstract, but is in fact diabolically difficult and fraught with uncertainty because of the many ways a government's intentions may be frustrated by factors that defy prediction. Imagine a transport analyst in August 2001, just before the 9/11 horror, trying to predict airline traffic volumes for 2002, or a tourism planner in early 2008, just before the economic meltdown, trying to predict visitor numbers and revenues for 2009 and beyond.

Sudden, wrenching changes in underlying conditions throw outcome projections up for grabs, and so do the cumulative effects of slower, long-term changes in social, economic, cultural, or security patterns. Implementation conditions and capabilities are further sources of uncertainty when projecting outcomes.

Sources of information for filling in the matrix include the following.

Past evaluation results

Some options will have been applied in other jurisdictions or at earlier times in history, and evaluation results from these episodes are treasures for outcomes projection. Analysts, however, need to remember that programs may behave very differently in different places and times and under different conditions. As financial investment houses tell their customers, 'past performance is no guarantee of future results'.

Evaluation findings become more valuable the more the studies are repeated and the findings replicated. Organisations such as Policy Hub in the United Kingdom and the Campbell Collaboration in the USA (modelled on the Cochrane Collaboration's library of evidence-based medicine) endeavour to collect and synthesise research findings to identify robust patterns of results across diverse settings.

Research findings

Program evaluation is only one form of policy-relevant research, and it may crowd out other valuable sources of research-based evidence.

To illustrate this point, take the case of hand-washing. For a hand-washing awareness campaign to be effective, three effects need to occur. First, the campaign has to increase actual, as distinct from intended or reported, hand-washing. Secondly, the increased hand-washing has to reduce bacterial exposure. Thirdly, the reduction in bacterial exposure has to reduce illness. Existing research provides pretty good benchmarks for estimating the size of the second and third causal connections: the effectiveness of hand-washing in reducing bacteria and sickness-based absences has been well proven. The first step in the logic – changing actual behaviour – will be difficult to predict without direct testing of the campaign by running a pilot program and evaluating the impact on hand-washing frequency. However, there is research showing that people do not wash their hands as often as they report in surveys, which suggests that actual hand-washing behaviour should be measured by direct observation rather than survey results.

Analogies

Past evaluations need not have studied an identical program to be useful. Findings from evaluations or other research studies may be applied across policy areas using analogical thinking.

For example, Thaler and Sunstein (2009:69–70) describe a study in which a sample of households received information about their weekly energy consumption compared with their neighbours' average consumption. The information changed behaviour quickly and dramatically. Those with high relative energy use cut it back significantly after seeing where they ranked relative to their neighbours, while those with low relative consumption tended to increase toward the local average. The latter result, however, which is known as a boomerang effect, disappeared when householders with low relative consumption were given 'an emotional nudge', in the form of a smiley-face emoticon, along with the data about their usage. This simple 'reward' of approval (that is, praise) was sufficient to reinforce their low energy-consumption behaviour and prevent them from creeping up toward the average. Consistent with this, the higher-than-average users who received a frowning emoticon alongside the comparative data reduced their energy use even more dramatically than those who received data alone.

What might these findings contribute, by analogy, to the designers of the hand-washing education campaign mentioned previously? If the program designers can devise a way to communicate approval and disapproval for good and bad hand-washing behaviour, then perhaps they can project higher overall impacts with more confidence. The insights from the energy program evaluation thus speak to both policy design and outcomes projection in a wide variety of policy areas associated with behaviour modification.

Quantitative modelling

Policy outcomes can be modelled econometrically if enough data is available to establish reliable patterns. For example, changes in parking meter fees might be regressed against volumes of traffic entering a central business district, and the resulting correlation coefficient may be used to predict how a further change in fees would affect traffic congestion.

The main glitch in any modelling venture is usually the problem of omitted variable bias. A robust model of traffic flows, for example, would need to include data on all major explanatory factors, including weather, special events, employment and residential patterns, economic conditions, and so on, in addition to parking fees, to generate accurate estimates of impact. Comprehensive models with high predictive power are the diamonds of the policy world – rare and valuable.

Scenarios

Where hard evidence is lacking, analysts can use their own knowledge, experience, and powers of reasoning and imagination to build plausible scenarios of the way particular options might be expected to unfold – sometimes called alternative or potential futures – and then evaluate these scenarios against the criteria. As Saliba and Withers (2009: 127) have observed, scenarios function like 'mental windtunnels' in which policies or program ideas can be tested by changing the conditions inside the windtunnel (that is, altering features of the scenarios) and observing how the outcomes change in response.

Scenarios can take the simple form of stories, and are best produced in groups to ensure that a wide range of perspectives and factors are taken into consideration. Multiple scenarios can be built for each policy option to describe likely impacts under various conditions. It is often wise to build scenarios before filling in the outcomes matrix even when other forms of evidence are available, because scenarios can expose less obvious risk factors.

Consultation

Analysts and advisers can project outcomes based on the more or less informed opinions of experts, community leaders, program clients, citizens, or stakeholders as to how various policy options would be likely to perform. Comparing opinions across groups is always enlightening.

Actual impacts will usually fall between the extremes predicted by interested parties.

Whatever methods are used, outcome projections need to be checked for sensitivity to assumptions, and when the results are reported, the uncertainties regarding projections should be acknowledged. Policy teams in charge of projecting outcomes need to stay alert to defects in projection methods, including incomplete literature reviews, disregard of the limits of anecdotal evidence, loose-fitting analogies, scenarios hijacked by wishful thinking, and lopsided consultation. Above all, humility is needed at this stage of the policy analysis process.

Beware of overly confident outcome projections and false precision. When you do not have enough information to address all of the interior boxes, you must resist the temptation to fill them on the basis of hunches and popular wisdom. It is better to leave some boxes blank than to guess wildly. Do not project beyond the available knowledge. Trust your instincts, but explain your reasoning. The outcomes matrix requires the best possible efforts to predict effectiveness at the policy formulation stage.

Compared to what?

It is nearly always advisable to compare proposed policy changes to the existing arrangements under current policy. This can be done by labelling the first column in the matrix 'current policy' and measuring the projected outcomes of all other options against the baseline of current conditions.

Participatory matrix-building

Virtually any analytical technique can be adapted to a participatory approach. In the case of the outcomes matrix, the most thorough participatory processes begin at the beginning, with the choice of options and criteria to be included in the shell of the matrix. Decisions must be made at an early stage about who will be invited to participate in the exercise – all interested parties, representatives of key stakeholder groups, randomly chosen citizens? Once the participants have been selected or self-selected, they need to be engaged step by step in the production and interpretation of the matrix. These steps include constructing options to be assessed, selecting criteria by which to assess them, projecting the outcomes for each option against each criterion, weighing up the trade-offs when no single option appears to be a winner on all counts, and finally, determining the details of a recommended policy option. Proctor (2009) describes a process known as deliberative multi-criteria evaluation, which allows multiple actors with different interests and values to work together via citizen juries to collectively frame a complex issue and arrive at an agreed recommendation.

Strengths and weaknesses of the outcomes matrix

Policy issues that are relatively easy to structure in a matrix are not necessarily easy to solve. The impacts of the options may be difficult to predict or difficult to measure against the chosen criteria. The options' total scores across all criteria may be too close to identify a clear winning option. In some cases, there may simply be no options worth pursuing. Any of these and other complications can cause a well-structured policy problem to stubbornly defy solution. Nonetheless, advisers are expected to deliver recommendations, and the well-constructed outcomes matrix often proves useful in structuring recommendations because it illustrates trade-offs between criteria.

The matrix is the nerve centre of an applied problem-solving approach to policy analysis, for it is where means (policy instruments) and ends (goals as expressed in criteria) are tested against projected realities (predicted outcomes). Policy scholar David Weimer (1998:115), an enthusiast for the goals/alternatives matrix, has argued that constructing matrices is the most important of all policy craft skills because (1) it provides an organising framework for analysts bewildered by the welter of complexities and short turnaround demands that typically accompany each new project, and (2) it 'imposes a discipline on analysts that helps them avoid many common pitfalls: failure to consider the full range of relevant values in comparing alternatives, failure to anticipate unintended consequences, and failure to identify potentially desirable alternatives'.

Our experience with the matrix is more mixed. On one hand, as Weimer points out, it is a welcome organising tool and an aid in filtering and sorting the mass of information that will accumulate on analysts' desks and in their heads at the start of a project. Policy teams can find it useful to engage in brainstorming exercises at the beginning of a policy analysis and then organise the results of the brainstorm into matrix-derived categories: criteria, policy options, likely outcomes, side effects, and problem features. The matrix provides a certain discipline, as Weimer notes, by insisting that all options be judged against a consistent set of standards and all impacts predicted with as much rigour as possible.

On the other hand, we have observed three common traps associated with the matrix. The first is the options straitjacket. Complex issues generally require multi-pronged policy interventions, which do not fit easily into boxes. The matrix forces the analyst to package each option in a discrete form, and this bundling process often obscures the very features of policy design that are most interesting. Selected options thus tend to be reduced to unsophisticated stereotypes, such as more government or less government, looser or tighter regulatory controls, centralised or decentralised purchasing, commercialisation versus government provision, and so on. The resulting one-dimensional options array often leads junior analysts into a false sense of comprehensiveness and frustrates more experienced analysts who want to portray the richness of policy combinations.

In the case of drug policy, for example, we would expect policy options to vary in multiple dimensions, depending on whether they emphasise demand- or supply-side, education- or treatment-oriented, community- or individual-based, targeted or whole population, and short-term or long-term options. Fitting these dimensions into a single matrix is practically impossible, but analysts will often struggle mightily to make them fit. The resulting spectrum tends to focus solely on the dimension of legal status and runs from prohibition to decriminalisation to legalisation, with a stray 'education and treatment' category tacked on at the end. This is where the discipline of the outcomes matrix becomes a straitjacket, because the resulting analysis misses a wide range of possible behaviour-modification and community-based interventions that could be used under any legal regime. It also misses subtleties such as calibrating the intensity and focus of drug law-enforcement activities or tailoring implementation to local contexts.

In the case of industry policy, the outcomes matrix tends to produce roughly three bundles of options, including two politically unrealistic and logically flawed 'straw men' – protectionism versus laissez-faire – and one 'ringer', often described vaguely and inoffensively as a facilitative or enabling role for government. Nearly all of the interesting questions in this policy space either fall between the cracks in this array or focus on the details of the last bundle of options. When this occurs, analysts may discard the first two option bundles – the extremes of protectionism and laissez-faire – which looks like a reasonable move, except that it risks focusing the subsequent analysis too narrowly.

The second common trap associated with the matrix is closely related; let's call it the multiplier problem. We have noted that optimal policy choice in many cases involves combining instruments into packages designed to exploit the synergies between instruments. Adding various combinations of instruments to an analysis either multiplies the columns in the matrix exponentially or forces the analyst to choose a limited

Table 4.3 Outcomes matrix for recycling

Criteria	Options			
	Cluster A	Cluster B	Cluster C	Cluster D
Decrease in rubbish volumes	Excellent	Moderate	Moderate	Poor
Cost-effectiveness	Moderate	Excellent	Poor	Moderate
Impact on low-income neighbourhoods	Low	Low	Low	Low

number of packages or clusters of instruments, sometimes arbitrarily.

Clusters of instruments are often the best answer to a policy problem, but they cause severe headaches for the analyst when it comes time to project outcomes. Will the outcomes for each cluster equal the simple sum of the individual instrument's projected impacts, or will the instruments in each cluster interact with each other to ratchet up outcomes? If the answer is multiplicative, then the analyst is left in the unenviable position of having to estimate the size of the multiplier effect; hence, the multiplier problem.

In the absence of solid information about the likely interactions of instruments within a policy cluster, we have seen far too many policy teams resort to instincts and hunches when filling in the matrix, resulting in something like table 4.3, which illustrates the third common trap – low-information outcomes projection.

Variations on this general approach include arbitrarily chosen numeric scores (1, 2, 3); red, green, and amber lights; or groupings of ticks, crosses, and/or asterisks in place of the word labels. (It is worth noting here that the last row of table 4.3 can be omitted from the analysis because it does not help distinguish between better and worse options. It should only be retained if the decision-makers asked to see it.)

A matrix like this can be produced quickly, but should decision-makers use it to inform their choices? The answer depends entirely on what stands behind the content inserted in the interior cells and the methods used to derive these 'scores'. The matrix shown in table 4.3 may be based on sound reasoning and common sense in the absence of data, in which case the scores deserve some attention. This cannot be determined from the display above, however, and some decision-makers may lack the time or patience needed to read explanations in the text of the accompanying paper. When pressed, some policy teams will include more information in each cell to explain some of the reasoning behind the scores, and this improves the value added by the matrix hugely.

Unfortunately, the low-information approach to outcomes projection often relies on stabs in the dark rather than logic or data, and when dressed up in the pseudo-rigour of a matrix, these guesses may exercise more power over decision-makers' judgments than they deserve. How, then, should analysts project outcomes for multi-pronged policy options, or when very little data is available for rigorous analysis? Weimer says that matrices with qualitative predictions are useful for informing short turnaround decisions, but this amounts to an invitation for analysts' unexamined biases to be systematically woven into the analysis. In our experience, matrices produced in haste tend to contain a lot of personal biases and conventional wisdom about policy options' impacts because this is easily assembled. When analysts are forced to produce policy information off the tops of their heads, it is often better to forego the matrix and present the results in outline form or as a series of bullet points to avoid the problem of dressing up hunches to look like analysis.

Despite the three traps, outcomes matrices are frequently useful tools for organising and focusing analysis, and discussing the traps sheds light on the situations in which matrices are most appropriate. The matrix works best when policy issues are easily structured, like the examples above of the swimming pool location decision and the ACCC decision. In these cases, the options are clearly defined and distinct; the criteria are easily articulated; and outcomes projections can be grounded in logic and information. In short, the matrix works well to display clear choices.

LOGIC TESTING

A New Zealand Treasury official once boiled down the flaws in policy work practice to two verbs: over-promising and under-explaining (Hawke 1993). Policy advice that inflates the likely benefits of a proposed policy (over-promising) and fails to describe exactly how the benefits will be conjured and the risks managed (under-explaining) usually needs a stiff dose of reality testing. When good data is available, as described above, sound projection techniques constitute such a test. In the absence of data relevant to projection, however, other methods are needed.

A technique known as intervention logic or program logic supplies one such method. We refer to it here as logic testing to move away from its traditional role as a tool of post-implementation evaluation and stress its value for assessing options before policy choices are made. Logic testing works by scrutinising the chain of connections that constitute a policy option's rationale – its theory of how the selected outputs are expected to produce a desired outcome.

In chapter 1, we defined a policy as a proposition regarding how public authority may be used to establish policy instruments that serve public purposes expressed as results. It is essentially a hypothesis as to how a particular course of government action (X) is expected to generate a desired outcome (Y). 'If a law is passed banning dangerous dog breeds (X), then there will be fewer serious dog attacks (Y)', proclaim the hypothetical supporters of such a policy option, and the central challenge for the policy analyst is to investigate the truth of that claim.

Intervention logic works by breaking a policy hypothesis into its component parts, revealing the chain of cause-and-effect steps that support the hypothesis, and then testing each step against logic and evidence. In the case above, for example, the logic of banning dangerous dog breeds contains only two main steps: (1) Banning certain identifiable breeds will reduce their numbers significantly; (2) Reducing the numbers of these dogs will reduce the number and severity of dog attacks. Articulating these two steps immediately exposes the assumptions behind the policy proposal, namely, that most dog attacks are committed by particular breeds of dogs, that these breeds are readily identified, and that a ban will be effective in changing dog owners' choices of breed. When a policy has been subjected to this unpacking and scrutiny, it becomes difficult to over-promise its benefits or under-explain its mechanisms of action.

Logic testing is a relatively simple and non-technical, but potentially powerful tool for exposing the strengths and weaknesses of a policy proposal. It can be used by anyone interested in understanding and influencing policy development from inside or outside government. Here is how it is done.

The main chain

Logic testing starts with a basic question: How is this policy meant to work? The answer to that question is then diagrammed in whatever form you find most useful.

Sue Funnell's diagramming approach stacks boxes on top of each other to illustrate the chain of intended effects. The bottom box describes the relevant policy or program in its essential form. The top box articulates the ultimate aim of the policy or program. The middle boxes describe intermediate outcomes necessary for achieving the final result. Figure 4.1 illustrates this using the case of microfinance programs, which offer small loans to help low-income households start or

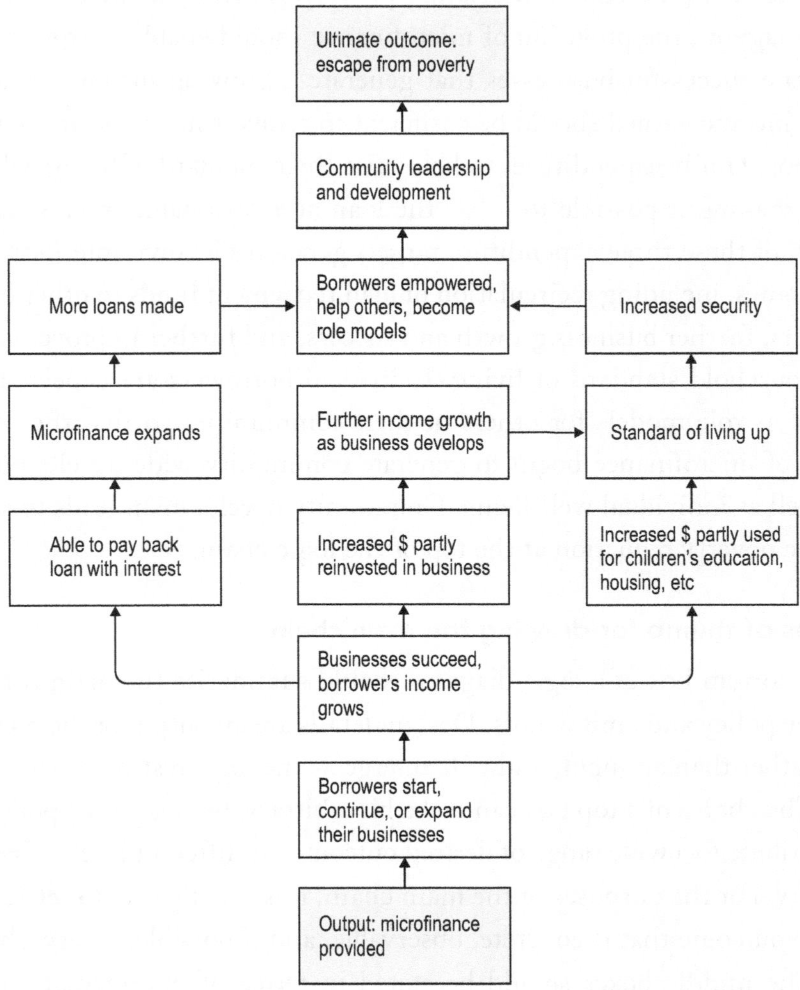

continue businesses and escape the poverty trap. The microfinance movement began in Bangladesh in the 1970s and has spread rapidly around the world. Many loans are tiny by any standards – less than $100 – as are the businesses which they support.

Figure 4.1 outlines the three-pronged mechanism behind this policy innovation and how it is meant to link the program to the outcome, or the means to the end of alleviating poverty. Starting at the bottom of the diagram, the provision of microfinance should enable borrowers to operate successful businesses that generate a growing income stream. The income earned should be sufficient to reinvest in the business and support family expenditures to help raise their standard of living, while also making it possible to repay the loan at a reasonable interest rate. Each of these three expenditure targets generates its own intermediate outcomes, including recirculation of loan repayment funds to other borrowers, further business growth and success, and further improvements in household standard of living. Individual borrowers are expected to serve as role models for others in their communities so that the benefits of microfinance begin to generate community-wide development as well as individual well-being. Community development leads to systemic poverty reduction at the top of the logic chain.

Rules of thumb for drawing the main chain

The bottom box of a logic diagram should summarise the main thrust of the policy and omit details. Design details are an output of the method rather than an input, and will emerge as the logic testing proceeds.

The choice of a top box can feel a bit arbitrary, because most policies contribute to a wide range of desired outcomes at different levels of generality. For the purposes of the main chain, it is usually best to settle on a top outcome that is concrete, observable, and if possible, measurable.

The middle boxes should be stated in terms of intermediate outcomes rather than processes or management steps. A process diagram would include items such as hiring staff, finding office space, determining eligibility criteria, or updating a website. These are not policy outcomes, so do not belong in the logic diagram. Logic diagrams should stick with real effects and impacts, things that actually happen to someone or something; not inputs, processes, or plans.

A policy's logic often consists of several strands, which should be illustrated separately, as in figure 4.1.

Approach the main chain charitably and with an open mind. Present the policy's promised logic, which evaluators sometimes call the theory of change, even if it differs from what you think would actually happen if the policy were implemented. The main chain is about a policy's intentions and aspirations rather than its probable effects. It represents the official best-case scenario. The reality check comes later.

Assumptions and risks

Now list the various factors that need to be present for the chain of outcomes to unfold as intended. These are the assumptions or suppositions behind the logic. Although they determine the strengths and weaknesses of the main logic chain, they are often taken for granted.

Every policy rests upon assumptions concerning the suitability of its instruments to the situation (Cato, Chen & Corbett-Perez 1998). In the case of dog attacks, the assumptions have to do with the proportion of all attacks attributable to particular breeds, the identifiability of these breeds, and the likely effectiveness of a breed ban. Likewise, welfare-to-work programs assume that jobs are available that suit the skills of beneficiaries; tax breaks for attracting industries assume that businesses are mobile and make location choices partly on the basis of taxes; devolution assumes that lower levels of government can absorb new functions effectively. In a logic testing model, key assumptions will slot in at particular links in the chain, as shown in figure 4.2, which uses a simplified version of figure 4.1 to show where in the main chain a sample of assumptions would be inserted.

If the assumptions underpinning the policy prove robust, then the policy is likely to succeed in achieving its aims, but if the assumptions prove false, the policy is likely to fail. As figure 4.2 illustrates, the main threats to the success of microfinance include borrowers who misuse

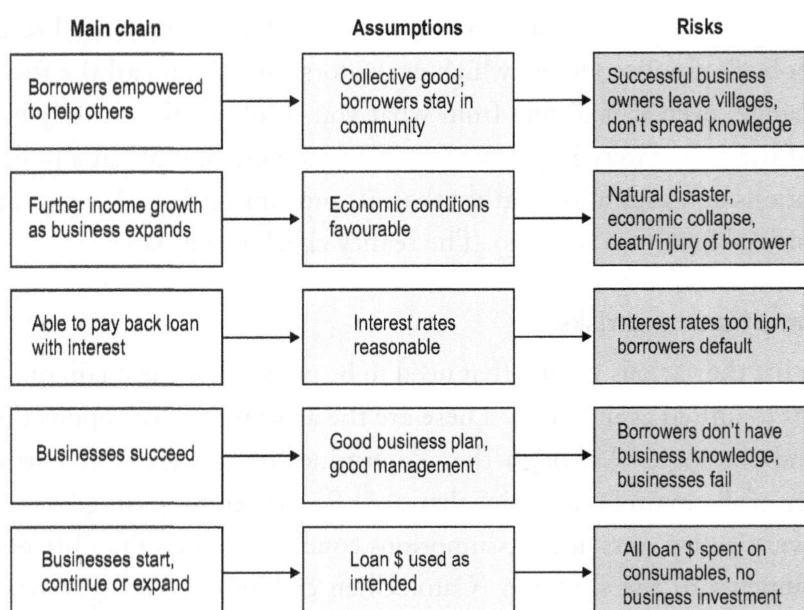

the money, shoddy business planning and management, excessive interest rates, unfavourable changes in economic conditions such as a downturn in the local business cycle, and the increased mobility of successful borrowers.

Risk analysis follows almost automatically from the identification of assumptions. In this context, risks are just the flipside of the assumptions. They are the unhappy outcomes that are likely to occur if the assumptions prove false. Risks include both (1) factors that might derail progress along a chain of outcomes, and (2) factors that might cause even a successful policy chain to generate unwanted side effects or unintended consequences. A chain of risks such as that in figure 4.2 often adds up to an argument *against* the intervention in question – what might be called the dismal logic, opposition logic, or worst-case scenario. Risks need not sink a policy idea, however. Instead, they can be used to point toward modifications in the policy's design in order to eliminate or minimise them.

Reality check

Policies rarely live up to either their supporters' rosy predictions or their opponents' dire warnings. Actual experience nearly always falls somewhere between the best- and worst-case scenarios, which means between the main chain and the chain of risks. In order to formulate useful, realistic advice, policy analysts need to assess the assumptions behind the proposed policy and make educated guesses about the relative probabilities of success or failure at each step along the chain of outcomes. This is where evidence often proves most fruitful, helping policy teams assess assumptions and risks. In the case of dog attacks, for example, data may be available to answer the question of how many attacks can be attributed to the so-called dangerous breeds.

Evidence plays a different role in the intervention logic model than it does in the outcomes matrix. In the matrix, the only evidence that counts is direct evidence concerning the likely impact of an option on a stated criterion. Logic testing, in contrast, can make use of many types of evidence, as long as each sheds light on one of the steps in the chain and the plausibility of the assumptions along the chain. A logic diagram complete with assumptions and risks creates the scaffolding for building richly evidence-informed policy.

Remedies

Some of the risks and weak links in a policy logic diagram may be remediable by design modifications, such as using smiling and frowning emoticons to boost the impact of information in changing people's energy consumption. Policy analysts should craft these design modifi-

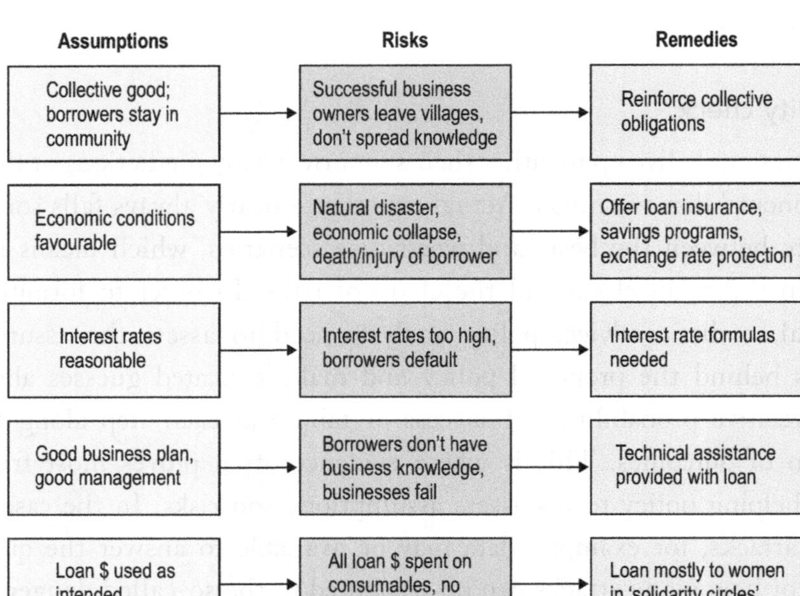

cations and formulate them as options for policy-makers. Consulting widely with relevant actors in operational agencies, stakeholder organisations, and communities can produce new ideas for remedies. Figure 4.3 shows a few design-based remedies in the far right column to address the risks of microfinance.

All of the program modifications featured in figure 4.3 come from actual microfinance programs such as the original, Grameen Bank, which started in Bangladesh. Starting with the bottom remedy box on the right, Grameen Bank's controversial policy of loaning mostly to women was a direct response to concerns that some male borrowers would abscond with the loan money or spend it on themselves rather than investing it in the family and the family business. In addition, the 'solidarity circles' refer to Grameen's practice of organising borrowers into small local groups for purposes of mutual support and peer pressure. Because Grameen's rules prevent the bank from making additional loans to any member of a group in which someone has fallen behind on repayment, group members are motivated to keep themselves and each other on track with repayments. The top remedy box refers to a set of principles that Grameen Bank uses to promote community orientation and obligation among borrowers.

Participatory logic testing

Intervention logic diagrams can be very useful in structuring group discussion about a particular policy. Meeting facilitators can begin with an existing backbone diagram of current policy or a selected policy proposal and invite participants to comment on its strong and weak links, identify its risks, and suggest possible remedies for its flaws, thereby helping the group to design and redesign the policy as they go. Alternatively, the facilitators can begin with a blank whiteboard and work with a group to develop and critique logic backbones for policy options that they suggest.

Policy developers working inside or outside of government often fret about the risks of exposing a new policy idea to public comment too early in its development. Although public service guidelines for consultation strongly encourage the practice of floating new policy ideas with the people who would be most affected by them, including key stakeholder groups and the general public, this kind of option testing usually occurs at the later stages of policy development when government is confident of its proposals. Earlier exposure of a policy idea runs the risk of equipping stakeholders to murder the idea in its infancy, but this may be balanced by the fact that early feedback can be incorporated into policy design to make the proposal both more effective and more acceptable in its final form.

Strengths and weaknesses of logic testing

Logic testing is a versatile method of policy analysis. It can be applied at the beginning of an analysis to identify flaws in current policy and spark creative thinking about alternatives. It can be applied later in the analysis to reality-test an option before recommending it for adoption. It can be used to shape policy design by showing where special arrangements are needed to manage risks. Logic diagrams also make excellent visual aids for both internal briefings and external consultation sessions. A well-designed logic diagram depicts the policy's main features in a single view. Although it broadcasts the policy option's risks and weaknesses for all to see (a potential problem if Official Information Act or Freedom of Information requests ensue), it also illustrates how the policy's design features address those risks.

Logic testing often recommends itself when the outcome matrix falls short. For example, it can help the analyst build a coherent, multi-dimensional cluster of instruments – a policy package – by starting with a single, dominant policy idea and then connecting various instruments as needed in the 'remedy' column to address the weak points – the wobblier assumptions and nastier risks – of the policy's logic. Instead of attempting to calculate future outcomes in an environment of high uncertainty, it can generate specific lists of the risks of each option, leaving the decision-maker to judge whether those risks are more or less likely to eventuate. Logic testing works especially well in the domain of responsive policy, when the main outlines of a policy have been decided and the task is one of designing the details. It works well when just a few dominant options are being considered and copes when the boundaries between those options are fuzzy and overlapping.

Whereas the outcomes matrix splits policies into their component parts (instruments and purposes), logic testing considers them as wholes and examines their integrity. The logic diagram focuses attention on the all-important question of whether the policy in question actually holds together: whether its instruments are well suited to its purposes. Logic testing, properly applied, is every bit as hard-nosed as the outcomes matrix, and at least as capable of illuminating values and consequences. It can, in fact, be used to produce information that is subsequently fed into a matrix.

Logic testing's distinctive defects arise from the limitations of the two-dimensional page. It does not remind analysts to consider roles for non-state actors when designing solutions to problems, most of which contain public and private elements. It does not lend itself to comparing more than two options, side-by-side, at a time. It does not facilitate analysis of interactions across many different packages of policies. It also struggles to incorporate multiple criteria and, therefore, works best when there is a single main policy purpose to be served – the ultimate outcome, which is placed at the top of the main chain. Other values and criteria (or their opposites) may be dealt with as risks to the chain, but this puts them in a subordinate role. The outcomes matrix is a better tool for systematically comparing different criteria side by side.

Like the outcomes matrix, logic testing imposes discipline on the analyst, who is expected to unpack the policy chain comprehensively and approach the identification of assumptions and risks impartially. As with the outcomes matrix, however, biases can always creep into the process, causing the analyst to overlook key risks or weak spots in the logic when the policy being diagrammed is favoured. One can build a main chain that links almost any intervention to any ultimate outcome. Sometimes, policy teams will find they have talked themselves into supporting a proposal in the process of constructing the main chain, but subsequent steps in the process – exposing assumptions and risks – should recharge their critical faculties. Leaps of logic are most common at the top of a logic chain, where there can be a tendency to make massive assumptions about causation: presto, problem solved! Particular caution is needed at this point in the process to ward off self-deception.

SYSTEMS MAPPING

Neither the outcomes matrix nor logic testing approaches provide clear guidance for matching policy options to the problems they are meant to address. Neither can fully accommodate the need to examine how a variety of different policy interventions might interact to produce intended and unintended results. Both of these fundamental tasks require tools with greater range. What is needed is a systems approach.

Chapter 2 introduced the idea of systems in the context of a policy-generating system – an intricate web of actors and institutions whose influence over policy development waxes and wanes as interests and circumstances continually change. The policy system includes everything from parliament to your local council; from the Business Roundtable to the local volunteer crime patrol; and from the *Sydney Morning Herald* to your best-loved or most-despised political blogger – as well as the interactions among these players. Pathways through the policy system take many different forms. Systems-based thinking is a vital antidote to the cycle models of policy development, which, despite their many uses, tend to oversimplify policy development processes and overlook the diversity of policy development trajectories.

This section focuses on a different type of system, which we will call the problem–solution system in order to focus attention outside the world of policy-making toward the larger world in which economic, social, cultural, and environmental issues hatch, grow, evolve, multiply, interact, and sometimes die a natural death without any government intervention at all. Problem–solution systems are potentially as deep and wide as human life itself, and therefore an important role for policy workers is to draw boundaries around these systems for purposes of analysis. Such boundaries need to include key factors known to contribute to the problem being analysed, and should exclude those factors that play a more marginal, purely background role.

Where possible, it is often useful to begin any large-scale policy analysis job by sketching a systems model of the relevant factors at play. Problem–solution system models allow us to map what we know and identify what we need to find out. The purpose of the model is to map available knowledge of the main influences and drivers that characterise the actual world into which policies and programs inject their resources and rules. For example, what causes rates of crime generally, or re-offending specifically, to rise and fall? What factors contribute to successful business start-ups? What are the characteristics of patients who are most likely to follow medical advice about managing disease, and why are they more co-operative? Why do some taxpayers happily comply with tax laws of their own volition while others have to be jollied along or coerced to comply? Huge advances in policy thinking can occur when analysts better understand the factors that influence whatever behaviours and outcomes are of interest.

Because problem–solution systems take many different forms, there is no such thing as a generic system template into which any issue's content can be poured. It is possible, however, to identify the main components of most system models, which include:

- factors or variables that are known to cause or contribute to the policy problem in question, whether directly or by creating incentives and disincentives, enablers and obstacles
- relationships between these variables
- relevant features of the physical, economic, social, legal, or cultural setting
- trajectories of the problem's impacts.

Quite a lot of policy analysis effort is spent trying to understand how to influence the behaviour of workers, businesspeople, computer hackers, consumers, farmers, fishermen, families, identity thieves, suicide bombers, tourists, drivers, and the leaders of other countries, among others, and how to break negative cycles of behaviour while reinforcing positive cycles. Understanding the systems that perpetuate these cycles – key variables, incentives, and disincentives, enablers and obstacles – is central to designing the right policies. Likewise, policy sometimes seeks to control physical settings (for example, building a seawall or planting mangroves to reduce beach erosion) and prepare for uncontrollable events, such as natural disasters or accidents.

Causal loops

There are many ways to map a problem–solution system. Figure 4.4 illustrates one such technique, often referred to as a causal loop diagram. The core message of figure 4.4 is that drug abuse and the personal and social problems associated with it form a vicious cycle with deep socio-economic and psychological roots. It should be noted that this system map looks only at the demand side of the drug system; a full analysis would model the supply side as well as describing the interconnecting influences between demand and supply. The label 's' in the diagram indicates a positive correlation between factors – a relationship in which factors tend to move in the same direction (hence, 's' for same); these factors, such as the amount of harmful use and the social problems it generates, tend to rise and fall together. If the diagram contained any negative correlations – factors tending to move in opposite directions (when one rises, the other falls, and vice versa) – they would be marked 'o' for opposite (Maani and Cavana 2000).

The heart of the drug problem system is 'harmful drug use' itself, which refers to patterns of use that lead to dependency, addiction, or drug use in settings where harm is most likely, such as at school or work, while caring for children, or while driving or performing skilled jobs. The label 'harmful use' is not meant to imply that some forms of use are entirely benign or that recreational drug use should be condoned. It does recognise, however, that many people pass through a

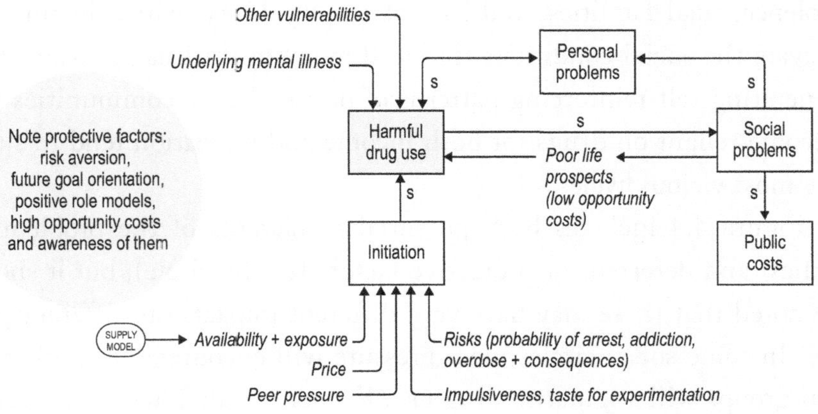

stage of drug experimentation without any significant damage, and a few may engage in occasional use over a long period without suffering severe problems. It should be noted, however, that even infrequent, recreational drug use in safe settings supports the black market and creates social norms that draw in more users, some of whom will be more vulnerable to addiction and patterns of abusive use than others. Recreational drug-taking is therefore never free of social impacts altogether and nor is it free of risks. Only in hindsight can it be shown that particular episodes of drug experimentation proved benign. Those who support legalisation of drugs will reply that drug experimentation and light use would be safer if government could regulate drug production and distribution. In addition, they will argue that black markets are entirely the fault of policy-makers, not drug users, and the harms associated with them could be eliminated at once by legalising drugs such as cannabis. All of these positions are hotly contested.

Whatever one thinks about the general debate over drug policy, it must be acknowledged that abusive patterns of use tend to create or worsen personal and social problems, such as child neglect, domestic violence, road fatalities, and lack of employability, which in turn aggravate the social conditions that lead many to start using drugs, thus generating self-reinforcing patterns of harm. Whole communities that become reliant on drugs for both income and recreation tend to suffer the most vicious cycles.

Figure 4.4 includes both potential accelerants of the problem (in italics) and deterrent or protective factors (in the circle), but it should be noted that these may have very different impacts on different people. In some social circles, peer pressure will encourage use; other social groups will stigmatise drug use. For some individuals and groups, knowing about the risks associated with drug use will enhance the thrill; others will be repelled by the risks. Likewise, family disapproval will act as a deterrent for some and an accelerant for the more rebellious.

Risks associated with drug use may influence individual decision-making, depending on whether and how the individual perceives them. Key risks include the probability of being caught combined with the magnitude of the legal consequences if caught, the probability of overdose, and the probability of addiction. Knowledge of these risks may alter behaviour, but only if individuals calculate probabilities and consequences accurately and realistically. The ability to do so varies dramatically, especially among young people.

Opportunity costs play a large role in the overall drug demand system. People who suffer the bad luck of being born and raised in poor, drug-infested areas tend to have constricted horizons and fewer visible opportunities for a better life. Because their opportunity costs are relatively low, they are highly vulnerable to the temptations of both using and selling drugs, and less susceptible than their more advantaged counterparts to the deterrent effects of strict anti-drug laws: at the end of the day, what have they got to lose? The opportunity costs of drug dependency for a university graduate with good social connections will be far higher than the opportunity costs for a high-school dropout living in a depressed rural area. In addition, young people who grow up in drug-infested communities encounter drugs and drug users regularly, and are therefore more likely to see drug-taking as normal rather than deviant.

Various personal characteristics, such as an impulsive personality or underlying mental illness, aggravate the risks of initiation leading to dependency and self-destructive behaviour, whereas other factors protect against harmful use. Traits such as risk aversion or future goal orientation are clear protective factors everywhere that they are found, and positive role models with high prestige among the target population can help promote these traits.

Vicious and virtuous cycles

A diagram such as figure 4.4, which contains only 's' relationships, is known as a reinforcing loop, or more colloquially, a vicious or virtuous cycle. Many stubborn policy problems involve vicious, reinforcing loops.

Take income inequality, for example. In the absence of big economic reversals or policy interventions, the rich tend to get richer while the poor get poorer, because the rich can reinvest their income in land, businesses, and education, all of which generate more income, while the poor must spend everything to live. The poor also lack human capital and job opportunities, which makes it harder to eat well, go to the doctor, and pay for good housing. When their physical and mental health deteriorates, it becomes harder still to keep a job, which may lead to borrowing and a spiral of debt. Poverty is transmitted intergenerationally when the children in poorer neighbourhoods receive lower-quality education and grow up in social networks with mostly unemployed role models. In societies that tie basic services to income, the reinforcing loop of poverty becomes ever more entrenched. Although these patterns are well-known, policy-makers and those who seek to influence policy frequently seem to lose sight of them.

Economic growth also follows the pattern of a virtuous, reinforcing loop. Increasing productivity brings increasing wages and disposable income and higher rates of savings and spending, which fuel investment, generating job growth and higher productivity for another turn of the cycle. The contrary is also true: when productivity remains stagnant, so do wages, leaving workers with less to spend. Businesses suffer. Savings and investment decline. More people are laid off. The cycle persists.

Some reinforcing loops create a spiralling effect. Only if the spiral reaches a tipping point, or an external shock occurs, will the cycle be broken. In the case of income inequality, for example, the cycle may be broken if the poor revolt and demand greater redistribution or if a new technology arises to shake up the income distribution. Where economic growth is concerned, a well-performing economy may continue to grow until inflation rears its head. A recession may last for a decade or more, but if underperforming businesses are weeded out and other businesses can find ways to stimulate productivity, growth will restart. Lowering interest rates and pouring fiscal stimulus funds into an ailing economy – deliberate external shocks – can help break a recessionary cycle by stimulating spending and investment.

Policy interventions can be designed specifically to break off vicious cycles or encourage virtuous ones. The most powerful interventions do both, directly or indirectly. For example, anti-poverty programs that combine cash assistance with effective employment-oriented interventions for healthy people of working age are more likely to have a lasting impact on poverty rates than either strategy alone.

Some causal loops contain a natural balancing element. For example, if a country is running a trade deficit (importing more than it exports), the value of its currency is likely to decline, making its goods cheaper overseas and imports dearer, which helps correct the trade imbalance. If interest rates subsequently go up, however, demand for the country's currency will go up, which may inflate the relative value of the currency, causing another trade deficit as the country's goods become more expensive overseas. Amid complexity, these general patterns can be observed.

Value-adding practice in systems mapping requires careful attention to both the reinforcing and balancing elements within a problem-solution system. The core of this approach is an understanding of how the key factors within the system interact with each other to create and perpetuate the problem or prevent the opportunity from being realised.

Alternatives to causal pathways

There are many ways to graphically illustrate systems thinking, and analysts should aim to develop their own hybrid approaches to fit their situations.

One alternative to the causal pathways is the fishbone diagram illustrated in figure 4.5, which helps to identify root causes of a problem, rather than focusing on symptoms. The typical fishbone diagram includes at least four areas of focus (material, equipment, people, processes), but there can be more, depending on the issue. The causes in each category can be identified through brainstorming and then clustered into groups, which become the major bones or categories of analysis.

Smaller bones may branch off from the major bones, showing particular features of each category. To derive these smaller bones, try adopting the why-question loop of a small child: to every answer about why something happened, ask why that next thing happened. Usually the bones with the most branches will be the most important places to seek policy solutions, but all the major bones should be explored, and a plan

Figure 4.5 Fishbone diagram of hospital waiting lists

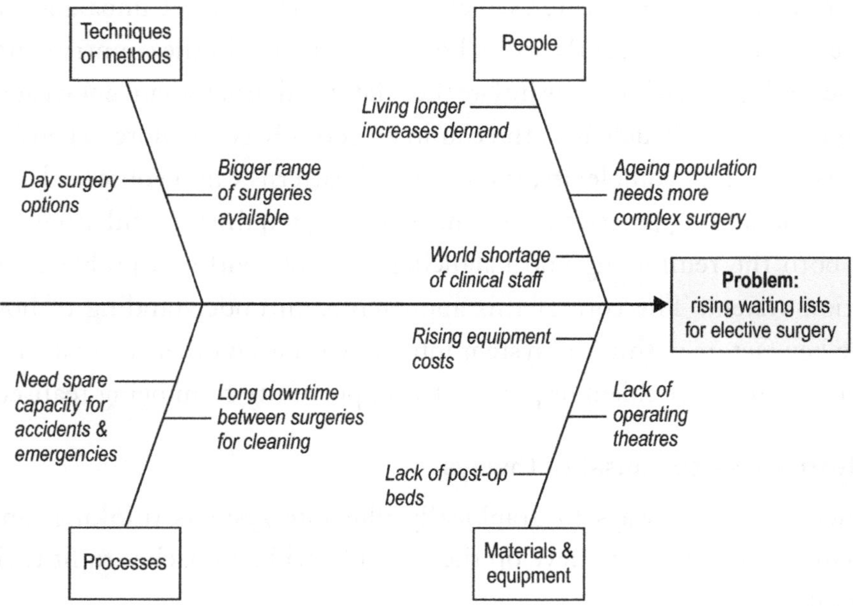

of action can then be developed to address the causes.

Other illustration tools include webs, hubs and spokes, decision trees, and, where relationships among factors are not well understood, elementary mindmaps with factors located somewhat arbitrarily.

Conventional policy options

A systems diagram begins by assembling what is known about a problem and its setting. Bridging from the problem stream to the solution stream requires plugging various possible interventions into the problem system and projecting their impact. Figure 4.4 suggests that policy intervention can focus on five broad mechanisms for change:

- preventing entry into the negative cycle

- breaking negative cycles that feed the problem (for example, increasing the risks of arrest to deter use or assisting users to quit through education or treatment)
- boosting protective factors
- cultivating alternative cycles of behaviour with better outcomes
- minimising the harms associated with the negative cycles without trying to stop the cycles altogether (for example, keeping injecting drug users safe from AIDS).

Choices between prevention and treatment are endemic to policy-making. Drug policy offers a classic case of this dilemma, of course, but so does biosecurity: should the bulk of biosecurity resources be focused on screening incoming goods to intercept pests, or on containment strategies once new infestations (inevitably) occur?

The fifth dot point above, often referred to as harm minimisation, begins with the assumption that a certain level of problem behaviours will always persist and government efforts to eliminate these behaviours altogether may generate more harm than good — for example, by driving problems underground, prompting black markets, and feeding organised crime. Rather than preventing problem behavior, harm minimisation efforts seek to introduce balancing elements into the negative cycles that appear later in the chain of causation.

Seat belt and airbag requirements are well-known examples of harm minimisation. These policies do not try to control the causes of crashes, such as speeding and drink driving. Instead, their aim is to reduce the probability of serious injury or death when a crash does occur. Their effectiveness can be credited to a comprehensive, evidence-based understanding of the physical forces operating within a car as it strikes an object at speed. Thank you, crash dummies.

In the drug policy case, interventions traditionally have focused on the second of the five general categories of mechanisms above — breaking the negative cycles of harmful drug consumption – using instruments of education, treatment, and law enforcement. The variables illustrated in the systems map help analyse these interventions.

The first traditional instrument of drug policy, education, assumes that people who use and misuse drugs lack good information about the risks associated with this behaviour and that their behaviour can be influenced by filling these information gaps, and in some cases by shocking people into absorbing the information. Figure 4.4 reveals this to be a reasonable assumption, because risk is listed as a contributing factor to both initiation and harmful use. As noted earlier, however, knowledge of risk is likely to affect some individuals more than others. Individuals with poorer life prospects or more impulsive personalities are probably less likely to take risk information into consideration when making decisions about drug use; some potential users will be attracted by risk.

Education-based policy interventions try to plug into the systems diagram at the point where risk influences behaviour to block the negative, reinforcing loop. For education-based interventions to succeed in penetrating the system, they need to tailor their messages to the relevant characteristics of the audiences they intend to target – including people's life prospects, peer influences, and relevant personality characteristics.

In economic terms, public education campaigns generally seek to alter people's tastes and preferences for some harmful activity. They do so either by conveying information, which assumes that people rationally arrive at their tastes, or through the emotional shock value of certain images and stories, which are meant to create aversions to the targeted behaviour. Evaluation results indicate that public awareness campaigns can help create and reinforce certain social norms (against drink driving, for example), generate greater understanding and tolerance of particular conditions (such as mental illness), and stimulate those in need to seek assistance (by calling a helpline, for example). If the goal of a public awareness campaign is to change tastes and preferences, then the factors influencing those tastes – knowledge, experience, personality, peer group, family background, geographic location, familiarity, risk aversion, etc – need to be well understood, and the public awareness campaign needs to target those variables that it can manipulate most effectively.

Alongside public education, governments have traditionally funded individual drug treatment programs to help addicts get clean and restart their lives. The policy mechanism at work here is neither information nor emotional shock, but direct provision of services to address the individual's, and in some cases the family's, personal problems. A government may not operate these treatment programs directly, but even when it uses third-party contractors, the policy mechanism is the same. Treatment interventions try to plug into the top loop of the systems diagram in figure 4.4 to break the self-reinforcing cycle between harmful use and personal problems. They should also aim to boost protective factors. Theories and practices of treatment vary hugely across practitioners and different types of drugs, which means that government purchasing of treatment services should be guided by evidence of effectiveness.

Plugging policy options into the system map

The most discussed drug policy intervention is, of course, enforcement of prohibition laws. Prohibition is often characterised as a supply-side intervention, but it also seeks to influence demand via the mechanisms of street price and social stigma. Figure 4.6 shows how an intervention's mechanisms of change can be plugged into a problem–solution systems map.

Increased drug enforcement aims to drive up street prices, which is expected to dampen demand for drugs at both the initiation and graduation stages of use. Many police departments track the street prices of

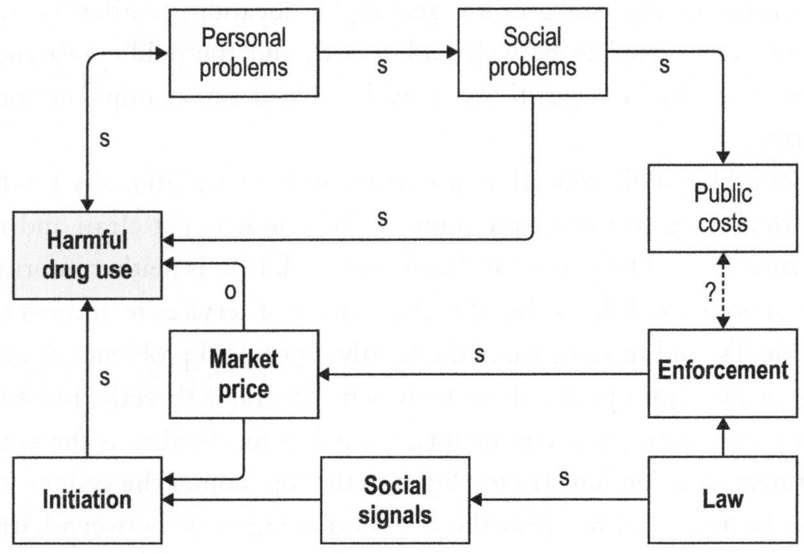

illegal drugs in order to measure their own performance against this theory. At the same time, the illegal status of drugs is meant to deter naturally law-abiding people from trying drugs via social stigma attached to breaking the law and fear of getting caught. As noted earlier, these social signals are likely to have very different impacts on individuals with different characteristics.

Drug prohibition is an attractively simple and logical theory, and we will never know how effective it has been unless we discover another planet that is identical to Earth in every detail except drug laws. Prohibition has been in place in so many countries of the world for so long that we have no way of reliably predicting how drug use patterns would have evolved under different rules. It is not an exaggeration to speak of longstanding, planetary drug policy frameworks. More than

170 countries, including Australia and New Zealand, are signatories to three United Nations conventions on narcotic drugs dating from 1961 to 1988, which require signatory countries to maintain prohibition policies.

The concept of decriminalisation or depenalisation (which refers to the removal of criminal penalties for use and possession of illegal substances) was invented in part so that countries could continue to fulfil their duties under the UN conventions, that is, maintain official policies of prohibition, while adjusting the severity of penalties to the realities of drug use and the goals of harm reduction. Some jurisdictions, including some states of Australia, have decriminalised cannabis to varying degrees, often substituting civil for criminal penalties, and have experimented with loosening rules around other drugs, but these policy changes are too narrow and too recent to tell us much about the role that cannabis and other, harder drugs would have played in society had they been more freely available for the past hundred years.

When contemplating changes in the legal status of a particular drug or changes in enforcement, two issues are central: how would the change alter consumption patterns? Would the change in patterns cause net harm to increase or decrease? Answering these questions requires a huge exercise in complexity taming due to the large number of variables involved, which include substitution and complementarity among drugs and alcohol, economic incentives, impacts on neighbourhoods, developments in countries that supply drugs, social and recreational fashions, demography, evolution of organised crime organisations, public attitudes, and many others. What-if scenarios of drug law reform all hinge on the hypothetical scope and distribution of these drugs' popularity in the absence of strictly enforced prohibition. If people were free to choose their own drug-taking patterns without threat of arrest, how many would calculate the risks accurately and respond rationally? How many would underestimate the risks and find themselves in deep trouble? How would these patterns vary among people with different characteristics? How would the resulting patterns of drug use and harm be distributed by ethnicity, gender, age, and income, and how would they affect long-term social inequalities?

In the absence of clear counterfactuals – prohibition v legalisation – we must fall back on logic and systems thinking to judge the strengths and weaknesses of the theory behind prohibition. Flaws evident in figure 4.6 include the following.

First is the predictable problem that an increase in the street price of a drug may lure more sellers into the market, particularly if these sellers are relatively relaxed about the risks of being arrested and convicted. More sellers translate into greater availability and exposure, which could increase initiation. Thus, even if law enforcement is successful in achieving its goal of driving up prices, it may not have the desired impacts on consumption. Moreover, higher street prices combined with higher risks associated with sale and purchase may benefit the more sophisticated drug operations, including those owned by organised crime syndicates, and intensify competition between them, including violent confrontations over turf.

A second flaw is the more complex problem of law enforcement's direct and indirect impacts on drug use itself and its downstream harms. If more enforcement discourages addicts from seeking treatment, due to fear of arrest, then it may perpetuate harmful use. If increased enforcement discourages injecting drug users from obtaining clean needles, then it may contribute to the spread of AIDS and other blood-borne diseases. If addicts have low price elasticity of demand for a drug, then higher street prices will increase their costs without significantly reducing their consumption. This may lead to more property crime by addicts who need to finance their habits as well as the social problems associated with deeper poverty. Prohibition itself, of course, generates black markets with all of their unsavoury accompaniments, including the use of violence to settle business disputes and a lack of product oversight.

The problems with prohibition do not necessarily lead to the conclusion that it should be scrapped. Studying an intervention paradigm such as prohibition in the context of the problem or opportunity system opens the mind to policy adaptations that can be used to address an intervention's basic flaws. For example, drug addicts can be encouraged to seek treatment even in the presence of prohibition with assurances of protection against arrest. Their treatment-seeking behaviour may depend more on the availability and quality of treatment and the opportunities they would face in life if they could beat their addiction than it does on fears of arrest.

System-based policy design

A good problem-system map records all of the known causal and contributing factors to a problem so that interventions can be tailored to address them. In addition, such a map can be used to examine current policy and adjust existing programs, as discussed earlier, to take better account of multiple factors that aggravate the problem as well as factors that protect against the problem.

Whether focused on old or new interventions, this process of policy adjustment and readjustment highlights the *design* element of policy work, in contrast with the *choice* element. Designing begins with a rough outline of a policy instrument and then adds, subtracts, and alters features in order to customise the instrument for the job it has to do within a given problem system. Value-added designing works with the problem stream's currents rather than against them. It cultivates protective factors, cushions against risks, pushes on the softer areas of the problem system, softens up the harder bits, and works with key actors whenever possible. The best policy and program designs use education only where information is known to have an impact on behaviour, incentives only where these are known to align with existing motives, and regulation only where rules can be crafted to produce more compliance than resistance. The best designs apply law enforcement selectively and strategically, but also fairly. The best designs acknowledge different characteristics and needs of different target groups and cater for these.

Take drug law enforcement, for example. It is often portrayed as a binary function – you can either have more or less of it – but police agencies have demonstrated that effective changes can be made in enforcement activities without altering the law itself. The same enforcement resources can be deployed very differently depending on the model of policing being used. For example, hot-spot policing focuses police patrols and other activities on high-risk areas, such as neighbourhoods with open-air drug markets. Evaluations of hot-spot policing suggest that it can be effective in preventing drug-related and other forms of crime in these areas, and need not displace crime elsewhere.

Another model, problem-oriented policing (POP), focuses police attention on investigating problems and their deeper causes, rather than simply closing cases. It involves the police in working with citizens to help design solutions to problems rather than always dealing with the aftermath of problems. Evaluation results have been generally positive for problem-oriented policing initiatives, but the idea continues to evolve. Community policing offers yet another variation on a theme. All of these adaptations in policy and practice follow from an increasingly systemic understanding of how negative social conditions arise, become embedded, and spiral into drug-related and other crimes.

Drug courts, a relatively recent policy innovation operating in parts of Australia, divert felony drug offenders from prison into intensive treatment, rehabilitation, monitoring, and supervision programs with the goal of lowering recidivism, improving their employability, facilitating their reintegration into the community, and reunifying them with their families. The ultimate purpose of drug courts is to break the cycle of substance abuse, crime, family breakdown, and community deterioration. Whereas traditional courts tend to rely on the mechanisms of punishment, deterrence, and incapacitation to change or block behaviour, drug courts focus on altering other positive and negative contributing factors as well – including psychological and personality-related vulnerabilities, risk awareness, peer messages, support networks, and opportunity costs. Access to treatment and rehabilitation-oriented services alongside frequent drug testing and strict supervisory arrangements is meant to combine the best of the coercion, diversion, and restoration models of criminal justice. This policy innovation acknowledges the systemic complexity of drug use.

Drug court programs apply many of the traditional treatment methods used in other programs, but the 'clients' face a different incentive structure thanks to their particular niche in the system – that is, their status as offenders. In theory at least, the offenders' strong desire to stay out of prison alters their incentives and makes them more receptive to the suite of intensive interventions on offer. The policy mechanism in operation here is complex and multi-layered to reflect the nature of the underlying problems. Evaluations to date have shown significant impacts from drug court programs on recidivism, but mixed effects on other outcomes. In New Zealand, drug-court principles have been introduced into regular court systems without establishing separate institutions; these programs' impacts beg to be evaluated.

Participatory systems mapping

Systems-thinking tools can help supply both analytical methods and participatory processes. Any group with a whiteboard can undertake a team exercise in systems mapping, as long as the person holding the whiteboard pen listens well, includes all contributions, and is good at seeing connections between factors. Group-based systems mapping works best when the assembled group includes people from the operational, policy, research, and evaluation sides of the issue, as well as the policy's target groups, where appropriate. It also helps if organisational boundaries can be temporarily ignored so that people are selected for the team based on their knowledge of and experience with the problem rather than their institutional roles. Such processes can be organised and hosted by either government departments or non-government organisations.

A participatory systems-mapping exercise may proceed in roughly five steps to produce a causal pathways diagram. First, label the problem and place this in the centre of the board (for example, harmful drug use, problem gambling, low national savings rates, rising juvenile offending, bank failures, traffic congestion, or any other). Second, ask people to list variables that they know or suspect to be causes of the problem, or at least contributing or aggravating factors. Third, ask people to suggest relationships among the variables, which can be depicted as lines, arrows, loops, or broken wires. Fourth, ask for variables that people know or suspect to be protective factors against the problem and list these – perhaps on a separate board. After the group session, a smaller team will need to tidy up the pathways diagram and produce a draft for comment by the participants.

The internet offers a different model for participatory systems mapping using the 'wiki' model. This approach starts by setting up a website where participants in the process can be given editing rights to an emerging systems map. The website designers need to provide at least a skeleton of the systems map to prime the process, but the full map will be the product of many contributions. Ideally, the website would use software that allows contributors to add, remove, or shift variables on a branching diagram rather than simply adding items to a text-based list. The visual depiction of relationships between variables is vital to systems thinking.

Website hosts operating a wiki model need to make decisions about who will be able to view the website and who will be granted editing access. The process can be opened up to everyone, like the Wikipolicy site of the Toronto *Globe and Mail*, which seeks to gather fresh, new ideas about policy and stimulate debate about proposals (but without any diagramming). Alternatively it can be restricted to the public service intranet, to a particular department, or to a team of people selected from relevant departments within government and key stakeholder organisations outside of government. Rules of engagement should be developed to anticipate possible editing wars, in which people with opposing views battle over the wording of a variable or its place in the map, and other inappropriate uses of the website.

Group-based whiteboard exercises and wiki-style exercises can use many different visual templates for systems thinking. Causal pathways are just one. Fishbone diagrams, described above, also work well. Many others can be found in the management and operational research literatures.

Thus, a systems map can be developed co-operatively and interactively within large or small groups, or in the solitary confines of a single adviser's head. Either way, a systems map can substitute for the problem-definition statement required by the standard model of policy analysis. Availability of the map helps liberate departmental planners, policy designers, and operational managers to think comprehensively and strategically about a complex problem and to avoid framing problems too narrowly too soon.

Strengths and weaknesses of systems mapping

Unlike either of the other approaches discussed above, the problem–solution systems map focuses on the world outside government and, therefore, helps the analyst think about roles for non-state actors in policy design. A well-executed systems map helps the policy team see how different types of interventions – regardless of who carries them out and how – correspond with different threads in the web of relationships and impacts.

The best policy analysts and advisers in our experience gradually and iteratively build their own system-oriented mental maps of the terrain within their policy areas. Although these individual maps tend to be tacit and undeclared, they are invaluable because they constitute one's personal intellectual capital or stock of knowledge. Mature mental maps generally include not only features of the problem situation but also a comprehensive picture of the full range of policy instruments available for addressing a particular policy issue, all of it based on the available research and evaluation evidence. The array of available instruments, in turn, sits alongside an historical picture of how various policy approaches have evolved over time in response to political pressures (or in their absence), which in turn includes a rough overlay of where key actors and institutions tend to be positioned relative to available policy options and the evidence that supports them. Every policy analyst in an organisation need not be required to demonstrate this breadth and depth of knowledge, but junior analysts should be working in teams that are managed by experienced analysts who possess such maps. Junior analysts might think of their career goals in terms of the steady accumulation of this kind of body of knowledge – the development of their own maps.

Mental maps of the policy-making and problem–solution systems are an important part of what makes it possible for public service policy officials to serve both current and future governments reliably, for the map allows the adviser to place current policy priorities and preferences in a larger context that crosses international, historical, and ideological borders. In some policy areas, the presence of these maps has generated innovations that cut across political stereotypes – for example, time-limited welfare regimes that also emphasise generous provision of social services and fair application of exemptions. It is challenging, but not impossible, to find ways of integrating the best of what is offered by left and right into new policy paradigms. This type of innovation is most likely to occur when policy designers are both deeply engaged with the current government's values and priorities and also aware of where today's favoured policy ideas sit in the larger sweep of policy history.

Mental maps can add value at the organisational level if they can be transferred from brain to paper (or, better yet, to interactive electronic form) and shared. The core business of strategic planning may be described in terms of steadily building and revising an organisation's map of its own problem–solution world and how it and other relevant institutions might influence behaviour and outcomes in that world in the past and future.

Hazards associated with problem–solution system mapping include being buried alive by complexity and creating a false sense of completeness. The art and craft of systems mapping requires a delicate balance between wallowing in endless details and prematurely closing the system. As with the other two approaches canvassed in this chapter, system mapping detached from evidence can become a vehicle for pushing the analyst's or department's preferences and biases.

CONCLUSION

This chapter canvassed three disciplines for avoiding self-deception in policy advice. All are methods of exercising reasoned, practical judgment, which can help anyone working in the policy realm combat self-deception by reminding them of the grounds for drawing sound conclusions about policy claims – namely, common sense and evidence. The outcomes matrix relies on evidence to project likely outcomes of different options, but also requires common sense to validate the projections and compare results. Logic testing relies heavily on a common-sense unpacking of the proposed policy's intentions while also drawing heavily on evidence to test assumptions and identify risks. Problem–solution systems use both common sense and evidence to map the factors that create and perpetuate policy problems and test options against them. These three approaches are complementary, and the next chapter discusses an overall crafting approach to policy work in which they can be combined and recombined.

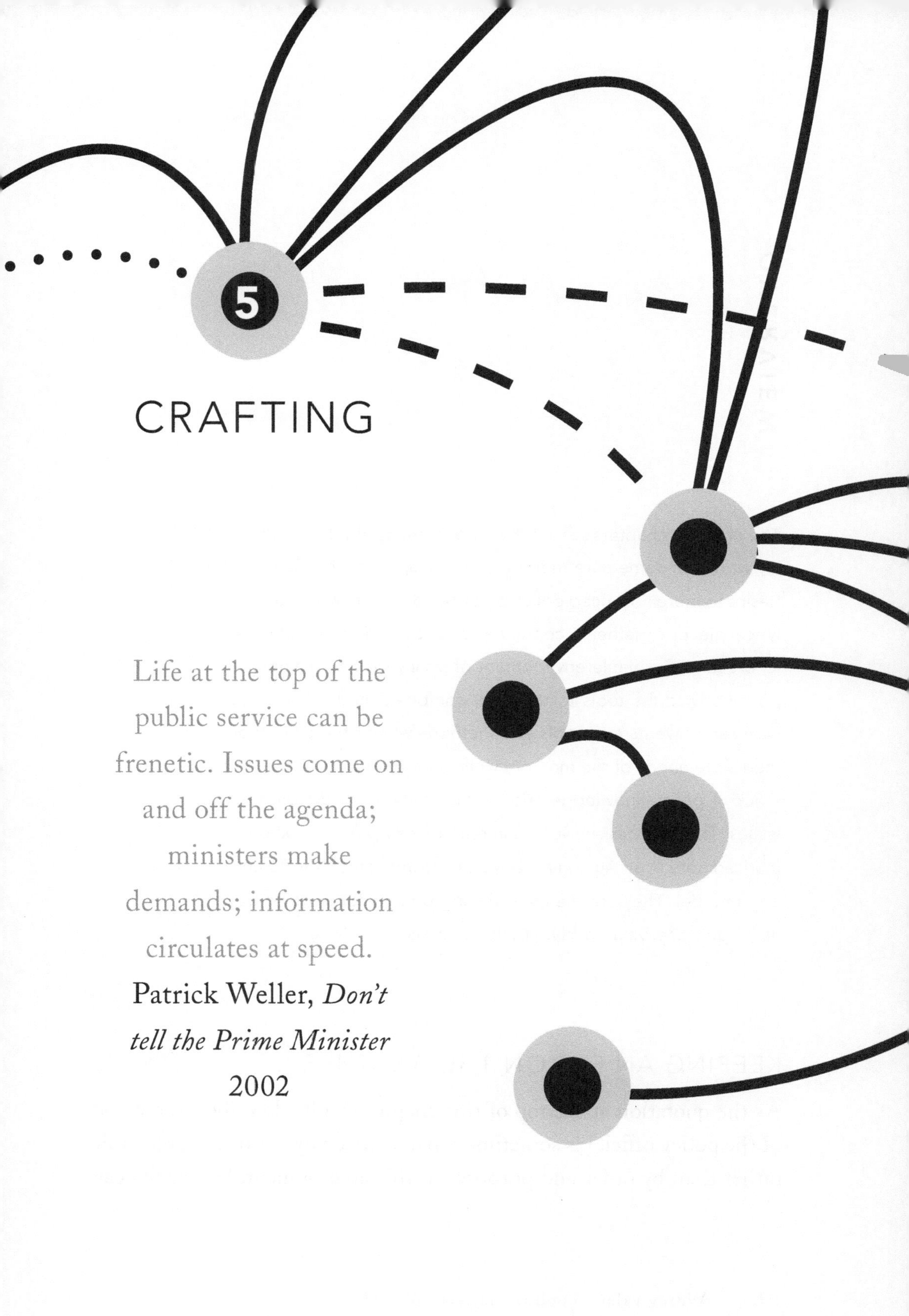

5

CRAFTING

Life at the top of the
public service can be
frenetic. Issues come on
and off the agenda;
ministers make
demands; information
circulates at speed.
Patrick Weller, *Don't
tell the Prime Minister*
2002

The previous chapters set out the fundamentals of value-adding policy work and some core methods. This chapter pushes beyond the basics to more advanced policy practice, focusing on fitting the analytical pieces together in context and adapting advice to the frenetic, precarious, volatile environment of policy-making. Value-adding policy advice fits tools to the task, combines methods in creative ways, and invents new tools and methods when others fall short. It meets the needs of the moment while also contributing to society's stock of policy knowledge and its capability for addressing future issues. The chief tasks involved in high-quality policy work are summarised here in an Australia–New Zealand version of the Dutch hexagon model. They are the essential ingredients for systems-based, fit-for-purpose, value-adding policy analysis and advice.

KEEPING AN EYE ON THE WEATHER ...

As the quotation at the top of this chapter vividly describes, the world of the policy official is sometimes characterised by confusion and panic rather than by order and purpose. In this environment, bad habits can easily form; good practice can be difficult to discern and even more difficult to put into action. Nevertheless, public servants working in policy units are expected to deliver policy analysis and advice that is accurate, timely, informed by the past, prescient of the future, easy to administer, politically palatable, co-ordinated across departments, embraced by communities, fit for the minister's purposes, locally adaptable, incisive, strategic, and overflowing with enduring benefits for stakeholders and the public. And they are expected to do so as inexpensively as possible, on a moment's notice.

Can standards of good practice in policy work be reconciled with the stark realities of policy-making? A core message of this chapter is that the competing imperatives of policy work cannot be resolved by any single model of 'the policy-making system', because policy is the product of multiple, interlocking systems embracing randomness and chance as well as purposefulness. To add value, a policy model must take account of the intricate web of interactions between key actors, institutions, norms, rules, and feedback mechanisms within the policy system. Perhaps most importantly, policy analysts and advisers need to understand the larger problem-solution system in which each issue resides, touching everything from family life, community ties, local ecosystems, and national culture to the economy (local, national, regional, and global), cyberspace, and the biosphere – all of which the policy-making system seeks to adapt to its purposes.

These larger forces relentlessly mould the contours of the policy landscape, the way that atmospheric elements such as wind, moisture, and temperature carve the physical landscape. They obey complex interacting laws and are predictable to a very limited extent. Policy analysts and advisers cannot control these forces, and so they must learn to adapt to the policy equivalent of short-run storms and droughts (such as a flu epidemic) or changes of season (such as the normal ups and downs in the business cycle), and long-run climate trends (such as population ageing). And they must learn to keep a weather-eye out, looking beyond their domains and communities of interest, observing and reading the social, economic, technological, cultural, and environmental forces that swirl around policy.

We prefer this three-dimensional image of landscape and atmosphere to more conventional depictions of the policy-making environment as a set of concentric circles. In the two-dimensional, concentric models, various key institutions such as the executive, legislative, and judicial branches, and the various levels of government, typically occupy the inner spaces, and the larger realm of social and economic forces typically fills the outermost circle. Concentric models cannot capture the complexities of interacting systems, the great shocks and trends that mark one era as different from another. These mighty forces of equilibrium and upheaval are all bigger than policy, but they often require attention from policy-makers. Policies occasionally influence the direction and strength of these forces, mostly at the margins but sometimes dramatically, as for example when wars are declared. The forces themselves often have profound effects on policy outcomes, as when a recession swamps a welfare-to-work program, sky-high world milk prices cause farmers to shift land and assets into dairying, the invention of the internet requires governments to rethink basic principles such as privacy and security, a period of high fertility eventually strains state school resources, or rising sea levels require whole island communities to be moved.

Much of the time, government policy is competing with these other, stronger forces of stability and change, and for that reason, expecting large, independent policy impacts is often hopelessly naïve. Maintaining a broadly critical and well-informed view of the inside game (how policy is made within government), the outside game (how things work in the 'real' world), and the vast interface between the two, helps ground analysts and advisers in reality and helps them spot opportunities for progress.

LEARNING

Static policy cycle models fail to take account of learning's tendency to shake up policy systems. Although the word carries positive connotations, learning is not automatically positive; con-artists, thieves, and drug lords are just as likely to learn from experience and continually improve their techniques as are athletes, philanthropists, and policymakers. Whether positive or negative in its effects, learning tends to disrupt cycles by causing people to clear new paths, meet new people, and invent new things.

Chapter 2 catalogues some of the systemic changes that have, gradually, and sometimes precipitously, transformed Australia and New Zealand's policy-making environments over the past twenty years. Many of these changes have their roots in learning and adaptation on the part of key actors. Government and opposition politicians are continually learning new methods of outfoxing each other, ducking media punches, and selling their parties' message directly to voters. Editors and journalists are continually learning more cost-effective ways of gathering and reporting news, and searching for better ways to compete with the rapidly expanding domain of web-based news services. All of this learning and adaptation has induced shifts in roles, relationships, and patterns of behaviour within the policy system – changes that should be reflected in day-to-day policy work.

The best policy teams in our acquaintance continually observe and adapt to such breaks and turns. They take a multi-systems approach to their work, consciously or unconsciously, which helps them discern patterns of change inside and outside government and build them into their mental maps, as described in chapter 4. Cultivating an integrated, multi-system perspective can help officials understand the comparative advantages and disadvantages of their own role in the government's decision-making system, and how to use it to coax a bit of order out of the chaos. They are well equipped with an understanding of systems and other resources to look ahead, anticipate problems and opportunities, and advise accordingly.

The fact is that many policy developers from all sectors in Australia and New Zealand find ways to deliver good policy analysis and advice much of the time, despite the frequently frenetic policy-making environment. When they resolve the tensions between real and ideal practice successfully, they do so not by wishing away the maddening intricacies and intrigues of politics and society, but by finding patterns amidst the confusion. They continually adapt to a changing policy landscape and weather patterns, treating them not as disruptions to, but as part of, the policy system.

COMPLEX PROBLEMS AND OPPORTUNITIES

Think of climate change, the economic meltdown of the late 2000s, terrorism, inter-generational poverty, obesity, and ethnic discrimination. What these issues have in common is complexity, contentiousness, and intractability. Rooted in problems both hopelessly entrenched and explosively unpredictable, such issues cannot be untangled, but neither can they be solved with a single, bold stroke. Often, the best that governments can do is to help people and communities anticipate and manage the impacts of complex, intractable problems. Beyond coping, governments also may facilitate the search for opportunities within problems – such as the creation of jobs in new industries that arise to address environmental threats – and help citizens pursue these silver linings.

Many policy analysis textbooks describe policy issues that unfold sequentially and submit to rational analysis, such as where to build a swimming pool (see chapter 4). We call policy issues such as these 'straightforward', because of their clearly discernible options with relatively predictable trajectories, widely agreed purposes, and uncontroversial criteria. Straightforward issues are not necessarily easy to solve, and indeed they may involve agonisingly difficult choices. But the choices are clear, and it is up to the policy-makers to face them without flinching. Surprises are always possible, of course, even in relatively tame situations – our local council might discover archaeological remains on the preferred site for a new swimming facility, for example – but shocks such as this do not change the nature of the problem; they simply constrain the choice among existing options.

Complex policy issues, like Rittel and Webber's (1973) 'wicked problems', are anything but straightforward. Their options involve overlapping and sometimes clashing design choices; their purposes and criteria are disputed; and the policy impacts of the options defy prediction. Complex issues are the juvenile delinquents of the policy world – erratic, obstinate, hot-headed, and sometimes dangerous. They are the Hydras of policy advisers' nightmares: chop off one head and another grows back. Break up a telecommunications monopoly, and watch investments in telecom infrastructure shrink. Cut the supply of heroin through better border control, and watch demand for illegal homemade drugs increase. Take one step forward and two steps back – the trade-offs between options in a complex issue analysis typically look unattractive at best, and occasionally unconscionable.

Key actors often disagree about the nature of these many-headed problems because they view the problems from different vantage points and therefore see only parts of the scene, never the whole. Complex problems shift and grow in multiple directions simultaneously because the many people, groups, and institutions involved in the problem continually react to changes in their environments and to each other's behaviour, and these micro-reactions often add up to massive shifts in macro patterns. The end result may be a self-reinforcing, spiralling problem propelled by multiple, interacting factors, as for example when the vicious cycle of poverty, isolation, and loss of traditional livelihoods combines with the vicious cycle of drug abuse, violence, and family breakdown to stunt indigenous development.

Some complex problems have a hidden tipping point, which means that the whole situation deteriorates rapidly when key factors reach a critical threshold; for example habitat loss in an animal community may trigger extinction, and job losses in a human community may lead to a rapid downward spiral of outmigration and haemorrhaging opportunities. Other complex issues tend to oscillate rather than tip. For example, bus lanes make bus travel faster and more reliable, which attracts more passengers and reduces road congestion. The resulting improvements in driving conditions eventually make driving more attractive, however, which may cause bus patronage to drop again, eventually leading to worse road congestion and another wave of public transport improvements. Up and down go the indicators, back and forth goes the public's attention.

The impacts of interventions are hard to predict when many interacting variables crowd the problem space. The probability of unintended outcomes, positive or negative, therefore increases with complexity.

Complex opportunities behave similarly to complex problems, but in reverse. They involve virtuous rather than vicious cycles and self-reinforcing strengths, as when improvements in education lead to more economic opportunities, which propel social, cultural, and environmental progress. They, too, can be volatile, coming and going without warning, for example when shifting international conditions expand and shrink markets for exports.

Complex issues require modifications to the usual methods and frameworks of policy analysis and advising, as explained by the Australian Public Service Commission (2007):

> Traditional policy thinking suggests that the best way to work
> through a policy problem is to work through an orderly and

linear process, working from problem to solution ... The
handling of wicked problems requires holistic rather than
linear thinking. This is thinking capable of grasping the big
picture, including the interrelationships between the full range
of causal factors and policy objectives.

Complex, wicked issues force the policy official to move beyond the basics of policy work explored in the last chapter, and find ways of combining and adapting approaches to gain leverage over the complexity. These issues shift the appropriate analogy from curing a diagnosed disease to managing chronic illness, sometimes without a precise diagnosis to guide treatment. They force closer intertwining of the problem and solution streams of policy so that the 'treatments', which often involve multiple interacting policy instruments, can be continually adjusted.

LAYERED ADVICE

Whether or not a particular issue can be treated as straightforward or complex often depends on which level of the issue is under examination. For example, advisers might be asked for specific recommendations about the relative merits of three pre-selected interventions for heroin addicts: supervised injecting facilities, methadone maintenance programs, and needle exchange programs. Although the larger problem of heroin addiction sits within a massively complex system of overlapping social, psychological, and economic variables with a large number of possible intervention points, the immediate policy task is relatively tame because the range of options and criteria has been constrained. An overall strategic policy direction – harm minimisation – has already been determined in this example, as have the particular instruments to be considered, and the evident goals (maintaining functionality for users and reducing heroin-related crime, social nuisances, and public health problems, such as the spread of HIV). The remaining tasks therefore lie on the boundary between responsive and operational policy.

Policy work is done in multiple domains of analysis corresponding to the three points of the policy triangle introduced in chapter 1 (figure 1.1) – strategic, responsive, and operational policy – and their zones of overlap. Figure 5.1 begins to identify tools of analysis and advising as they relate to policy domains. Most tools can be applied to all of the domains, but fit best at the intersections between domains, as shown in figure 5.1.

Starting at the top of the triangle, party officials play key roles in high-level, strategic direction-setting because many such decisions are made during election campaigns. As time passes between elections, however, senior public servants increasingly contribute to direction-setting processes as new issues storm the agenda, crises break out, existing policy directions come under external pressure, and governments that have long been in power begin to run low on new ideas. Policy analysts and advisers working in private business, community, or special-interest organisations often invest much effort trying to influence high-level direction-setting processes before and after elections. They use many of the same methods as their counterparts inside government, although the professional requirements for balanced analysis are less stringent.

Once an overall policy direction has been determined, policy work within an organisation focuses on activating the vision and moves into the domain of responsive policy. When regulatory reform of the financial markets is on the agenda, for example, further decisions will be needed in the domain of responsive policy: which specific activities will be included, how subsequent market outcomes will be monitored, whether additional policy instruments will then be needed to address other market failures, and so on. Useful tools in this domain include tables such as 3.4 to match policy instruments to types of problems. They

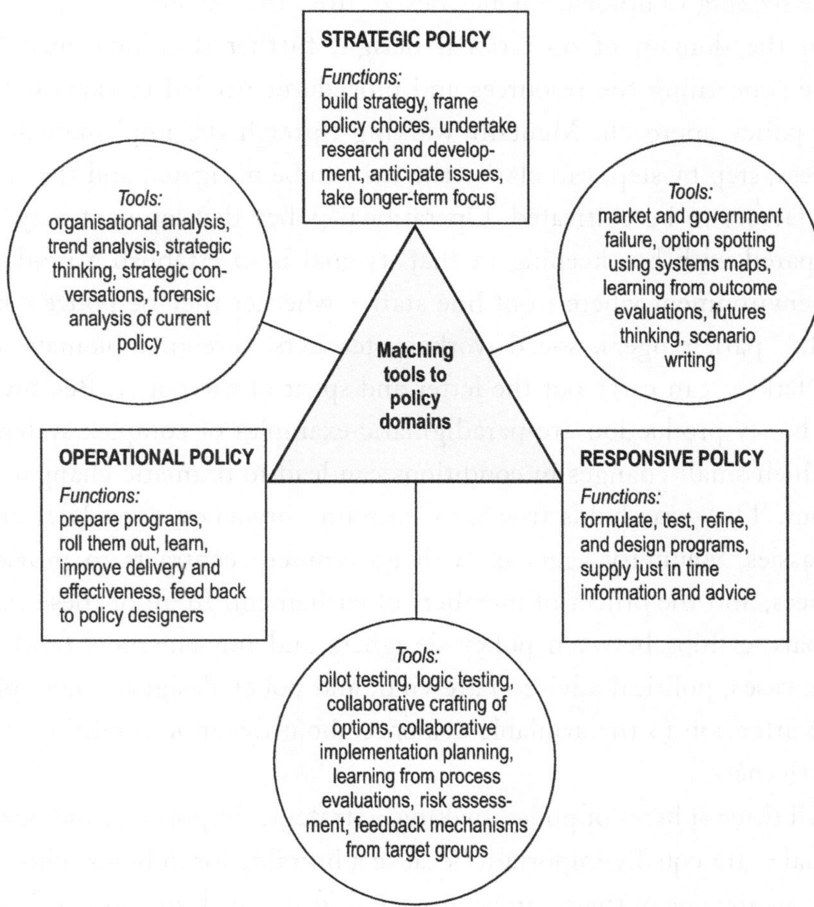

constitute a stock or bank of options from which ideas can be withdrawn and applied in context. Other methods of crafting options use system maps, dialogue with stakeholders and operational agencies, and creative combinations of existing policy ideas (policy cross-breeding). Responsive policy work also requires rigorous testing of policy ideas and attention to risks before making recommendations. All of these methods can be used equally by policy designers inside government and those seeking to influence policy design from the outside.

In the domain of operational design, further decisions must be made concerning the resources and procedures needed to carry out a new policy approach. Mentally walking through the implementation process, step by step, can clarify the risks to be mitigated and the success factors to be cultivated. Operational policy development may be compared with bee-keeping in that its goal is to establish a productive environment where front-line staff – whether they be police constables, park rangers, social workers, teachers, foreign diplomats, or tax clerks – can carry out the letter and spirit of the policy. Bee hives and honey production are paradigmatic examples of complex systems in which small changes in conditions can lead to dramatic changes in output. The same holds true for Centrelink branches, consulates and embassies, voluntary agencies with government contracts to provide services, and the offices of members of parliament. In all of these cases, partnerships between policy designers and implementers (and in some cases, political advisers) are vital, and policy designers must pay close attention to the available evidence about dynamic conditions for effectiveness.

All three spheres of policy-making – strategic, responsive, and operational – are equally important because admirable (or dubious) choices made in any one of them can be unwound (or rescued) in another. Take the deinstitutionalisation of the mentally ill, a well-intentioned policy that spread throughout the developed world from the 1960s to the 1980s. Deinstitutionalisation is now widely considered an implementation failure, but the blame for this debacle ought to be spread among all three spheres of policy development.

The initial idea was a good one. The deinstitutionalisation movement sought to liberate the mentally ill from the overcrowding, under-resourcing, abuse, and neglect found in many mental hospitals earlier in the twentieth century. This was to be done by replacing the allegedly harmful and isolating institutions with more modern, humane, community-based programs that would help reintegrate patients into society. In practice, however, the first part of this two-part plan raced ahead of the second part, leaving many highly vulnerable people in treatment limbo. Shutting down the old asylums turned out to be quite easy compared with the political and budgetary challenges of establishing sufficient, effective community-based programs to serve the needs of the previously institutionalised. In some jurisdictions, large numbers of former patients thus fell through the cracks of the patchy new system, and too many of them eventually experienced re-institutionalisation in homeless shelters, prisons, and sub-standard shared-housing facilities.

The term 'deinstitutionalisation' has become almost synonymous with 'policy fiasco' for all of these reasons throughout the developed world, and yet the problems could have been alleviated in any sphere of policy-making, given sufficient risk analysis, leadership, and political will. In the domain of high-level planning, the deinstitutionalisation strategists should have understood the diversity of mental health needs and capacities more fully and built a more responsive framework for deinstitutionalisation, rather than embracing the clean-sweep, all-or-nothing reform message. At the level of responsive policy design, one might argue that lags in developing community-based programs should have been expected, and deinstitutionalisation time-frames could have been adjusted accordingly. More assistance could have been provided to local agencies for starting up and expanding community-based services. In the domain of operational policy, leadership was needed to combine the efforts of private-sector, third-sector, and government-based programs to create the best community safety nets possible for the mentally ill.

Dedicated individuals in each policy level anticipated problems and tried to prevent disaster, but many were stymied by financial, political, and organisational barriers, and by the urgency of shutting down the worst institutions as quickly as possible.

EMERGENT POLICY DESIGN

The saga of deinstitutionalisation is not only a classic example of systemic failure, but also a vivid reminder that most complex policy interventions cannot be implemented successfully in one go. Where effective community-based mental health programs were established, they took years, and sometimes decades, to evolve in response to local needs. Infusions of external resources can speed the process, but trial-and-error learning is needed to shape such programs to their local contexts; this takes both time and a policy structure that can accommodate learning. Had the early deinstitutionalisers accounted for the predictable lags in their policy designs, the screening and releasing of patients could have proceeded incrementally, in step with the evolution of community-based services. Granted, politicians who want to claim victory over policy problems may resist incremental policy designs, which make less of a media splash and take time to produce outcomes. Policy advisers who recommend gradual or emergent options need to make their case forcefully and anticipate obstacles to later stages of reform as public attention waxes and wanes and politicians resist spending money on yesterday's issues.

Many of the best policy options include this emergent feature; they explicitly encourage learning and adaptation, a quality that Bardach (2005, p. 33) calls 'improvability'. Large-scale federal benefit reforms in the USA in the 1990s, for example, set targets for the states regarding employment levels among their welfare caseloads; but states were free to determine the best mix of services and interventions to achieve the targets, based on trial-and-error learning as well as accumulating research results. Community-based strategies in general tend to follow this learning-based template, with central government taking the role of facilitating the development of home-grown solutions to problems and the sharing of ideas between communities.

As organisations learn how to address the varying needs of different groups within their realms of responsibility, they may construct new frameworks for policy development. The regulatory pyramid, an idea developed by John Braithwaite and Ian Ayres (1992), is one example of such a framework, built from accumulated knowledge about differences between client groups. Although the pyramid focuses on regulatory policy design, its basic principles apply more broadly.

The concept of the regulatory pyramid begins with the carefully documented observation that individuals who fail to comply with regulations do so for many different reasons. Understanding these reasons allows regulators to tailor their activities to specific target groups for maximum effectiveness with minimum resort to coercion. Regulatory case management is the craft of knowing where on the pyramid to place a particular client at a particular time, which set of pre-enforcement or enforcement interventions to apply, and when. It is interesting to note that the reasons for non-compliance tend to be similar in different regulatory areas.

In the mid-1990s, the Australian Tax Office (ATO) built its tax compliance model on the foundations of the Ayres–Braithwaite pyramid, and several other countries' tax departments quickly followed suit. Figure 5.2 depicts one version of the model.

The base of the pyramid represents naturally compliant targets who are generally happy to follow rules to the best of their abilities. This is typically the largest category and the easiest to deal with, because the best way to maximise compliance with this group is to make the process as painless as possible. Threatening clients in this category with harsh

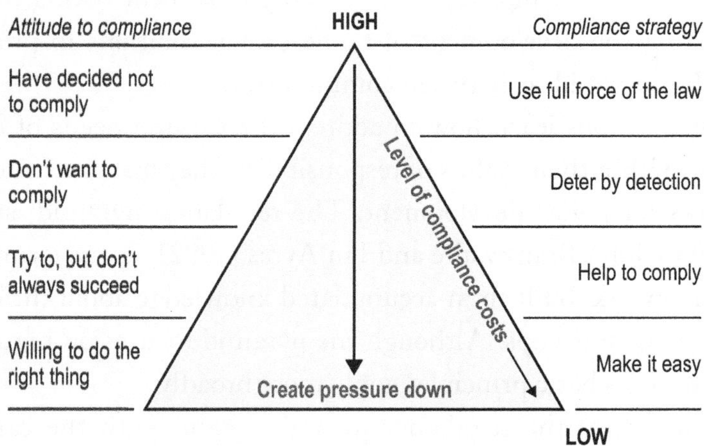

sanctions for non-compliance is overkill; not only is it wasteful of enforcement resources, but it also might generate backlash and create resentment and resistance where none existed previously.

The next largest group on the pyramid consists of people who generally want to comply, but sometimes find it hard to do so, because they are lazy, they face particular obstacles, or the process is too difficult. Additional assistance may be needed for this group, but threats may worsen non-compliance by causing these clients to fear the agency.

Some target individuals simply do not want to comply, because they disagree with the rules, feel that they should be exempt, or prefer to duck obligations whenever possible. Responses to this group, which occupies the middle of the pyramid, should be in moderate enforcement mode, typically involving visible detection efforts. Members of this group who perceive a reasonable probability of being caught are often motivated to comply in order to avoid confrontation with authorities. This may be true even if the consequences of detection are less than severe.

The smallest group of non-compliers – the incorrigibles – sits atop the pyramid, and consists of people who cannot be assisted, cajoled, or threatened into complying. Full-scale detection and enforcement activities with meaningful penalties are needed to make this group pay or obey and to warn potential incorrigibles of the consequences of non-co-operation.

The more cases handled at the base of the pyramid, the better, for reasons of both efficiency and justice. Prosecuting regulation breakers and tax cheats is expensive not only in financial terms, but also in the use of the state's coercive power. Both money and the threat of force should be used as sparingly as possible in liberal democratic societies. Therefore, agencies using a responsive regulation model will often begin by classifying a new case at the bottom of the pyramid, then escalate interventions as necessary, until compliance is achieved. Applying the pyramid concept to a particular regulatory environment requires continuous learning about the particular clients involved and their patterns of behaviour. Good practice emerges when improvability is built into the policy design.

ADAPTING METHODS

The three approaches to policy work introduced in chapter 4 allow endless variations and combinations. Variations on the problem–solution system map, for example, include the following.

Simulation exercises may take the form of informal role-playing, more structured gaming, or simulations using high-tech computer software. What these techniques have in common is the goal of creating a space within which actors (avatars) representing key figures associated with a policy problem (from investment bankers to drug buyers and sellers to drivers on a motorway) can be observed interacting with their environment and with each other under specified conditions. By varying the conditions, those running the simulation can test the impacts of policy changes on the outcomes of these multiple interactions. How will investment bankers react to changes in information disclosure rules, and how will other parts of the system react to their cumulative actions? How will individual drivers respond to the introduction of toll booths on a particular stretch of road, and what will be the flow-on effects for traffic patterns and other modes of transport around the region? Of course simulation 'testing' is only as good as the accumulated knowledge and wisdom of the person who designs the exercise.

Opposition channelling means playing devil's advocate – trying to imagine what a policy option's opponents would say about it. Political advisers are paid to do this for purposes of political strategy, but non-political planners, designers, and implementers can use similar techniques. The core idea behind this technique is to counter the natural tendency of policy advisers to protect their ideas from criticism and to use the arguments of critics as windows into a policy idea's potential flaws. Policy proposals can then be adjusted to remedy the flaws. No proposal can be made opposition-proof or risk-immune, but policies can be improved considerably through careful designing in response to hard-nosed critique. This technique overlaps with worst-case scenarios and the component of intervention logic focused on risk assessment and remedy formulation, both of which share with opposition channelling the purpose of spotting flaws in a proposal. All of these techniques can be used together, for example by examining an intervention logic backbone through the eyes of the opposition and writing a worst-case scenario based on what would happen if all of the opposition's warnings came true.

Outcomes matrices can be adapted to co-ordinate with the results of other exercises, including systems mapping, logic-testing, and ana-

Table 5.1 Alternative outcomes matrix

Criteria based on systems map and logic testing	Options			
	1 Extend banking regulation framework to non-bank financial firms	2 Deregulate financial industry (or facilitate self-regulation)	3 Break up large financial institutions that are 'too big to fail'	4 Prohibit credit default swaps
Does the option address the failures evident from problem scoping?	Yes – it addresses information asymmetry about product risks and problems of sub-rational 'bubble' psychology that perpetuate price spirals, but may create false sense of 'safety', leading to moral hazard			
Does the option recognise key system connections?	Yes – it is based on role of unregulated and lightly regulated institutions in aggravating system-wide financial vulnerability			
Soundness of basic logic	Good. The parallel or 'shadow' banking system engages in many of the same activities as banks and should therefore be regulated similarly			
Risks identified in main chain	Based on questionable assumption that existing regulations are effective in preventing banks from assuming excessive risk			
Availability of design features to mitigate risks	Regulatory reforms to improve effectiveness should precede extension of rules to shadow banking system			
Projected side effects, good or bad	Possible dampening effect on product and business model innovation in financial industry; costs will be borne by customers and taxpayers; note potential impacts on international business			
Projected impacts on other criteria of interest	May be biased against smaller companies who cannot afford compliance costs			

NOTE This is not a thorough analysis of option 1 and is presented for illustrative purposes only. Consultation with experts would be needed to complete the matrix for all options 1–4, and other options would need to be considered as well.

lysing likely side effects. Table 5.1 illustrates one version of a combined approach, using several policy ideas being debated internationally in the wake of the 2008–09 financial crisis. Many other versions of the alternative matrix are possible. This approach to comparing options puts less pressure on outcomes projection methods, and makes the role of analytical judgment more explicit. It highlights the need for balanced argumentation – 'on the one hand, on the other hand' – in the practice of policy analysis.

Logic diagrams also can be adapted to suit different purposes. For example, figure 5.3 illustrates what we call a top-down version of intervention logic, which can be used to generate policy options rather than test them. Like the version of intervention logic introduced in chapter 4, top-down logic modelling starts with a simple but challenging question: how are desired outcomes naturally produced? In other words, in the absence of government intervention, where do outcomes such as economic competitiveness, social harmony, and environmental sustainability come from? Figure 5.3 begins to answer this question in the case of healthy body weight – an outcome of great interest to health ministers and officials fighting obesity in both Australia and New Zealand.

A top-down logic exercise may begin with a brainstorm to elicit the economic, behavioural, physical, cultural, or other factors that contribute to the desired outcome. The only rule at this stage of top-down logic diagramming is that policy options should be kept out of the discussion. The factors proposed can be organised to show chains of causation. In figure 5.3, for example, the formula that determines body weight is shown to be simple, consisting of calories consumed (dietary intake), calories expended (exercise), and the rate at which calories are burned (metabolism). The behaviours associated with the first two factors – dietary intake and exercise – are themselves products of two simple but often hard to control sub-factors, access and choice. Access is determined by the relationship between the costs (in both time and money) of exercising and obtaining and preparing food, on one side of the ledger, and the income available (in terms of time and money) on the other side, in combination with availability – some foods may not be available at any reasonable cost in some areas. Of course, the logical simplicity of healthy body weight does not make it an easy goal to achieve. Choice appears to be the most complex and multi-dimensional variable in this logic model, and figure 5.3 only begins to list the factors that influence choice.

A good top-down logic model should reveal opportunities for effective intervention. Options may target any point on the diagram. For example, price controls, subsidies, or tax concessions on fruits and vegetables, and/or taxes on 'junk' food would lower the economic costs of healthy food compared to unhealthy food. Public education campaigns

Figure 5.3 Top-down logic diagram

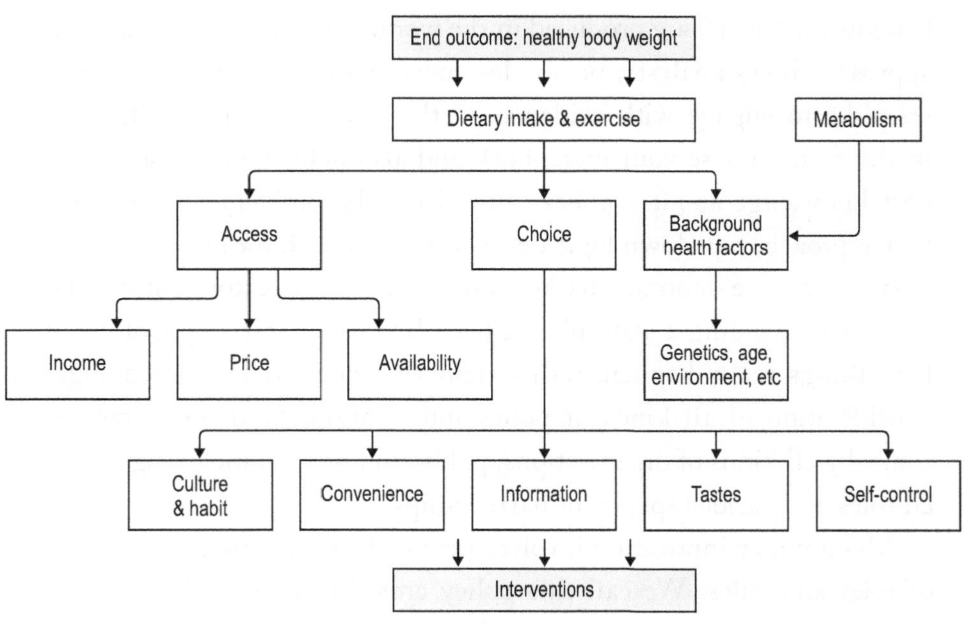

might be introduced to influence choice via information, with more advanced social marketing techniques applied to altering people's underlying tastes and preferences. Underlying health issues can be addressed through the health care system.

Top-down logic diagramming resembles systems mapping, with the main difference between the two being the feedback loops that characterise systems. In addition, problem–solution systems typically focus on the factors that are causing or contributing to a problem, whereas top-down logic models typically look at how positive outcomes are produced. These two roles can easily be swapped, with systems modelling of pathways to positive outcomes and top-down logic diagrams of wicked problems. A top-down logic model may evolve into a systems map as the number of central factors increases and feedback loops are added.

BEYOND PUBLIC–PRIVATE

Top-down logic has the advantage of focusing on the realities of how benefits (or harms) are produced in the world outside government. This approach forces analysts, policy designers, managers, and implementers alike to engage with evidence on the ground, at the coalface, or in the field (choose your metaphor), and also helps them organise expert knowledge about a policy issue. Like the problem–solution system approach, top-down logic de-centres the search for policy options; it avoids a state-centred, market-centred, or third-sector-centred bias while also avoiding a state-phobic bias. Because it starts by looking at how things really happen, rather than who does what, it encourages consideration of all kinds of policy interventions (and non-interventions) by all kinds of organisations, public and private, including blended roles and various species of partnerships.

Much policy innovation involves people devising new combinations of roles and rules. We call this policy cross-breeding. Public–private and public–public partnerships, covenants and voluntary agreements, community trading enterprises, self-regulation, and decriminalisation are just a few examples of cross-bred policy solutions that break down artificial and dysfunctional boundaries. The new combinations arise when people stop worrying excessively about who (market, government, or NGO) should intervene and focus on what needs to be changed. Focusing first on what needs to change – rules, incentives, resources, distributions, alliances, rights, etc – often leads to creative ideas about who should work together to achieve the change.

COMBINED APPROACHES

The analytical approaches canvassed in chapter 4 are natural complements. They should be pursued together when time and resources will allow. In theory, this is a relatively clear-cut matter of

- mapping the key factors in a problem–solution system
- plugging various policy options into the system using logic diagrams
- analysing the assumptions and risks associated with these options
- projecting the options' overall chances of success against selected assessment criteria
- recording the results of the analysis in an outcomes matrix for ease of comparison.

In practice, interweaving analytical approaches is a mighty challenge, but nearly always worth the effort.

Consider the global financial crisis of the late 2000s, a prime example of cascading market and government failures, tipping points, behavioural anomalies, and bewilderingly intricate international connections between actors, institutions, and the larger forces of economic order and disorder. The first big, visible domino to fall in this drama was

Bear Stearns, a New York-based investment bank and securities trading firm that had been an early and enthusiastic trader of mortgage-backed securities. When the value of the mortgages underpinning these securities declined steeply in 2007, the firm ran into strife. It finally collapsed in 2008, in part because of self-fulfilling rumours about its lack of liquidity and collateral, which may have been fuelled by the news of a government bailout loan. Once the rumours took hold and investors' confidence was lost, the only recourse was to sell the company at a huge discount to JP Morgan Chase.

Bear Stearns' demise shook international market confidence to its roots, reducing banks' willingness to loan not only to customers but also to each other. Subsequent bank failures in the USA and Europe led to a full-blown credit crisis, which depressed international trade and global economic output, contributing to steep declines in stock market indexes, currency crises, fluctuating commodity prices, recession, business failures, layoffs, declines in non-profit fundraising, reductions in community-based assistance to low-income households, family instability, and personal stress in all its manifestations.

The rise of mortgage-backed securities – arguably one of the main precursors to the economic meltdown – appears to have resulted from a market failure with colossal potential for systemic harm, but it does not seem to fit any single category of market failure clearly. Information asymmetry certainly plays a role, because the risks associated with these securities often were not communicated accurately to investors. Moral hazard (that is, an increase in risk-taking behaviour by people who know they are insured against, or otherwise protected from, the consequences of that behaviour) has also been implicated in two forms. First, investment firms passed risks along to groups of investors by bundling and re-bundling their mortgage-backed debts for sale to creditors in a perverse game of pass the parcel. Second, if the large investment firm leaders assumed that government would bail them out in case of collapse, then policy-generated moral hazard may have distorted their risk tolerance. Governments' failure to anticipate the collapse may be due to two additional categories of failure – lack of co-ordination among key actors and lack of any system-wide picture of the national or international banking and investment industry.

Thus far, in practice, governments have responded to the financial crisis and its aftermath with various combinations of bail-outs, fiscal stimulus packages, and regulatory schemes to impose more discipline on financial firms. Large-scale public borrowing has been necessary in some cases to fund the new policies, and its systemic impacts are yet to be seen.

Predicting the impacts of these multiple interventions on the economy requires a clear understanding of how the instruments will interact with each other and how businesses and individuals will respond to the policy changes. The whole picture needs to be grasped as fully as possible in order to predict with confidence how any specific piece of the picture is likely to evolve.

In order to draw such a picture, policy teams would need to begin by inventorying all of the key factors, only some of which were noted above. They include the submerged icebergs of systemic risk lurking beneath various financial products and financial institutions' practices; the interdependency of the banking, insurance, private equity markets and other financial institutions and parts of the economy; the roles of central banks and multilateral institutions such as the World Trade Organization and World Bank; the systemic barriers to the free flow of information; the incentives and disincentives holding all of these factors in place; and the points of entry to the system where changes could most easily be introduced. A diagram of the main points of interconnection between these factors would amount to a problem–solution system map.

An initial set of policy options can be developed using the problem frameworks introduced in chapter 3. For example, stronger disclosure rules and changes in risk assessment protocols are a natural step to addressing information asymmetry, and increased capital requirements for financial institutions are a natural remedy for moral hazard (forcing those institutions to insure themselves up to a point). Both options were being discussed widely in 2009. The problem frameworks mentioned here provide insights into the problem, but do not capture its complexity in full as experts continue to debate a long list of causes and contributing factors to the meltdown, including, among many others, deregulation of financial institutions, failure of securities rating agencies to perceive systemic risks, failure of regulation to keep pace with financial institutions' innovations, central bank policies, and US federal government efforts to expand home ownership in the 1990s along with other precursors to sub-prime lending. A problem–solution map that includes these factors would point to additional options beyond those indicated by the problem frameworks.

Logic diagrams could then be drawn to assess the policy options' probable effectiveness, and to reveal other possible intervention points. The process of scrutinising the options through logic testing would reveal risks, which would point to additional options for addressing those risks, so that policy options would snowball. The resulting options would not simply form a list of alternatives, however, because some options would build on others synergistically and some would be tied to other options as remedies for unavoidable flaws in the overall design.

Once clusters of policy options began to emerge, they could be displayed in an alternative outcomes matrix. This would enable analysts to compare the option clusters side by side, and consider their merits and demerits against assessment criteria. Insights gained from the logic-testing exercises could be used to complete the internal cells of the matrix, as illustrated in table 5.1.

As a final step, the preferred clusters of options could be plugged back into the systems map by asking 'what if' questions: for example, how would various parts of the system respond if new policies required a freer flow of information or higher capital requirements for banks? This exercise prompts a policy team to look ahead and think systematically about chains of reactions and their likely impacts within a whole system or a set of overlapping systems.

THE POLICY WORK HEXAGON

Figure 5.4 offers a simple typology of the main families of tasks and functions that constitute value-adding policy analysis and advice. Together, these six families of activities add up to a fundamentally system-based, externally focused, and fit-for-purpose mode of policy work.

The shape of the typology – a hexagon – is borrowed from Mayer et al (2004), who distinguished six roles and associated styles of policy craft in the Dutch policy system: research and analyse, design and recommend, advise strategically, mediate, democratise, clarify values and arguments. Their framework links particular roles to particular kinds of work done by analysts (including desk-based or field-based) and clarifies the relative importance of relationships with decision-makers, stakeholder groups, and citizens in the Dutch governance system. The hexagon model of Mayer et al is a useful device for macro-mapping policy work, including the interface with clients and customers. It recognises the imperative for policy analysts to understand how different tasks require different roles, methods, resources, and relationships between analysts and advisers, decision-makers and citizens.

This hexagon differs from its Dutch cousin in several important ways. First, it is a starter model only. It should be tailored to reflect differences in the social, political, and governance contexts between Australia and New Zealand and between the various jurisdictions in each country. It also needs to be continually revised to capture the constant changes in the local, state, national, and international policy environ-

Figure 5.4 The Australia–New Zealand policy hexagon

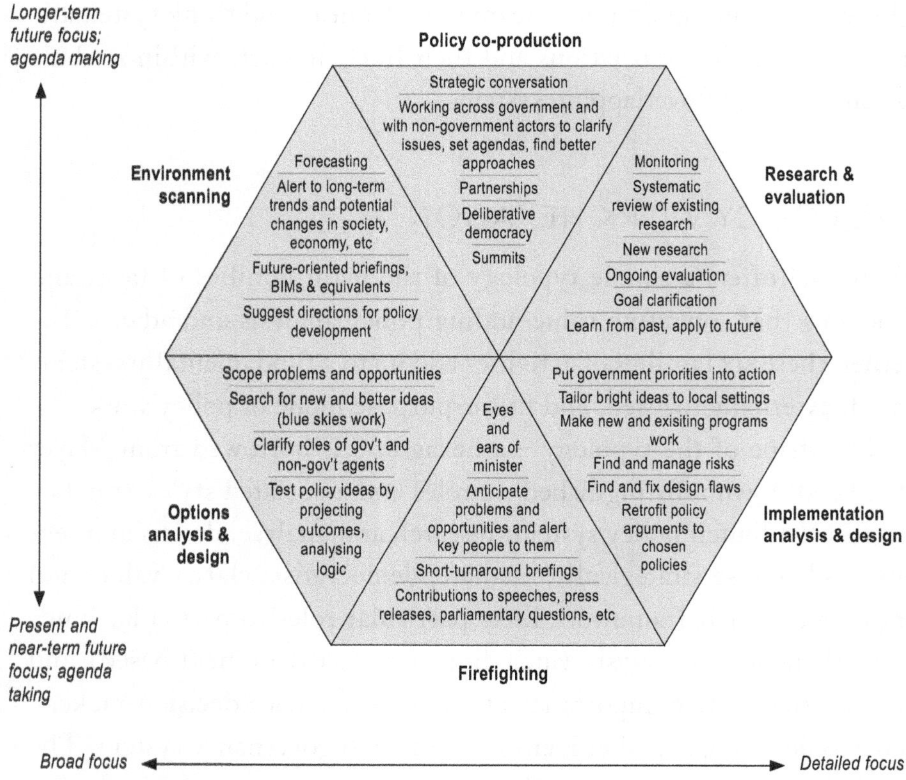

ments. A different version of the hexagon might be constructed for each jurisdiction.

Unlike the Dutch original, our Australia–New Zealand hexagon does not purport to describe what policy workers actually do, although some of the activities it records are undertaken regularly. The Australia–New Zealand hexagon is largely prescriptive or normative; it sets out the core activities that constitute value-adding policy work and encourages policy teams in virtually any setting to build their capabilities in these six areas. The Australia–New Zealand hexagon does not adopt the Mayer et al distinction between desk-based and field-based work, because every one of the six roles in figure 5.4 requires a mixture of both types of activity, though in varying proportions. Nor does figure 5.4 distinguish between orientations toward objects and subjects or between idealistic and pragmatic imperatives, as the Dutch hexagon does, because all of these elements ought to mingle freely in each of the roles.

What Mayer et al refer to as the 'democratising' role of policy officials does not appear as a separate item in our hexagon. This is because, in this part of the world, consultation and other engagement activities falling under that banner generally serve policy-specific purposes, such as engaging with stakeholders to help plan implementation or jointly framing community problems in search of fresh solutions to them, rather than serving a broader agenda of democratisation. It is entirely possible that a government one day will wish to expand and empower citizens comprehensively through the policy advising function, but we are not there yet. Neither does the Dutch category of 'values clarification and debate' appear as a separate item in the Australia–New Zealand hexagon because, here again, we see values debates typically occurring simultaneously with options and implementation design exercises, or as part of a co-production process, rather than on a separate track.

The axes of the Australia–New Zealand hexagon focus on the distinction between what we call agenda-making and agenda-taking activities. In figure 5.4, the work being done in the top half of the hexagon tends toward a long-term focus and may, under the right circumstances, influence not only the choice and design of particular instruments and groups of instruments, but also the content of the policy agenda itself. Environment scanning, research activities, and deep engagement initiatives with multiple actors (co-production) may lead governments to add, discard or reprioritise issues. It is important to note, however, that the agendas being set in the top half of the hexagon do not necessarily constitute strategic, big-picture, direction-setting policy. They are just as likely to concern operational policy, and therefore, do not fit neatly into a conventional, clockwise policy cycle in which implementation follows decision-making, which follows agenda-setting. Cycle models cannot cope easily with the idea of an operational policy agenda.

Policy work located in the bottom half of the hexagon is more likely to take the agenda as given – whether it is strategic or operational – and focus on pursuing it by producing policy options and implementation plans and by responding swiftly and effectively to day-to-day demands for information and argumentation. Each element of the hexagon is discussed in turn below, in no particular order.

Policy co-production

In a representative democracy, policy officials are never entirely free to throw open the policy-making doors to the public, but effective problem-solving sometimes requires not only consultation, but also active engagement with the people directly affected by a policy problem. Although relationship-building is not always considered a core component of policy work, it is often the most fruitful source of fresh ideas for addressing entrenched problems and can also be useful in helping to overcome people's resistance to change. In cases where deep engagement is needed, the policy task will not fit neatly into any formulaic model because there are no clear prescriptions for how ministers, public servants, and the people with the greatest stake in an issue should jointly thrash things out. Co-production means not only commenting on pre-selected policy proposals, but jointly framing the problem (or opportunity), building a systems map together, and jointly undertaking the options exploration and analysis. A wide range of public, private, and community-based organisations can play important roles in these activities, but these roles and the details of the processes can be difficult to specify in advance. Chapter 4 described how three approaches to policy analysis could be adapted for use in participatory policy development processes.

Although loosely defined and highly variable, the process of policy co-production must not break free entirely from its moorings in representative democracy. Public servants involved in the process need to keep the government of the day's priorities in mind, while also learning about the directions in which other organisations would like to see government moving. Co-production calls upon the government adviser to build constructive relationships with people outside the usual circles of parliament, the executive, established consultancies, and peak interest groups, which requires both flexibility and perseverance – but to do so without straying too far from the government's stated interests.

Co-production processes can be risky for government, because at least some of the potential players will be hard to control – as will be the policy products and the outcomes. Local communities and communities of interest do not always welcome government officials with open arms, and neither do the members of a community always agree with each other about the best way forward. Thus, analysts and advisers who take on policy co-production or partnership-type projects may get bogged down in disputes. Advisers involved in co-production processes need skills and instincts for acknowledging and defusing conflict.

Policy summits can be used to good effect when co-production processes are required, although the use of summits for window-dressing purposes has raised suspicion about this tool. Nonetheless, there are good examples in Australia and elsewhere of structured engagement progressing policy work, as long as officials are committed to following up on a summit's findings. Co-production processes may reveal that home-grown solutions to the problem are already being practised at the local level, in which case the main role for government may be to help communities share their solutions.

Co-production qualifies as a core activity in the hexagon by contributing to an outwardly focused systems understanding. It puts policy developers and those who wish to sway them in dialogue with the people who inhabit the problem–solution system, whose actions and reactions determine the system's evolution and impacts. It helps keep policy development grounded in reality, and can gradually build capability for broad collaboration not only among policy teams but also among community leaders and citizens, who will gradually learn how to work with government. One specific capability to be developed is that of adapting technology to facilitate public engagement and collaborative policy development.

Policy work in co-production mode looks for opportunities to increase coherence and synergy between related and interacting policy areas, which requires regular contact with cognate agencies inside and outside government. This sort of strategic work requires adaptive leadership and sharp understanding of government's priorities. It requires experienced advisers who can spot overlaps between community interests and governmental priorities. It helps government shape its agenda to meet emerging problems and opportunities.

Environment scanning

King Arthur had Merlin the wizard, and the Old Testament's Pharaoh had the divinely inspired Joseph, but today's government leaders must rely on ordinary human beings to help them anticipate problems and opportunities. Toward this end, the set of activities under the heading 'environment scanning' ranges from technical exercises in economic forecasting to street-level intelligence gathering. Ministers' interest in these activities will depend upon their own policy horizons, with very long-term problems and opportunities occasionally falling off the radar until events or changes in public consciousness force leaders to pay attention. Environmental issues often follow this sort of trajectory, with a slow, gradual build-up of awareness eventually leading to flurries of official activity. This pattern occurred in developed countries in the 1960s and 1970s, resulting in the establishment of new environmental ministries and the passage of landmark environmental laws in most countries, and it appears to be occurring again regarding climate change.

In addition to monitoring long-term emerging issues, ministers need good information about the economic, social, cultural, and environmental conditions in which current programs and policies are operating. This kind of information makes a continuous-improvement approach to program performance possible; incremental adjustments can be made as needed to keep programs relevant to evolving needs, and more dramatic policy shifts can be made when the accumulating changes begin to overwhelm current capacities. Close, constructive working relationships between policy and operational units can help ensure that environmental scanning information flows where it is most needed, and that the right kinds of information are being collected in the first place.

Monitoring and scanning activities sometimes shade into research when they focus more closely on particular populations or variables of interest, in which case officials will find themselves moving toward the right side of the upper hexagon, where research and evaluation functions reside.

Research and evaluation (R&E)

Policy officials are expected to stay current on the research and evaluation (R&E) literature in their policy fields, as well as undertaking new research to fill gaps in the literature or to test the applicability of international findings to their own jurisdiction. The resources available for research and evaluation will vary between governments and departments depending on fiscal abundance and the relative value placed on these activities. High interest in 'evidence-based' (or 'evidence-informed') policy tends to favour R&E. Within the R&E budget, allocations for various types of studies also will vary, depending on needs and public management fashions.

Evaluation spending is often justified in terms of a quasi-medical model, where choice of policy 'treatment' should depend largely on measured results from 'clinical trials' or their closest policy equivalent – that is, summative or outcomes-based program evaluations. Other forms, such as formative or process evaluations, worry less about replicating the medical evidence model, and focus on collecting useful data about early successes or failures in a program's implementation in order to spot opportunities for adjustments. Because this latter kind of evaluation can provide results early in the life of a new policy or program, it can help guide its development. Where formative and process evaluations serve this sort of feedback and learning function, it becomes clear that the conventional policy cycle's distinctions between policy formation, implementation, and evaluation are drawn too sharply. These three phases of the cycle often overlap to the point of blurring into each other.

Research is not always entirely separable from evaluation, but can often be distinguished by its focus on describing and explaining phenomena of interest to policy-makers apart from programmatic impacts – such as the rates of, and reasons for business investments in some areas and not others, criminal re-offending and rehabilitation, more and less successful settlement of new immigrants, declines and resurgence in fish stocks, trade surpluses and deficits, changes in pollutant levels, and so on. Whereas evaluation studies tend to focus specifically on separating out (and understanding) government's impact on a group of people or a section of the economy, society, or environment, research studies may focus as much if not more attention on understanding non-government variables.

R&E studies may be undertaken directly by government policy officials, or they may commission others to do the work, such as university staff or private consulting firms – which adds research contract management to the portfolio of many policy officials. One of the most challenging parts of the public service R&E portfolio involves communication of findings in ways that are useful for policy-makers. Departments that sponsor large volumes of research need to invest in what might be called summation and translation services – in other words, people whose job it is to find coherent patterns of findings across multiple studies, compare these findings with the international literature, and then explain clearly and concisely to ministers what research means for policy.

The R&E job also may include systematic reviews of current policies and programs, which again requires summation and translation of large quantities of disparate evidence about the target program and its past performance and future prospects. Such reviews may be prompted by the impending expiration of a major piece of framework legislation or by government's decision to make a particular policy area a priority for review. These policy processes may involve high-profile advisory committees, who may be required to nurture ties with interested stakeholders and communities or to maintain an arm's-length relationship between the review process and the government.

Systematic reviews require both breadth of knowledge of the policy environment and a detailed knowledge of current policy mechanics. Working knowledge of evaluation processes is needed here, and both systems modelling and logic modelling can be very useful. The interface between R&E, policy, and operations/management should inform this type of policy work, and so good intra-departmental relationships again become vital to good practice. A sophisticated understanding of intergovernmental relations and relationships with contractors and other key players in the communities and stakeholder groups will also boost effectiveness in these tasks. In addition, systematic reviewers need to understand the international context for policy in the relevant area, including international agreements and other arrangements that constrain policy options.

Firefighting

Formal education and training almost never prepare policy teams for this part of the job. Yet virtually all policy workers, irrespective of whether they are public servants, private consultants, or issue advocates, encounter demands for quick-turnaround policy services. Such tasks may include fending off media and opposition attacks on current or proposed policies, supplying bits of data and analysis for use in speeches and press releases, and, in the case of government policy officials, providing answers to parliamentary questions. When a policy position is under attack, policy teams may be asked for defensive information that will justify the beleaguered policy, or for ideas about rehabilitating or patching up a damaged program. In some cases, the best response to crisis is to call for a full-scale policy review, rather than take the risks associated with hasty analysis and decision-making when real changes are needed.

Good practice combines clear understanding of government's priorities and vulnerabilities, willingness to think about the public fortunes of a policy once it leaves the policy shop, a capacity for quick responses to demands for information and arguments, and the ability to manage crises when necessary. Analysts faced with these tasks need access to good intelligence about what is happening on the ground in order to judge whether criticism is real or gratuitous. This means monitoring immediate impacts, eliciting feedback from affected constituencies and operational staff, and staying in touch with local communities. In addition, policy firefighters need strong skills in forensic policy analysis (that is, analysis of why previous policies went wrong), cost estimation, and judging of organisational capability to respond to proposed modifications. Good relations with operational staff and communities are very useful. Forward-thinking analysts will try to anticipate crises by keeping an ear to the ground. Note the potential for close collaboration between public servants and ministerial and special advisers in this category of tasks.

Options analysis and design

This category includes a broad continuum of activities from blue-skies-type exploration and brainstorming of policy ideas to critical scrutiny of each option's likely impacts, and artful tailoring of a program to fit local conditions.

A 'blue-skies' approach to policy options is based on challenging conventional policy thinking and discovering alternative approaches. Active participation in both international policy communities and local communities helps put the blue-skies adviser in touch with the wider world and with new ideas, exotic and home-grown. Other rich sources of ideas include the problem–solution systems map, which should point to intervention opportunities. Analysts may begin by thinking about how the system needs to change in order to address the policy problem or opportunity, then talk about who is most likely to bring about that change, and how government may or may not be helpful. They may look for policies that plug in to a systems model at critical points to break up negative cycles of behaviour, to channel energy more productively, or to encourage positive cycles.

When scoping options, analysts should try looking beyond ideological stereotypes and simple binary choices (centralise–devolve, privatise–nationalise, regulate–deregulate, and so on) and consider different combinations of familiar elements. 'What works' in the relevant policy area from the perspectives of the political right, left, and centre? Can these features be blended into a new hybrid approach?

Options analysis and design may proceed à la carte – it is common practice to pick and choose clever policy ideas from across jurisdictional boundaries. Where states within a federation are concerned, such sharing should happen easily because the policy will be transferred between similar social, cultural, economic, and physical settings, so similar impacts and outcomes can be expected. But more care is needed about generalising a policy's benefits across national boundaries. When abstracted from the larger policy system and culture in which it normally resides, a policy instrument may behave in unexpected ways and generate unanticipated side effects. Some of New Zealand's 1990s health reforms were taken directly from the Netherlands, for example, with little consideration of how they might settle in differently here. When borrowing ideas, analysts and advisers should be alert to options for tailoring the program to local conditions. A co-production approach to generating policy options with stakeholders can help policy officials avoid the problems associated with à la carte policy transfer.

The enthusiasm of a blue-skies policy explorer eventually needs to be tempered by hard questioning from critics and risk-spotters, to improve the robustness of policy options by subjecting them to tough testing before recommendations are unveiled. Methods for testing options are discussed at length in earlier chapters. Often, the case for a policy option needs to be pieced together from bits of related evidence, and testing it will thus mean questioning not only the pieces of component evidence but also the coherence of the story that links them.

Implementation analysis and design

When a policy fails to meet its goals, policy designers should not be allowed to deflect all of the blame on to implementers and operating agencies, because policy designers should engage with those who understand implementation at the earliest possible stages of planning.

The implementation-planning function of policy work involves formulating and analysing potential plans for actualising a newly selected policy or repairing implementation problems associated with existing policies and programs. Depending on the situation, analysts involved in implementation planning work may or may not have opportunities to suggest significant modifications in a promised policy's designs. There is great skill involved in crafting such modifications to address the risks inherent in the selected policy without altering it beyond recognition.

Analysts need to pay careful attention to implementation risks at an early stage. Those risks that can be minimised through good policy design and implementation planning should be, and those that appear to be unmanageable should be brought to the attention of government either through public service policy officials or lobbying by outside organisations. Good relationships with ministers' offices and ministerial or special advisers are worth cultivating to improve receptiveness to implementation risks.

This category of policy work also involves attending to the various inconsistencies and unexpected effects that inevitably arise in every policy design, once program operations begin. Implementation design is a continual process, because the settings for policies and the ways they are implemented tend to shift almost constantly, requiring frequent tune-ups. The results of formative and process evaluations, described above, are helpful for determining where adjustments are needed.

The main goal of ongoing implementation design and redesign is to adjust the details of policy design to address anomalies and improve performance. When solutions are very simple and obvious, or when crises require immediate attention, this type of operational policy work may take the form of quick fixes. When more time is available and the situation is more complex, value-adding maintenance work will be based on performance reviews and consequent adjustments to operational or design features. This form of incremental learning requires close connections with and feedback from staff and other organisations involved in operations, including intergovernmental players and third-party contractors. In addition, advisers should be in touch with those directly affected by the policy, through key informants, for example, to gather their feedback and address their concerns. Implementation analysts need to understand the various co-production processes at work in their policy area.

No amount of good policy analysis and advice can guarantee success for any policy idea. Even highly promising policy ideas that are well implemented may fail to achieve their intended outcomes because of bad luck inside or outside government.

Nonetheless, good policy development work clearly increases the probability of success and ongoing improvement. Good policy work helps remove the 'bugs' from a policy program before it goes live and makes the most of the policy's strengths. This at least keeps the opposition and media at bay long enough to learn how the policy is working in practice and adjust it accordingly. At its best, the combination of wise political leadership, thorough policy design and implementation planning, effective and efficient operations, and good luck will lead to successful, well-supported programs that continue creating public value well beyond any single government's time horizons.

In order to produce value-adding policy analysis advice, policy teams need not only individual skills, knowledge, and character, but also a larger environment that supports and indeed demands high-quality policy work. The next chapter discusses the larger role of policy-making systems in nurturing value-adding practice.

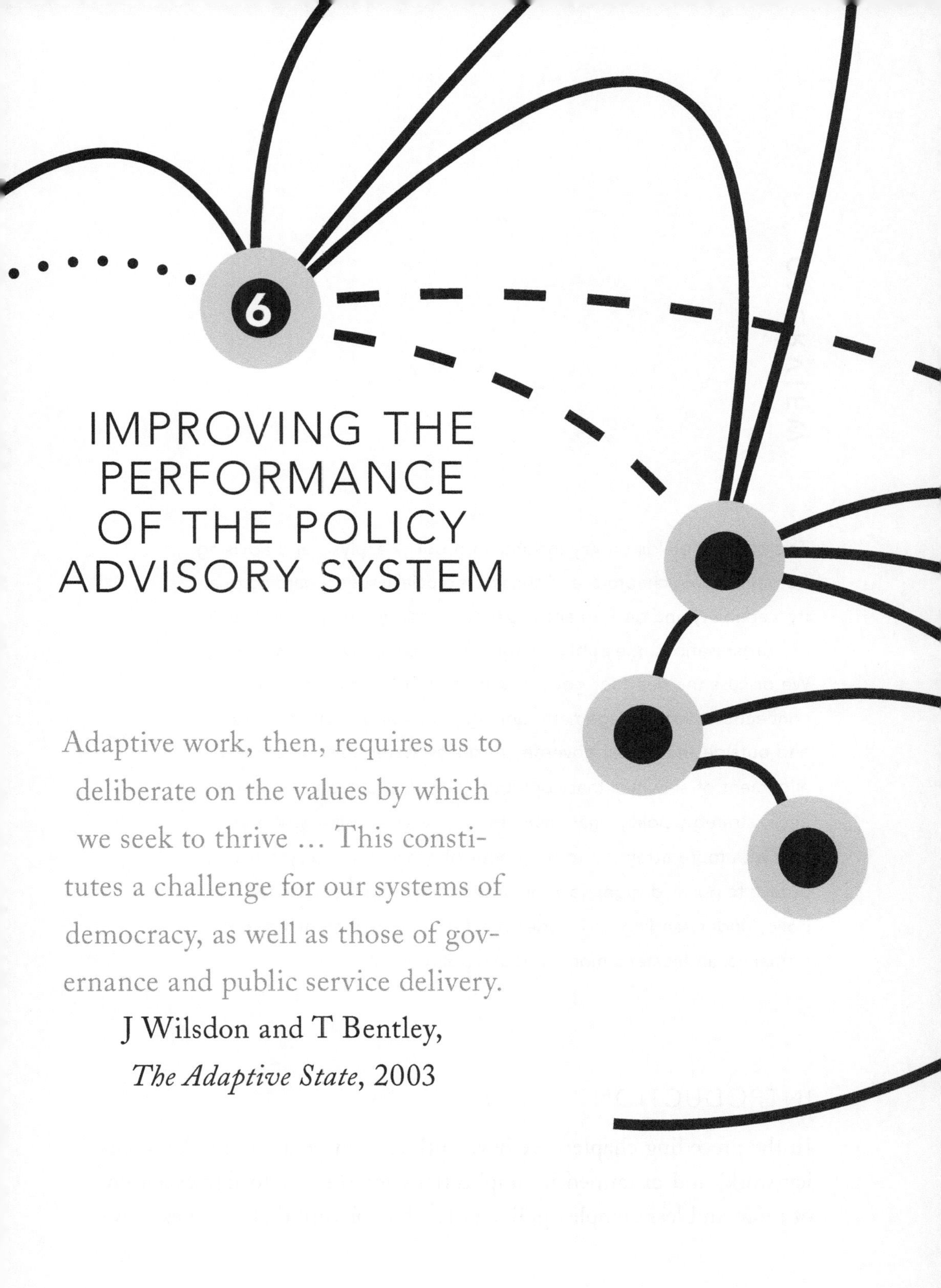

IMPROVING THE PERFORMANCE OF THE POLICY ADVISORY SYSTEM

Adaptive work, then, requires us to deliberate on the values by which we seek to thrive … This constitutes a challenge for our systems of democracy, as well as those of governance and public service delivery.

J Wilsdon and T Bentley,
The Adaptive State, 2003

This chapter builds on key insights into policy analysis and advising from preceding chapters, and considers crucial issues regarding quality, capability and performance as they pertain to analysts and advisers, organisations, the public sector and the policy system as a whole. We discuss the need for governments and their advisers to cultivate connections and engagement, among actors and institutions within and outside the formal government policy system, and improve the alignment of activities that contribute to policy outcomes – governance, strategy, policy, management and service delivery. We argue that with more attention to the rigour of analysis and a systems approach to policy design, governments and their advisers can facilitate policy understanding and leadership, lift the government's own performance, and foster a more engaged polity.

INTRODUCTION

In the preceding chapters we have outlined a systems approach to policy work, and examined its implications for the day-to-day execution of more and less complex policy tasks. The picture that emerges as we bring together broad and narrower views of policy practice has clear implications for the current debate about quality in policy advising and the capabilities needed to improve the performance of the policy advisory system, which we explore further in this chapter.

Starting broadly, it is clear that the environment in which policy is developed has changed in recent history, as has the policy agenda, necessitating change in policy practice. The change is a matter of kind as well as degree; governments more and more often must develop strategies for dealing with complex, multi-faceted, multi-sectoral problems, which can be managed but not solved definitively. Managing them requires policy design tailored to the specific context. Standard-issue generic policy solutions will not suffice, and this has challenged the capability of policy advisory systems.

The question is whether and how Westminster-style policy advisory systems can adapt to this more demanding policy agenda and environment. Questions have certainly been raised about the public sector's ability and responsiveness in practice. Ministers and state-sector agencies in several Westminster-type governments, including those of New Zealand and Australia, have suggested that a policy capability gap exists in the public sector. The degree to which this reflects greater challenges and complexity, perception or actual performance is another matter.

Hard evidence as to capability deficits is hard to come by; but indisputably the perception that they exist has exercised academics and practitioners alike for some time. Substantial resources have been directed into evaluating the performance of the advisory system and the quality of its product, and various measures have been taken with a view to remedying perceived inadequacies and strengthening capability and performance.

We have mentioned research by Behm et al (2000) that suggested that public servants had strong 'transactional' skills but often lacked the 'transformational' skills to deliver proactive, long-term solutions. Terry Moran (2009) has also suggested that the public sector has deficient transformational skills and thus a limited ability to exert leadership:

> By and large, I believe the public service gives good advice on incremental policy improvement. Where we fall down is in long-term, transformational thinking; the big picture stuff. We are still more reactive than proactive; more inward than outward looking. We are allergic to risk, sometimes infected by a culture of timidity. We should take the Prime Minister at his word when he said in his speech to the SES last year – and I quote – 'We cannot afford a public service culture where all you do is tell the government what you think the government wants to hear'.

This is not a simple matter of older values and imperatives coming up against changing times: 'telling the government what you think it wants to hear', timidity and risk-aversion fly in the face of the traditional Westminster principle of offering 'frank and fearless' advice to ministers.

These issues are not new, and in recent years many governments have worked to lift the strategic and operational policy capability in their public sectors. Since the early 1990s, for example, the UK public service has invested heavily in strategies for building policy capability, and undertaken to modernise the mechanisms and methods of policy-making. Many of the principles underpinning the reform program are essentially those behind the systems approach to policy work set out in the preceding pages of this book: policy that is forward-looking, innovative, flexible, creative, and soundly based on evidence and evaluation; an outward orientation, and readiness to learn from other sectors and jurisdictions; a strategic approach to governance, funding and delivery; inclusive policy-making, drawing on experience and expertise from a broad range of stakeholders; and joined-up policy-making to ensure alignment at every level (Bochel & Duncan 2007).

The systems focus implicit in these developments has been complemented by an approach to organisational capability and performance that has put strategy and policy, service delivery and leadership on equal footing in the performance assessment of public sector agencies. This integration of policy and management and leadership goals recognises that high performance by public sector agencies must ensure that these activities are aligned, in order to carry out the strategic intent of the government.

OPEN SYSTEMS PERSPECTIVE

Contemporary policy agendas are increasingly dominated by intractable issues, which require comprehensive approaches, and often co-operation and support from outside the formal policy-making system. We have suggested that positioning intractable issues in a wider systems context is essential, as it expands the range of options and breadth of analysis, and thus the potential for creative policy responses.

An open systems approach draws information and ideas from communities as well as from professionals and subject experts from many fields and disciplines, framing issues so as to acknowledge and balance alternative perspectives. Unlike process models of policy development or those that assume the centrality of ministers or government, a systems approach focuses on understanding what is going on. It does not pre-judge the potential value of contributions by government and other actors; and it treats policy as hypothesis testing in the context of uncertainty about facts, mandates and causal connections. This approach allows a range of alternatives and contingent recommendations to be developed, linking options to divergent underlying values and intended impacts, and to alternative views about the relationships between 'problems' and possible 'solutions'.

Faced with intractable problems, governments have little to lose and often much to gain by seeking out fresh approaches to policy development, and involving external actors and institutions from both inside and outside of government and the public sector in defining, choosing and implementing policy options. The systems perspective also encourages policy makers to draw on international evidence from many fields and disciplines, and to exploit the potential for learning and beneficial policy transfer. This potential is considerable given the growing ease of access to international information, research and evidence. Sharing information to inform policy debate can also prevent the uncritical adoption of policy approaches and instruments, disregarding the need to adapt them to important differences in the context and institutional environment.

Crucially, a systems focus does not detract from the importance of public-sector decision-makers and their advisers and analysts in policy development. Indeed it can open up new potential and opportunities for the public sector. Systems approaches encourage policy professionals to anticipate the impact of international trends and other external forces on the domestic policy environment, and require them to cultivate analytical, crafting and negotiating skills to a high level.

Policy development in this more open and fluid environment is less technocratic; the mechanistic metaphor of applying 'levers' to procure predictable results becomes less apt, and policy work is seen as fundamentally concerned with designing something that is fit for purpose in a dynamic environment.

Policy effectiveness is premised upon a good fit between systems and the issues requiring analysis, and, we argue, below that policy quality and capability must also be seen in terms of the ability of systems and policies to respond and adapt to changes in the environment and the various state, societal and international forces.

LINKING STRATEGY, POLICY AND MANAGEMENT

While the theory and practice of public policy can be strengthened by looking beyond the confines of the institutions of government, constitutional and administrative structures and conventions also have a significant effect on the responsiveness of policy systems.

Policy work ranges from big-picture strategic policy at one end, to day-to-day regulatory or program policy at the other. A system-wide perspective on policy work can help make strategic connections between policy issues and sectors, and thus to foster alignment between sectors and portfolios, and between policy initiatives within particular sectors. The smallest regulatory and implementation tweaks contribute to the functioning of the system as a whole, for better or worse, even though a comprehensive systems perspective is not needed for day-to-day problem solving and responding to demands for practical timely advice.

There is a growing recognition of convergence, overlaps and interdependencies between policy, management, and leadership. It is difficult to wholly separate out policy capability from other kinds of capabilities – for service delivery, strategic thinking and planning, and leadership. In the United Kingdom, for example, a capability assessment tool is used to measure the capability and performance of government departments in terms of management, strategy and leadership skills, recognising the substantial overlap between strategy and policy skills.

Public sector reforms in Australia and New Zealand in the years since the mid-1980s have led to institutional separation between policy and service delivery in organisations and jurisdictions, which is compounded by overlaps in Australia's federal system. Recent trends in public management and policy, recognising that services are delivered in order to achieve desired policy outcomes, have pulled in the opposite direction, however, strengthening the connections between the two areas.

Public management reforms have delivered some advantages, in the form of emphasis on outcomes, and incentives for good organisational performance; but they have also contributed to a separation and fragmentation of strategic, policy and management roles. In particular the emphasis on organisational accountability has sometimes thwarted policy and managerial alignment within organisations and indeed across the public sector. Despite pressures for whole-of-government responsiveness, co-operation and collaboration between public-sector agencies remains elusive, particularly when many organisations and players are involved.

Good management needs good human resources systems to recruit and retain accumulated expertise and knowledge. The skills to model systems and clarify the policy logic underpinning options are essential to evaluating the results of interventions and thus to adapting and improving policy. Experimentation is critical, as is a culture that supports innovation, coupled with countervailing provision for recognising and managing risk.

Good alignment of governmental agencies and management of policy processes are needed to provide policy-makers with system-wide reach and vision. In some government agencies process and project management dominate policy work, creating incentives for staff to stay on a predictable track, rather than shift their focus in response to a changing environment. Thus they lack the agility to respond to shifting government priorities, challenges from citizens and stakeholders to existing approaches, or new information or evidence. A strategic perspective is needed in governance and management to recognise the limits of policy agencies' internal resources and to draw upon external expertise and resources where necessary, whether by tapping into international research and evidence or by seeking information and insights from local residents.

A systems approach can foster linkages and synergies between strategic and operational policy units in the public sector, and support whole-of-government approaches; it can also help recognise and exploit opportunities to work with others, expanding the capability of the system as a whole. Multi-agency and multi-sector approaches, however, require the development of new approaches to policy work, including shifts in attitudes and behaviours. Yet another re-structuring will not necessarily procure synergistic benefits to the policy system.

The UK *Strategy Survival Guide* (UK Strategy Unit 2000) has raised awareness of the overlap between strategy, policy and service delivery, their common focus on outcomes, and the benefits of feedback from citizens and stakeholder groups. The document makes useful connections between government and citizens, and clarifies the iterative nature of strategy and policy formulation, of which rigid cyclical or process models fail to take account. Strategic policy units have been established in various jurisdictions; and strategic plans and policy statements have been developed to guide policy development and improve alignment between medium-term and short-term policy settings.

Creating opportunities for strategic thinking and conversations involving citizens can help governments enhance their overall policy performance. Strategic thinking and conversation can help advisers and public sector leaders to explore patterns and trends and maintain awareness of and knowledge about the systems, structures and world-views that are shaping issues and events.

COMMUNITY ENGAGEMENT IN POLICY DEVELOPMENT

Policy design is no longer the prerogative of a nation-state and increasingly policy development draws freely on actors and institutions outside the formal policy system. An openness to consultation and co-production of policy is needed to maximise the chances of buy-in and thus of successful implementation. But models for use by policy practitioners are predominantly client-centred, only some acknowledging the roles of policy networks, policy communities and stakeholders in influencing policy design.

Partnerships between governmental organisations and policy networks are being used increasingly to achieve co-ordination and strategic direction. In social policy areas, where intervention seeks major behaviour changes, policy processes are incorporating engagement with citizens throughout the policy process, from the early stages of policy design, to implementation and evaluation. Approaches to policy and program design are more likely to deliver value if they secure buy-in in advance, and are connected with implementation and the subsequent monitoring of results on the other.

Once again, the government finally controls the agenda; short-termism will still prevail if the government of the day will not provide the resources and time to secure support from stakeholders before making commitments to a new policy direction, and consider its implications for other policy areas and alignment with medium-term strategies. In this respect short-termism can be a resourcing rather than a political issue.

Innovation is not the exclusive preserve of experts. Marsh (2001) has suggested that Australia's limited capacity for strategic conversations has constrained its performance in strategic policy development. While strategic thinking is sometimes used simply to mean a medium- to long-term perspective on issues, the term can be more usefully understood as a wholly different way of thinking, aimed at bringing a rich information base to bear on the critical assumptions that underlie traditional deliberative planning.

Strategic conversation with citizens and stakeholders provides opportunities to make connections between various events, issues and ideas, to explore patterns and trends, and to consider the systemic structures and dynamics and world-views that may have shaped current problems. Australia and New Zealand have experimented with policy summits, which convene individuals and sometimes organisations to share information and learning about policy issues. Some such events elicit a shared understanding and a willingness to work together on policy solutions; others simply serve as a forum for considering possible trade-offs and compromises where agreement is out of reach.

QUALITY AND CAPABILITY

There is no broad agreement as to what constitutes quality in policy analysis and advising, and thus what capabilities are needed to ensure it. The diversity of proposals for enhancing the performance of policy advisory systems will therefore reflect diverse views about the nature of problems and opportunities, approaches to policy work, and the clients for advice.

Policy analysis can be conceived as technocratic analysis of objective information and evidence or as an expression of political purpose or community values; its product can be judged in terms of fitness for purpose or of political responsiveness, of delivering on a mandate, or in terms of desired or actual results. Views of the content of policy work and the role of policy advisers inevitably shape understandings of quality and value, and it is scarcely surprising that there is no simple handbook for doing policy or assessing its quality. However, a shift in focus can be observed from inputs and processes toward outputs and outcomes and the relationship between them. There are debates about the proper roles of public servants and governments in policy development and the balance between representative and participatory democracy.

One solution to a perceived deficit in responsiveness by public sector advisers is the employment of politically appointed ministerial advisers, within or outside of the public service. This trend can polarise the political and analytical dimensions of policy, leading to perceptions of the political dimension as inappropriate interference on the one hand, or as the only game in town on the other. We argue that the political dimension is a legitimate and necessary consideration in policy analysis and advising, to be acknowledged in the crafting of policy advice rather than split off from it; and that conversely, diminishing or constraining the role of analysis disadvantages the policy system and compromises policy design and outcomes.

In the abstract, quality is an unproblematic concept, which can be defined as fitness for purpose; but in practice it must be decided whether this means responsiveness as judged by elected representatives, or something that can be assessed objectively with reference to professional standards, benchmarking and external review of advisory services. The appropriateness of proactive leadership by public service advisers and managers is vigorously debated, alongside the importance of client satisfaction. If the sole client is simply the minister or government, then responsiveness to immediate and implicitly political imperatives must dominate.

If we accept, on the other hand, that the clients for advisory work include ministers, future as well as current governments, and citizens and their descendents, the challenge is to determine how their distinct and sometimes divergent needs can all be served and reconciled. The strength of an apolitical Westminster-style policy advisory system is its potential to maintain institutional and tacit knowledge and undertake research and development to serve both current and subsequent governments. This inevitably means a degree of tension between the advisers and the recipients of the advice, at least on some issues.

CAPABILITY AND COMPETENCIES

There is little agreement in academic and practitioner literatures as to precisely what knowledge, skills and competencies are needed in policy analysis and advisory work to serve both current and future governments. At an individual and institutional level policy capability is relatively straightforward, at least in theory. Public sector analysts and advisers require the particular bodies of knowledge and the specific skills and competencies to allow them to deliver high-quality, value-adding advisory services, on an individual level. The New Zealand State Services Commission defines capability on an organisational level, as 'what an agency needs in order to deliver its outcomes now and in the future in a high quality, efficient and timely manner'. But strategies are also needed to maintain and improve the whole sector's capability and responsiveness.

The public services of Australia and New Zealand recruit large numbers of generalists, who in the course of their careers will each serve in a succession of different agencies and departments; finance ministries and subject areas such as transport, regulation, communication and justice require significant numbers of more technically trained specialists. In Australia, staff of the Commonwealth's Senior Executive Service are employed on contract, and encouraged to amass experience in operational and policy roles in a succession of agencies in the course of their careers, on the assumption that a comprehensive knowledge of the system is preferable to narrow sectoral or institutional expertise.

Desirable skills and abilities can be analysed and defined as 'competencies' linked to the requirements of particular roles or tasks. Inside government, assessments of quality assurance are made on the basis of internal and external policy audits and evaluations, and by formal or informal surveys, which incorporate feedback from ministers. Policy experts are also used to providing peer review of policy work or to oversee a process of self-review. The quality of policy advisory processes is routinely audited and various good practice guidelines and principles have been established to guide policy practice. The competencies specified for policy advisers often include general requirements such as understanding the public sector context, good communication, and administrative and managerial skills. The changing policy environment has led to the specification of more and more administrative and managerial skills, and less specificity about research and analytical skills and technical abilities or elusive qualities such as creativity and innovation in policy design.

Competency modelling is widely used in efforts to ensure a good balance of generic and specific skills; however, it typically emphasises organisational fit over job content, and can thus be too general to have practical use for assessing policy capability, especially on a systemic scale. Explicit capability requirements in the public sectors in Australia and New Zealand are focused on large occupational classes and senior management positions; and there is little attempt to set out sector-wide common approaches to capability and capacity. Capability requirements are often defined more specifically in departments, ministries or organisations. In New Zealand, the staff of departments and ministries are employed by their chief executives, who thus play a major role in defining the capabilities required.

Painter and Pierre (2005) define policy capability as 'the ability to marshal necessary resources to make intelligent collective choices about setting strategic directions for the allocation of scarce resources to public ends', which raises the issue of how 'necessary' can and should be defined. Bryson, Mallon and Merrit (2004) propose a concept of human capability that draws attention to the different levels and kinds of capability that are required – defining capability as the sustained ability to perform from a systemic perspective, analysing capability in terms of outcome, output and input, and recognising the linkages between individual and organisational capabilities.

All the kinds of ability and expertise that may be needed will not be found in a single generalist. Therefore, securing and maintaining policy capability in an organisation, sector or system means assembling complementary abilities possessed by diverse individuals into an appropriate balance. Generic public service capabilities – contextual, administrative and managerial skills – need to be balanced with the technical expertise in research and analysis demanded by complex problems.

Skill in the communication of technical material is crucial to policy capability in an increasingly complex environment. Then particular skills are entailed in merging individual capability in organisational capability. The New Zealand State Services Commission (2008) recommends that organisations consider capability in seven dimensions: leadership, people, culture, relationships, information and communication technologies and internal management systems, assets and structures. On a smaller scale, policy work of any substance is typically undertaken by teams rather than individuals; and on a larger scale we argue that a systems perspective means looking not just to alignment and co-ordination with other state sector entities, but also beyond the sector to procure the appropriate mixture of skills and knowledge for any task or project.

GOVERNANCE AND POLICY

Ultimately in the Westminster system the government is responsible for setting the policy agenda. In effect, policy will succeed or fail in the longer term as a result of the decisions a government takes in response to the advice it receives, rather than as a consequence of the advice itself. Even when a government is committed to particular policies, a public sector can contribute much value in developing implementation plans and undertaking risk analysis of proposals. Policy improvements do not necessarily take the form of strategic new initiatives.

Performance can be improved by applying insights from regular monitoring and review of policies, and more or less effective contributions made to outcomes in the implementation of a government's predetermined policy agenda.

Governments are only as good as their exercise of judgment in policy decisions. They can also, however, take steps to strengthen the contributions and alignment of the various institutions and actors in the larger policy system, and to maximise the potential of policy agencies to craft fit-for-purpose policy that is responsive not only to government but also to a complex and turbulent environment.

Because the government determines the agenda and authorises policy actions, the political dimension is a legitimate and necessary part of the policy advising response – not a nuisance whose effects should be reduced or eliminated. Policy work is of its nature client-centred, and the client, the government in the form of a particular minister or as a whole, is the source of policy authorisation. So public sector policy work will always involve responsiveness in reconciling political imperatives with policy outcomes – a further reason for considering the policy system as a whole rather than advisory arrangements in isolation.

Maintaining a medium-term as well as short-term focus to policy development is often difficult under pressure from media and popular sentiment, and short electoral cycles. Various steps have been taken to attempt to bridge this gap, such as the establishment of strategic policy units and the development of strategic plans or policy statements to guide longer-term policy development. Governments often develop jurisdictional or sectoral strategic plans setting out desired outcomes, goals and objectives as a device for gaining collaboration and co-operation inside and outside government and the public sector. They also engage in various priority-setting exercises, particularly when resources are under pressure, to ensure alignment between services and other outputs and outcomes. Strategic plans have been introduced in many states in Australia, for example, and ten-year long-term council community plans are mandated for local governments in New Zealand.

Some of these strategic plans provide largely high-level guidance and direction; some serve governments' marketing and branding purposes. Others are more specific, and include performance indicators and even links to the performance agreements of public sector agencies and senior public servants. Such plans at their best can provide strategic focus and co-ordination; but they can also lack specificity, and may be linked to performance measures that are unrealistic or applied to organisations with limited influence over the outcomes in question. The result then is a constraining rather than enabling effect upon the policy response.

POLICY ADVENTURISM OR POLICY LEADERSHIP?

Advice, however well researched, analysed and crafted, may be rejected, which raises issues about the need to balance various dimensions of policy advisory work, and especially about the interface between policy professionals and elected representatives. The common separation in the public administration literature whereby ministers 'make' policy and public servants 'administer' it is artificial and unrealistic. Moreover, it frustrates one of the most positive contributions of the Westminster system – its ability to have a professional public service that adds value and can serve both current and future governments, a public service that provides a repository of knowledge and understanding about issues which assists ministers and governments of whatever persuasion.

Academics and practitioners have debated whether a more proactive public service is consistent with Westminster advisory arrangements. There is a view that public sector managers and analysts should refrain from 'policy adventurism' (Wanna & Rhodes 2006) in a Westminster advisory system, and see their role as largely about implementation and responding to immediate imperatives rather than being concerned with policy creation. Reich, however, argues on the contrary that the policy advisory role is less about delivering to the public what they 'need', and more about assisting public deliberation about alternative futures and examining assumptions about individual and collective values.

WESTMINSTER RECONSIDERED

Certain factors can be observed to hinder the policy system from responding effectively to policy issues and challenges. They can be analysed as failures of focus: state-centricity, for example, directs undue attention to the internal motivations and accountabilities of government agencies, neglecting the value that may be derived from non-state sources in the wider system. The traditional focus of government policy agencies on inputs and process has meant a neglect of the crucial relationship of outputs to outcomes, and thus a failure to focus on the purpose and intended results that policies and services are supposed to deliver. And when the inevitable political pressures come into play, the focus of policy work becomes short-term political advantage rather than medium-term policy outcomes.

The Westminster policy advising system is open to these failures of focus and is a ready target, in general or in a particular instance, when policy fails to deliver. But such blame is in itself a failure of focus, being fixed on just one part of the policy system, which is, as we have demonstrated, much larger than the governmental agencies charged explicitly with policy advising.

For policy to be effective in securing outcomes that deliver value to citizens, the entire system must function well. Policy failures may be failures of analysis and advice for the reasons discussed above; but they may equally be down to defects or defaults in other parts of the system — to failures of governance (the obvious instance being political short-termism), failures of management (to take a strategic, outcomes-focused view), or even failures on the part of citizens and other stakeholders (such as apathy, or unwillingness to make concessions, accept trade-offs, or recognise impossibilities).

The Westminster tradition is sometimes criticised as insufficiently responsive to political imperatives. But we argue that it offers a particular strength in its capacity to integrate and reconcile policy and politics, whereas more explicitly politicised arrangements can entrench short-termism and render strategic policy-making well-nigh impossible.

This strength lies in the Westminster system's defining feature: career policy professionals charged with providing frank and fearless advice, combined with responsibility to the government. Because they serve successive governments, not just the incumbent, they are better placed than political advisers to consider longer-term policy outcomes. Because their work horizons extend beyond electoral cycles, they are equipped and motivated to undertake research and development with a long view and broad compass, looking beyond immediate need. And because the system was intended to foster careers, rather than short-term appointments, the public service advisory system can develop the broad knowledge base and intricate crafting skills that are needed to address increasingly complex and intractable issues.

Public-sector advisers must necessarily respond to the government's priorities; we argue that with more attention to the rigour of analysis and a systems perspective on policy design, the public sector can also facilitate policy understanding and leadership, lift its own performance, and foster a more engaged polity. The complexity of contemporary policy issues makes it imperative that decision-makers and their advisers look outward, beyond governmental and institutional boundaries, and often indeed beyond jurisdictional and national borders, rather than try to tackle them in isolation. They need to do so first of all simply to understand the big picture – the influences and causal factors at work in the problem–solution system, and the patterns and changes in the turbulent dynamics. Politicians and their advisers also need to keep an eye on the window so they are aware of what is happening outside, and are not caught out by changes in the weather; and so that they can respond with agility and ingenuity to new knowledge, ideas and inspiration.

Not just the windows, but also the doors need to be thrown open to two-way traffic, recognising that governments on their own are no longer equipped, if they ever were, to effect solutions to policy problems on their own. The doors of policy institutions need to admit input from actors and institutions outside the governmental inside game, by way of consultation and engagement in design, delivery and implementation; and their staff need to venture out to participate in the co-production of policy with various individuals and non-governmental organisations, rather than trying to go it alone in institutional isolation.

Lifting the capability of the policy advisory system depends to an extent on the market for free, frank and fearless advice. Risk aversion and a corresponding loss of appetite for frank and potentially unwelcome advice have grown in both Australia and New Zealand. The days when advising was a relationship between a single adviser and a minister are also over. Departments work to multiple ministers, and policies are often about balancing competing goals, with many clients in the decision frame.

The traditional Westminster advisory system is based on the idea that governments will be served best by a permanent cadre of advisers whose expertise, institutional memory and wisdom about policy is developed over years. Making an advisory system more innovative and transformational, while maintaining the clear benefits of the Westminster tradition, calls for a delicate balancing act, but the public sector can do more to encourage deliberation and decision-making on medium-term issues.

The provision of policy advice is an industry which, like any other, requires investment, innovation and risk-taking to improve its performance. Like other industries, the public sector needs ongoing investment in building the capability and performance of policy advisers and in research and development – without which the sector's comparative advantage as a provider of policy advice and analysis will suffer. Public sector policy leadership can be extended by building capacity in anticipation of future policy challenges and opportunities. Investment in futures research and environmental scanning may help maintain an appropriate balance between short- and medium- to long-term policy perspectives.

We have argued for a crafting approach to policy analysis and a proactive approach to policy advising, and for public sector leadership, where politicians work together with the public service and other sources of advice. This chimes with the wide vision Robert Reich articulates of the role and function of elected members and advisers:

> The core responsibility of those who deal in public policy
> – elected officials, administrators, policy analysts – is not
> simply to discover as objectively as possible what people want
> for themselves and then determine and implement the best
> means of satisfying their wants. It is also to provide the public
> with alternative visions of what is desirable and possible, to
> stimulate deliberation about them, provoke a re-examination
> of premises and values, and thus broaden the range of potential
> responses and deepen society's understanding of itself
> (1988:5–6).

His vision places responsibility upon elected representatives and policy professionals to exhibit policy leadership; and at the same time to throw open their doors and windows to new ideas, knowledge and perspectives; and to cultivate a purposeful, productive and genuinely mutual engagement with the polity.

BIBLIOGRAPHY

Abramson M, Breul J & Kamensky J (2006) *Six Trends Transforming Government*, Special Report Series, IBM Centre for the Business of Government, Washington DC.

Adams D & Hess M (2001) Community in Public Policy: Fad or Foundation? *Australian Journal of Public Administration*, 60(2):13–23.

Adolino JR & Blake CH (2001) *Comparing Public Policies*, CQ Press, Washington DC.

Advisory Group (2001) *Report of the Ministerial Advisory Group on the Review of the Centre*, State Services Commission, Wellington.

Agranoff R & McGuire M (2003) *Collaborative Public Management: New strategies for local governments*, Georgetown University Press, Washington DC.

Albrecht K (2003) *The Power of Minds at Work: Organizational intelligence in action*, American Management Association, New York.

Althaus C, Bridgman P & Davis G (2007) *The Australian Policy Handbook*, 4th edn, Allen & Unwin, Sydney.

Ammons DN (2002) *Tools for Decision Making: A practical guide for local government*, CQ Press, Washington DC.

Angwin D, Cummings S & Smith C (2007) *The Strategy Pathfinder: Core concepts and micro-cases*, Blackwell, Malden.

Argyrous G (ed) (2009) *Evidence for Policy and Decision-making: A practical guide*, UNSW Press, Sydney.

Aulich C, Halligan J & Nutley S (eds) (2001) *Australian Handbook of Public Sector Management*, Allen & Unwin, Sydney.

Australian National Audit Office (2001) *Some Better Practice Principles for Developing Policy Advice*, Canberra.

Australian Public Service Commission (2007) *Tackling Wicked Problems: A Public Policy Perspective*, Canberra.

Ayres I & Braithwaite J (1992) *Responsive Regulation, Transcending the Deregulation Debate*, Oxford University Press, Melbourne.

Baehler K (2002) Intervention Logic: A user's guide, *Public Sector*, 25(3):13–19.

—— (2003) Managing for Outcomes: Accountability and Thrust, *Australian Journal of Public Administration*, 62(4):23–34.

Baehler K & Bryson J (2008) Stress, Minister: Government policy advisors and work stress, *International Journal of Public Sector Management*, 21(3):257–70.

Bailey SJ (2004) *Strategic Public Finance*, Palgrave Macmillan, Hampshire.

Bakvis H (2000) Country Report: Rebuilding policy capacity in the era of the fiscal dividend: a report from Canada, *Governance*, 13(1):71–103.

Banks G (2009) *Evidence-based policy-making. What is it? How do we get it?* Productivity Commission, Canberra.

Bardach E (2009) *A Practical Guide for Policy Analysis*, CQ Press, Washington DC.

Baumgartner R & Jones B (2002) *Policy Dynamics Chicago*, University of Chicago Press, Chicago.

Behm A, Bennington L & Cummane J (2000) A value-creating model for effective policy services, *Journal of Management Development*, 19(3): 162–78.

Behn RD (2001) *Rethinking Democratic Accountability*, Brookings Institution, Washington DC.

Bevir M, Rhodes RAW & Weller P (2003) Traditions of Governance: Interpreting the changing role of the public sector, *Public Administration*, 81(1):1–17.

Birkland TA (2006) *An Introduction to the Policy Process: Theories, concepts and models of public policymaking*, M.E. Sharpe, New York.

—— (2007) *After Disaster: Agenda setting, public policy and focusing events*, Georgetown University Press, Washington DC.

Bochel H & Duncan S (2007) *Making Policy in Theory and Practice*, Policy Press, Bristol.

Borzel TA (1998) Organizing Babylon: On the Different Conceptions of Policy Networks, *Public Administration*, 76(2):253–73.

Boston J, Callister P & Wolf A (2006) *The Policy Implications of Diversity*, Institute of Policy Studies, Wellington.

Boston J, Levine S, McLeay E & Roberts NS (1996) *New Zealand under MMP: A new politics?* Auckland University Press, Auckland.

Boston J, Martin J, Pallot J & Walsh P (1996) *Public Management: The New Zealand Model*, Oxford University Press, Auckland.

Bovens M & 't Hart P (2005) *Understanding Policy Fiascoes*, Transaction, London.

Boyne GA, Meier KJ, O'Toole LJ Jr & Walker RM (2006) *Public Service Performance: Perspectives on measurement and management*, Cambridge University Press, Cambridge.

Braithwaite V (2006) *Ten Things You Need to Know About Regulation But Didn't Want to Ask*, Occasional Paper 10, Regulatory Institutions Network, Australian National University, Canberra, <http://demgov.anu.edu. au/papers/Braithewaite2006OP10. pdf>.

Briggs L (2005) *A Passion for Policy*, speech delivered at the ANZSOG/ ANU Public Lecture Series, Canberra, 29 June 2005.

—— (2007) *The Context and Challenges of Policy Advising*, speech delivered at the ANZSOG Executive Master in Public Administration course, Canberra, 12 June 2007.

Brudney J, O'Toole LJ Jr & Rainey

HG (eds) (2001) *Advancing Public Management: New developments in theory, methods and practice*, Georgetown University Press, Washington DC.

Brunner RD, Steelman TA, Coe-Jull L, Cromley CM, Edwards CM & Tucker DW (2005) *Adaptive Governance: Integrating science, policy, and decision-making*, Columbia University Press, New York.

Bryson J, Mallon M & Merritt K (2004) Opportunities and Tensions in New Zealand Organisations: The individual and the organisation in development. In Blumenfeld S & Lafferty G (eds), *Proceedings of the 11th Conference on Labour, Employment and Work in New Zealand*, Victoria University of Wellington, 275–80.

Bullock H, Mountford J & Stanley R (2001) *Better Policy-making*, Centre for Management and Policy Studies, London.

Callister P & Galtry J (2006) Paid parental leave in New Zealand: A short history and future policy options, *Policy Quarterly*, 2(1):38–46.

Canadian Task Force on Strengthening Policy Capacity (1996) *Strengthening our Capacity*, Clerk of the Privy Council & Coordinating Committee for Deputy Ministers, Ottawa.

Capper R, Brown A & Ihimaera W (1994) *Vision Aotearoa: Kaupapa New Zealand*, Bridget Williams Books, Wellington.

Cato B, Chen W & Corbett-Perez S (1998) Logic Model: A tool for planning and evaluation health and recreation prevention programs, *Journal of Physical Education, Recreation & Dance* 69(8):57–61.

Cheyne C, O'Brien M & Belgrave M (2005) *Social Policy in Aotearoa New Zealand: A critical introduction*, 3rd edn, Oxford University Press, Singapore.

Clough P & Nutbrown C (2002) *A Student's Guide to Methodology*, Sage, Hampshire.

Cochran CL & Malone EF (2005) *Public Policy Perspectives and Choices*, 3rd edn, Lynne Rienner, London.

Cohen M, March J & Olsen J (1972) A Garbage Can Model of Organizational Choice, *Administrative Science Quarterly*, 17:1–25.

Colebatch HK (2002) *Policy*, Open University Press, Buckingham.

—— (2006a) *Beyond the Policy Cycle: The policy process in Australia*, Allen & Unwin, Sydney.

—— (2006b) *The Work of Policy: An international survey*, Lexington Books, Maryland.

Colin J (1992) *New Territory: The transformation of New Zealand 1984–92*, Bridget Williams Books, Wellington.

Considine M (2002) *Public Policy: A critical approach*, Macmillan, Melbourne.

—— (2005) *Making Public Policy: Institutions, actors, strategies*, Polity Press, Cambridge.

Coyle G (2004) *Practical Strategy: Structured tools and techniques*, Pearson Education, Essex.

Cummings S (2002) *ReCreating Strategy*,

Sage, London.

Cunningham G (1963) Policy and Practice, *Public Administration*, 41.

Cyert RM & March JG (1963/1992) *A Behavioral Theory of the Firm*, 2nd edn, Prentice Hall, Englewood Cliffs, NJ.

Davis G & Keating M (2000) *The Future of Governance*, Allen & Unwin, Sydney.

De Leon P (1999) The Stages Approach to the Policy Process: What has it done? Where is it going? In Sabatier P, *Theories of the Policy Process*, Westview Press, Boulder, CO.

Dobel JP (2003) Teaching Resource: Memo writing, *Electronic Hallway*, retrieved at <ww.hallway.org>.

Dollery B, Garcea J & LeSage EC Jr (eds) (2008) *Local Government Reform: A comparative analysis of advanced Anglo-American countries*, Edward Elgar, UK.

Dror Y (1964) Muddling through: science or inertia? *Public Administration Review*, 27(3), cited in Parsons W (1995) *Public Policy*, Edward Elgar, Lyme.

Duignan P (2001) Approaches and Terminology in Programme and Policy Evaluation. In Lunt N, Davidson C & MacKegg K, *Evaluating Policy and Practice*, Pearson Ltd, New Zealand, 77–90.

Dunn W (2004) *Public Policy Analysis: An Introduction*, Prentice-Hall, New Jersey.

Durie M (2003), *Ngā Kāhui Pou Launching Māori Futures*, Huia, Wellington.

Durning D & Osuna W (1994) Policy Analysts' Roles and Value Orientations: An empirical investigation using Q methodology, *Journal of Policy Analysis and Public Management*, 13(4):629–57.

Dye TR (2001) *Top Down Policymaking*, Seven Bridges Press, New York.

Easton D (1965) *Framework for Political Analysis*, Prentice-Hall, New Jersey.

Eden C & Ackermann F (1998) *Making Strategy: The journey of strategic management*, Sage Publications, London.

Edwards L (2002) *How to Argue with an Economist*, Cambridge University Press, Cambridge.

Edwards M, Howard C & Miller R (2001) *Social Policy, Public Policy*, Allen & Unwin, Sydney.

Eichbaum C & Shaw R (2003) A Third Force? Ministerial Advisers in the Executive, *Public Sector*, 26(3):7–13.

Eichbaum C & Shaw R (2008) Revisiting Politicization: Political Advisers and Public Servants in Westminster Systems, *Governance*, 21(3):1–27.

Etzioni A (1967) Mixed scanning: a 'third approach to decision-making', *Public Administration Review*, 27:385–92, cited in Parsons W (1995) *Public Policy*, Edward Elgar, Lyme.

Fenna A (2004) *Australian Public Policy*, Pearson Longman, Sydney.

Fischer F (2003) *Reframing Public Policy: Discursive politics and deliberative practices*, Oxford University Press, New York.

Flyvbjerg B, Bruzelius N & Rothengatter W (1998) *Megaprojects and Risk and Anatomy of Ambition*, UK University

Press, Cambridge.

Forester J (1999) *The Deliberative Practitioner: Encouraging participatory planning processes*, MIT Press, Cambridge.

Fountain JE (1992) *Building the Virtual State*, Brookings Institution, Washington DC.

Frame J (1961) Faces in the Water, Pegasus Press, Christchurch.

Frederickson HG & Smith KB (2003) *The Public Administration Theory Primer*, Westview Press, Boulder, CO.

Funnell S (1997) Program logic: an adaptable tool for designing and evaluating programs, *Evaluation News and Comment*, 6:1.

Geva-May I (ed) (2005) *Thinking Like a Policy Analyst: Policy analysis as a clinical profession*, Macmillan, New York.

Goldsmith S & Eggers W (2004) *Governing by Network*, Brookings Institution, Washington DC.

Gregory R (2004) Political Life and Intervention Logic: Relearning old lessons? *International Public Management Journal*, 7(3):299–315.

Gupta DK (2001) *Analyzing Public Policy: Concepts, tools and techniques*, CQ Press, Washington DC.

Hague R & Harrop M (1998) *Comparative Government and Politics: An introduction*, 7th edn, Palgrave Macmillan, Hampshire.

Hall I & Hall D (2004) *Evaluation and Social Research: Introducing small-scale practice*, Palgrave Macmillan, Hampshire.

Hawke GR (1993) *Improving Policy Advice*, Institute of Policy Studies, Wellington.

Hede A & Prasser S (2007) *What Ministers Want: Towards Best Practice in Policy Advising*, Report to Institute of Public Administration, Australia, July 2007.

Heifetz R (1996) *Leadership with Easy Answers*, The Belknap / Harvard University Press, Cambridge MA.

Heinrich CJ & Lynn LE Jr (eds) (2000) *Governance and Performance: New Perspectives*, Georgetown University Press, Washington DC.

Helliwell J (2001) Social capital, *ISUMA Canadian Journal of Policy Research*, 2(1):11–87.

Heywood A (2002), *Politics*, 2nd edn, Palgrave Macmillan, Hampshire.

Hogwood BW & Gunn LA (1984) *Policy Analysis for the Real World*, Oxford University Press, Oxford, 12–19.

Hood C & Lodge M (2004) Competency, Bureaucracy and Public Management Reform: A comparative analysis, *Governance*, 17(3):313–33.

Horne D (1964) *The Lucky Country*, Penguin, London.

Howard C (2005) The Policy Cycle: A model of post-Machiavellian policy making? *Australian Journal of Public Administration*, 64(3):3–13.

Howlett M & Ramesh M (2003) *Studying Public Policy: Policy cycles and policy subsystems*, Oxford University Press, Toronto.

Hueglin TO & Fenna A (2006) *Comparative Federalism: A systematic inquiry*, Broadview Press, Peterborough.

Hughes OE (1998) *Public Management*

and Administration, 2nd edn, Macmillan, Melbourne.

Hunt S (2003) The Role of Government. In Hughes OE (1998) *Public Management and Administration*, 2nd edn, Macmillan, Melbourne, 71–93.

—— (2005) *Whole of Government: Does working together work?* Asia Pacific School of Economics and Government, Australian National University, Discussion paper No. 05/01.

Huxham C (2003) Theorising Collaboration Practice, *Public Management Review*, 5(3):401–23.

Ingraham PW & Lynn LE Jr (eds) (2004) *The Art of Governance: Analyzing Management and Administration*, Georgetown University Press, Washington DC.

James C (2002) *The Tie that Binds: The relationship between Ministers and chief executives*, Institute of Policy Studies, Wellington.

Jenkins-Smith H (1990) *Democratic Politics and Policy Analysis*, Brooks/Cole, Pacific Grove, CA.

Johnson G & Scholes K (1997) *Exploring Corporate Strategy*, Prentice-Hall, UK.

—— (2001) *Exploring Public Sector Strategy*, Prentice-Hall, UK.

Kahn AE (1993) *The Economics of Regulation*, MIT Press, Cambridge.

Kakabadse A & Kakabadse N (1999) *The Essence of Leadership*, International Thomas Press, London.

Keating M & Davis G (2000) *The Future of Governance*, Allen & Unwin, Melbourne.

Keating M (1996) in Uhr J & Mackay K (eds), *Evaluating Policy Advice: Learning from Commonwealth experience*, Federalism Research Centre, Australian National University, Canberra.

Keating K, Wanna J & Weller P (eds) (2000) *Institutions on the Edge? Capacity for Governance*, Allen & Unwin, Sydney.

Kettl D (2005) *The Global Public Management Revolution*, 2nd edn, Brookings Institution, Washington DC.

Kettl D & Fesler J (2005) *The Politics of the Administrative Process*, 3rd edn, CQ Press, Washington DC.

Kingdon J (1995) *Agendas, Alternatives and Public Policies*, Harper Collins, New York.

Kjaer AM (2004) *Governance*, Polity Press, Cambridge.

Kraft M & Furlong SR (2004) *Public Policy: Politics, analysis and alternatives*, CQ Press, Washington DC.

Ladley A & Martin JR (eds) (2005) *The Visible Hand: The Changing Role of the State in New Zealand's Development / Essays for Sir Frank Holmes*, Institute of Policy Studies, Wellington.

Lasswell HD (1951) The Policy Orientation. In Lerner D & Lasswell HD, *The Policy Sciences*, Stanford University Press, Stanford.

Lawrence E (1999) *Strategic Thinking: A discussion paper*, Public Service Commission of Canada, Ottawa.

Le Grand J (2007) *The Other Invisible Hand, Delivering public services through choice and competition*, Princetown University Press, New

Jersey.

Ledbury M, Miller N, Lee A, Fairman T & Clifton C (2006) *Understanding Policy Options*, Home Office Report 06/06.

Light PC (1999) *The New Public Service*, Brookings, Washington DC.

Lindblom CE (1968) *The Policy Making Process*, Prentice-Hall, Englewood Cliffs, NJ.

Lindquist EA (2001) Building Policy Capacity in Government: Evaluating recruitment strategies, *Public Sector*, 24(2)8–10.

Lindquist EA & Desveaux JA (1998) *Recruitment and Policy Capacity in Government: An independent research paper on strengthening government's policy community*, Public Policy Forum, Ottawa.

Local Futures Research Project (2006) *Local Government, Strategy and Communities*, Institute of Policy Studies, Wellington.

Lunt N, Davidson C & McKegg K (eds) (2003) *Evaluating Policy and Practice: A New Zealand Reader*, Pearson, Auckland.

Maani KE & Cavana RY (2009) *Introduction to Systems Thinking*, Pearson Education, New Zealand.

Maddison S & Denniss R (2009) *An Introduction to Australian Public Policy: Theory and practice*, Cambridge University Press, Sydney.

McCool D (1995) *Public Policy: Theories, models and concepts*, Prentice Hall, New Jersey.

MacGregor D, Leigh A, Madden C & Tynan P (2004) *Imagining Australia: Ideas for Our Future*, Allen & Unwin,

Sydney.

MacRae D & Whittington D (1997) *Expert Advice for Policy Choice*, Georgetown University Press, Washington DC.

Management Advisory Committee (2004) *Connecting Government: Whole of government responses to Australia's priority challenges*, Australian Public Service Commission, Canberra. Retrieved: 2007, from <http://www.apsc.gov.au/mac/ connectinggovernment.htm>.

Marsh I (2001) Can the Political System Sustain the Conversations Australia Needs? *Australian Journal of Management*, 25:153–70.

Marsh I & Yencken D (2004) *Into the Future: The neglect of the long term in Australian politics*, Griffin Press, Melbourne.

Marston G (2003) Tampering with the Evidence: A Critical Appraisal of Evidence-based Policy-making, *The Drawing Board*, 3(3):143–63.

Martin J (1988) *A Profession of Statecraft?* Institute of Policy Studies, Wellington.

—— (1996) The Impact of MMP on Policy Development and Advice, *Public Sector*, 19(2):17–22.

—— (2006) *Spirit of Service: A history of the Institute of Public Administration New Zealand*, Institute of Policy Studies, Wellington.

May P (2005) Policy Maps and Political Feasibility. In Geva-May I (ed) (2005) *Thinking Like a Policy Analyst: Policy analysis as a clinical profession*, Macmillan, New York.

Mayer IS & Bots P (2002) Dam the river

or go with the flow? Changing views on policy analysis in Dutch water management. Paper to *APPAM Fall Research Conference*, Dallas.

Mayer IS, van Daalen CE & Bots P (2004) Perspectives on Policy Analysis: A framework for understanding and design, *International Journal of Technology Policy and Management*, 4:169–91.

McCool D (1995) *Public Policy Theories, Models and Concepts*. Prentice-Hall, Upper Saddle River, New Jersey.

Meier K & O'Toole L (2001) Managerial Strategies and Behaviour in Networks: A model with evidence from U.S. public education, *Journal of Public Administration Research and Theory*, 11(3):271–93.

—— (2003) Public Management and Educational Performance: The impact of managerial networking, *Public Administration Review*, 63(6):689–99.

Miller R (2006) *New Zealand Government and Politics*, 6th edn, Oxford University Press, Hong Kong.

Ministerial Advisory Group (2002) Review of the Centre, State Services Commission, Wellington.

Minow M (2002) *Partners, Not Rivals: Privatization and the public good*, Beacon Press, Boston.

Mintrom M (2003) *People Skills for Policy Analysts*, Georgetown University Press, Washington DC.

Mintzberg H (1994) *The Rise and Fall of Strategic Planning*, Pearson Education, Essex.

Mintzberg H, Ahlstrand B & Lampel J (1998) *Strategy Safari: A guided tour through the wilds of strategic management*, Free Press, New York.

Moore M (1995) *Creating Public Value: Strategic management in government*, Harvard University Press, Cambridge.

Moran T (2009) Speech to the Conference of the Institute of Public Administration Australia, Canberra, 15 July 2009.

Moran M, Rein M & Goodin RE (2006) *The Oxford Handbook of Public Policy*, Oxford University Press, Norfolk.

Munger MC (2000) *Analyzing Policy*, Norton & Company, London.

Musso J, Biller R & Myrtly R (2000) Tradecraft: Professional Writing as Problem Solving, *Journal of Policy and Management*, 19(4):635–46.

New Zealand Treasury (2009) Treasury Quality Standards for Policy Advice, Statement of Intent 2009–2012.

Nicholson-Crotty S & O'Toole LJ Jr (2004) Public Management and Organizational Performance: The Case of Law Enforcement Agencies, *Journal of Public Administration Research and Theory*, 14(1):1–19.

Nicklaus J (2005) *Golf My Way*. Simon and Schuster, New York.

Norman R (2003) *Obedient Servants? Management freedoms and accountabilities in the New Zealand public sector*, Victoria University Press, Wellington.

O'Toole LJ Jr & Meier KJ (2003) Plus Ça Change: Public Management Personal Stability and Organizational Performance, *Journal of Public Administration Research and Theory*, 13(1):43–65.

OECD (2002) *Distributed Public Governance: Agencies, Authorities and other government bodies*, OECD, Paris.

Orange C (1987) *The Treaty of Waitangi*, Allen & Unwin, Wellington.

Painter M (2001) Policy Capacity and the Effects of New Public Management. In Christensen T & Laegreid P (eds), *New Public Management: The transformation of ideas and practice*, Ashgate, Aldershot.

Painter M & Pierre J (2005) Unpacking Policy Capacity: Issues and Themes. In Painter M & Pierre J (eds), *Challenges to State Policy Capacity: Global trends and comparative perspectives*, Palgrave Macmillan, Basingstoke.

Pal LA (2001) *Beyond Policy Analysis*, 2nd edn, Nelson, Ontario.

Palmer G & Palmer M (2004) *Bridled Power: New Zealand's Constitution and Government*, 4th edn, Oxford University Press, Melbourne.

Parker S & O'Leary D (2006) *Re-imagining Government*, Demos, London.

Parsons W (1995) *Public Policy*, Edward Elgar, Lyme.

—— (2004) Not Just Steering but Weaving: Relevant knowledge and the craft of building policy capacity and coherence, *Australian Journal of Public Administration*, 63(1):43–57.

Patapan H, Wanna J & Weller P (eds) (2005) *Westminster Legacies: Democracy and responsible government in Asia and the Pacific*, UNSW Press, Sydney.

Patton C & Sawicki D (1993) *Basic Methods of Policy Analysis and Planning*, 2nd edn, Prentice Hall, New York.

Peters BG (1996) *The Policy Capacity of Government*, Canadian Centre for Management Development, Ottawa.

Peters BG & Van Nispen FKM (1998) *Public Policy Instruments*, Edward Elgar Publishing, Northampton.

Podger A, Simic A, Halton J, Shergold P & Maher T (2004) Integrated Leadership System in the Australian Public Service, *Australian Journal of Public Administration*, 63(4):108–18.

Polidano C (2000) Measuring Public Sector Capacity, *World Development*, 28(5):805–22.

Pollitt C & Bouckaert G (2004) *Public Management Reform: A comparative analysis*, 2nd edn, Oxford University Press, Oxford.

Prasser S (2006) Providing Advice to Government, Paper to the *Senate Occasional Lecture Series*, Canberra, 24 February 2006.

Proctor W (2009) Multicriteria Analysis. In Argyrous G (ed), *Evidence for Policy and Decision-making: A practical guide*, UNSW Press, Sydney.

Productivity Commission (1999) *Australia's Gambling Industries*, Report No. 10, AusInfo, Canberra.

Prokhovnik R (2005) *Making Policy, Shaping Lives*, Edinburgh University Press, Oxford.

Quade E (1975) *Analysis for Public Decisions*, American Elsevier, New York.

Radin B (2000) *Beyond Machiavelli: Policy analysis comes of age*, Georgetown University Press,

Washington DC.

Reich R (ed) (1988) *The Power of Public Ideas*, Harvard University Press, Cambridge, MA.

Reuter P (1987) The (continued) vitality of mythical numbers, *Public Interest*, 75:79–95.

Ringeling R (2002) European Experience with Tools of Government. In Salamon M, *The Tools of Government: A guide to the new governance*, Oxford University Press, Oxford, 585–99.

Rittel H & Webber M (1973) Dilemmas in a General Theory of Planning, *Policy Sciences*, 4:155–69.

Roberts N (2000) Wicked Problems and Network Approaches to Resolution, *International Public Management Review*, 1(1):1–19.

Robertson D & Judd D (1989) *The Development of American Public Policy*, Scott-Foreman, Illinois.

Sabatier P (1988) An Advocacy Coalition Framework of Policy Change and the Role of Policy-oriented Learning Therein, *Policy Sciences* 21:129–68.

—— (2007) *Theories of the Policy Process*, Westview Press, Boulder, CO.

Saliba G & Withers G (2009) in Argyrous G (ed), *Evidence for Policy and Decision-making: A practical guide*, UNSW Press, Sydney.

Scott CD (2001) *Public and Private Roles in Health Care Systems*, Open University Press, Suffolk.

—— (2005) Value-adding Policy Analysis and Advice: New Roles and Skills for the Public Sector, *Policy Quarterly*, 1(3):489–94.

—— (2006) The New Zealand Policy Environment. In Colebatch & Radin (eds), *The Work of Policy: An international survey*, Lexington Books, Lanham.

—— (2008) *Enhancing Quality and Capability in the Public Sector Advisory System*, IPS Futuremakers Series, Victoria University, Wellington.

Scott G (2001) *Public Sector Management in New Zealand: Lessons and challenges*, Centre for Law and Economics, Australian National University, Canberra.

Shafritz JM (2004) *The Dictionary of Public Policy and Administration*, Westview, Boulder, CO.

Shah A (2005) *Public Services Delivery*, World Bank, Washington DC.

Shaw R & Eichbaum C (2005) *Public Policy in New Zealand*, Pearson, Malaysia.

Shergold P (2005) Government and Communities in Partnership: Sharing Responsibility, speech at *Government and Communities in Partnership Conference*, Melbourne.

—— (2007) speech at launch of the Management Advisory Committee Report, *Reducing Red Tape in the Australian Public Service*, Canberra.

Shippmann J et al (2000) The Practice of Competency Modeling, *Personnel Psychology*, 53:703–40.

Singer M (1971) The vitality of mythical numbers, *Public Interest*, (23):3–9.

Smith C (2005) *Writing Public Policy: A practical guide to communicating in the policy making process*, Oxford University Press, Oxford.

Sparrow MK (2000) *The Regulatory*

Craft, Brookings, Washington DC.

State Services Commission (1992) *The Policy Advice Initiative: Opportunities for Management*, State Services Commission, Wellington.

—— (1999) *Essential Ingredients: Improving the quality of policy advice*, Occasional paper No. 9, Wellington. Viewed 2006 at <www.ssc.govt.nz/display/document.asp?docid=2910>.

—— (1999) *High Fliers: Developing High Performing Policy Units*, Occasional Paper No. 22, State Services Commission, Wellington.

—— (2000a) Gaining through Training: Developing high performing policy advisors, Working paper No. 2, Wellington.

—— (2000b) Pieces of the Puzzle: Machinery of government and the quality of policy advice, Working paper No. 4, Wellington.

—— (2001–2004) Human Resource Capability Survey of Public Service Departments, Wellington.

—— (2005) *Goals for the State Services*, Wellington.

—— (2008) The Capability Toolkit: A tool to promote and inform capability management, <www.ssc.govt.nz/capability-toolkit>.

Stewart J (2009) *Dilemmas of Engagement: The role of consultation in governance*, ANU E Press, Australian National University, Canberra.

Stewart R (1999) *Public Policy: Strategy and accountability*, Macmillan, Melbourne.

Stokey E & Zeckhauser R (1978) *A Primer for Policy Analysis*, Norton, New York.

Stone D (2002) *Policy Paradox*, 3rd edn, Norton & Company, London.

Sundakov A & Yeabsley J (1999) *Risk and Institutions of Government*, Institute of Policy Studies, Wellington.

Sutherland J & Canwell D (2004) *Key Concepts in Strategic Management*, Macmillan, Hampshire.

Thaler R & Sunstein C (2009) *Nudge: Improving Decisions about Health, Wealth, and Happiness*, Yale University Press, New Haven.

Tiernan A (2005) *Minding the Minders: Addressing the Problem of Ministerial Staff*, paper to the Australasian Political Studies Association, Otago University, Dunedin.

—— (2007) *Power Without Responsibility: Ministerial staffers in Australian Governments from Whitlam to Howard*, UNSW Press, Sydney.

Tiernan A, Wanna J & Edwards L (2009) Competence, Capacity, Capability: Towards Conceptual Clarity in the Discourse of Declining Policy Skills, Occasional Paper.

Torgeson D (1992) Priest and Jester in the Policy Sciences: Developing the focus of inquiry, *Policy Sciences*, 25(3):225–35.

Turner S (2002) *Tools for Success: A manager's guide*, McGraw Hill, Berkshire.

Twomey A & Withers G (2007) Federalist Paper 1: Australia's Federal Future: Report for the Council for the Australian Federation.

Tyson J (2004) Case study: A voluntary environmental accord for the dairy industry (A) 2004–07, Australia and New Zealand School of Government, Melbourne.

Uhr J & Mackay K (eds) (1996) *Evaluating Policy Advice: Learning from Commonwealth experience*, Federalism Research Centre, Australian National University, Canberra.

UK Cabinet Office (1999a) *Modernising Government*, Cabinet Office, London.

—— (2000) Wiring it up: Whitehall's Management of Cross Cutting Policies and Services, London.

—— (1999b) Professional Policy Making in the Twenty-first Century, Strategic Policy Making Team, London.

Vasil R (2000) *Biculturalism: Reconciling Aotearoa with New Zealand*, Institute of Policy Studies, Wellington.

Vickers G (1965) The Art of Judgment: A Study of Policymaking, 1983 edition, Chapman & Hall, London; cited in Parsons (1995) *Public Policy*, Edward Elgar, Cheltenham, 360.

Viljoen J & Dann S (2003) *Strategic Management*, 4th edn, Prentice Hall, Malaysia.

Voyce E (1997) Providing Free and Frank Advice to Government: Fact or fiction? *Public Sector*, 20(1):9–17.

Wanna J (2003) Public Policy and Public Administration. In McAllister, Dowrick & Hazzan, *The Cambridge Handbook of Social Sciences in Australia*, Cambridge University Press, UK.

Wanna J & Tiernan A (2006) *Competence, Capacity, Capability: Towards conceptual clarity in the discourse of declining policy skills*, paper to the JCPA Forum Workshop, Australian National University, Canberra.

Weaver K & Rockman B (1993) When and How do Institutions Matter? In Kent & Rockman, *Do Institutions Matter?* Brookings Institution, Washington.

Weimer DL (1991) *Policy Analysis and Economics: Developments, tensions and prospects*, Kluwer Academic Publisher, Boston.

—— (1998) Policy Analysis and Evidence: A craft perspective, *Policy Studies Journal*, 26(1):114–29.

Weimer DL & Vining AR (2004) *Policy Analysis: Concepts and practice*, 4th edn, Prentice Hall, New Jersey.

Weller P (2002) *Don't tell the Prime Minister*, Scribe Publications, Melbourne.

Weller P & Stevens B (1998) Evaluating Policy Advice: The Australian Experience, *Public Administration*, 76:579–89.

White N (2007) *Free and Frank: Making the Official Information Act 1982 work better*, Institute of Policy Studies, Wellington.

Wildavsky A (1979) *Speaking Truth to Power*, Little Brown, Boston.

Wolf A (1997) *Building Advice: The Craft of the Policy Professional*, Working paper No.7, State Services Commission, Wellington, retrieved from <www.ssc.govt.nz/wp7>.

Woolcock M (2001) The Place of Social Capital in Understanding Social and Economic Outcomes, *IUSMA Canadian Journal of Policy Research*, 2(1):11–17.

WEB LINKS

Adding It Up: Improving Analysis and Modelling in Central Government	www.cabinetoffice.gov.uk/media/cabinetoffice/strategy/assets/coiaddin.pdf
Association for Public Policy Analysis and Management	www.appam.org
Australian Public Service Commission	www.apsc.gov.au
Australian Policy Online (APO)	www.apo.org.au
Brookings Institution	www.brookings.org
Department of Prime Minister and Cabinet, Australia	www.dpmc.gov.au

Cabinet Implementation Unit	www.dpmc.gov.au/implementation/index.cfm
Grameen Bank	www.grameenfoundation.org/
International Association of Public Participation	www.iap2.org
Ministerial Advisory Committee	www.apsc.gov.au/mac/connectinggovernment.htm www.aspc.gov.au/mac/connectingsummary.htm www.aspc.gov.au/mac/connectingguide.htm
Northwestern University library of international governmental organisations (IGOs)	www.library.northwestern.edu/govinfo/resource/internat/igo.html
Policy Hub	www.policyhub.gov.uk
Productivity Commission, Australia	www.pc.gov.au/
Rand Corporation	www.rand.org
Resources for the Future	www.rff.org
Strategy Survival Guide	interactive.cabinetoffice.gov.uk/strategy/survivalguide
The Urban Institute	www.urban.org
UK Cabinet Office	www.cabinet.gov.uk

INDEX

Printed and bound by CPI Group (UK) Ltd, Croydon, CR0 4YY

09/07/2026

14916234-0001